Face Recognition and its Disorders

Sydney
Schultz

Face Recognition and its Disorders

Sarah Bate
Senior Lecturer in Psychology, Bournemouth University, UK

palgrave
macmillan

First published 2013 by
PALGRAVE MACMILLAN

Palgrave Macmillan in the UK is an imprint of Macmillan Publishers Limited, registered in England, company number 785998, of Houndmills, Basingstoke, Hampshire RG21 6XS.

Palgrave Macmillan in the US is a division of St Martin's Press LLC, 175 Fifth Avenue, New York, NY 10010.

Palgrave Macmillan is the global academic imprint of the above companies and has companies and representatives throughout the world.

Palgrave® and Macmillan® are registered trademarks in the United States, the United Kingdom, Europe and other countries.

ISBN 978–0–230–29216–1   hardback
ISBN 978–0–230–29217–8   paperback

This book is printed on paper suitable for recycling and made from fully managed and sustained forest sources. Logging, pulping and manufacturing processes are expected to conform to the environmental regulations of the country of origin.

A catalogue record for this book is available from the British Library.

A catalog record for this book is available from the Library of Congress.

10   9   8   7   6   5   4   3   2   1
22   21   20   19   18   17   16   15   14   13

Printed and bound in Great Britain by
CPI Antony Rowe, Chippenham and Eastbourne

For Ava,
who grew within me while this book was written

Contents

List of Figures

Acknowledgements

I would like to thank those people who supported me throughout the production of this book. Thanks to my husband, Ben, for his unwavering support and advice; and to my parents, Ron and Pat, for the ongoing care and attention that they have given both to me and my own little girl, allowing me to complete this project. Finally, I would like to thank the editorial team at Palgrave Macmillan for their assistance throughout the writing and production process, particularly Jenny Hindley for her constant guidance and support.

Publisher's Acknowledgements

The author and publisher would like to thank the following for permission to reproduce copyright material:

Figure 1.1, taken from V. Bruce and A. Young (1986) 'Understanding Face Recognition', *British Journal of Psychology*, 77, 305–27. (Reproduced with permission from Wiley.)

Figure 1.2, taken from A. M. Burton, V. Bruce and R. A. Johnston (1990) 'Understanding Face Recognition with an Interactive Activation Model', *British Journal of Psychology*, 81, 361–80. (Reproduced with permission from Wiley.)

Figure 1.3, taken from A. M. Burton, R. Jenkins, P. B. J. Hancock and D. White (2005) 'Robust Representations for Face Recognition', *Cognitive Psychology*, 51, 256–84. (Reproduced with permission from Elsevier.)

Figure 1.4, taken from T. Valentine (1991) 'A Unified Account of the Effects of Distinctiveness, Inversion and Race in Face Recognition', *Quarterly Journal of Experimental Psychology*, 43A, 161–204. Reproduced with permission from Taylor & Francis Ltd.)

Figure 1.5, taken from M. B. Lewis and R. A. Johnston (1999) 'A Unified Account of the Effects of Caricaturing Faces', *Visual Cognition*, 6, 1–42. (Reprinted with permission from Taylor & Francis Ltd.)

Figure 1.6, taken from P. Thompson (1980) 'Margaret Thatcher: A New Illusion', *Perception*, 9, 483–4. (Reprinted with permission from Pion Limited, London, www.envplan.com.)

Figure 1.7, taken from R. Robbins and E. McKone (2007) 'No Face-Like Processing for Objects of Expertise in Three Behavioural Tasks', *Cognition*, 103, 34–79. (Reprinted with permission from Elsevier.)

Figure 2.1, taken from P. E. Downing (2007) 'Face Perception: Broken into Parts', *Current Biology*, 17, R888–R889. (Reprinted with permission from Elsevier.)

Figure 2.2, taken from M. I. Gobbini and J. V. Haxby (2007). 'Neural Systems for Recognition of Familiar Faces', *Neuropsychologia*, 45, 32–41. (Reproduced with permission from Elsevier.)

Figure 3.1 reprinted with kind permission from Paul Ekman.

Figure 4.1, taken from I. Gauthier, M. Behrmann and M. J. Tarr (2004) 'Are Greebles Like Faces? Using the Neuropsychological Exception to Test the Rule', *Neuropsychologia*, 42, 1961–70. (Reprinted with permission from Elsevier.)

Figure 5.1, taken from R. M. Bauer (1984) 'Autonomic Recognition of Names and Faces in Prosopagnosia: A Neuropsychological Application of the Guilty Knowledge Test', *Neuropsychologia*, 22, 457–69. (Reprinted with permission from Elsevier.)

Figure 6.1, taken from H. D. Ellis and M. B. Lewis (2001) 'Capgras Delusion: A Window on Face Recognition', *Trends in Cognitive Sciences*, 5, 149–56. (Reproduced with permission from Elsevier.)

Figure 11.1, taken from R. T. Schultz (2005) 'Developmental Deficits in Social Perception in Autism: The Role of the Amygdala and Fusiform Face Area', *International Journal of Developmental Neuroscience*, 23, 125–41. (Reproduced with permission from Elsevier.)

Figure 14.1, taken from Y. Lee, B. Duchaine, K. Nakayama and H. Wilson (2010) 'Three Cases of Developmental Prosopagnosia from One Family: Detailed Neuropsychological and Psychophysical Investigation of Face Processing', *Cortex*, 46, 949–64. (Reproduced with permission from Elsevier.)

Figure 14.2, taken from R. Le Grand, P. Cooper, C. J. Mondloch, T. L. Lewis, N. Sagiv, B. de Gelder and D. Maurer (2006) 'What Aspects of Face Processing are Impaired in Developmental Prosopagnosia?', *Brain and Cognition*, 61, 139–58. (Reprinted with permission from Elsevier.)

Figure 14.3, taken from L. Garrido, B. Duchaine and K. Nakayama (2008) 'Face Detection in Normal and Prosopagnosic Individuals', *Journal of Neuropsychology*, 2, 119–40. (Reprinted with permission from Wiley.)

Figure 14.4, B. Duchaine, L. Germine and K. Nakayama (2007). 'Family Resemblance: Ten Family Members with Prosopagnosia and Within-Class Object Agnosia', *Cognitive Neuropsychology*, 24, 419–30. (Reprinted with permission from Taylor & Francis Ltd.)

Figure 14.5, taken from B. Duchaine and K. Nakayama (2006) 'The Cambridge Face Memory Test: Results for Neurologically Intact Individuals and an Investigation of its Validity Using Inverted Face Stimuli and Prosopagnosic Subjects', *Neuropsychologia*, 44, 576–85. (Reprinted with permission from Elsevier.)

Figure 14.6, taken from A. Young, D. Perrett, A. Calder, R. Sprengelmeyer and P. Ekman (2002) 'Facial Expressions of Emotion: Stimuli and Tests (FEEST)'. Thames Valley Test Company. (Reprinted with kind permission from Andy Young and Paul Ekman.)

Figure 14.7, taken from S. Baron-Cohen, S. Wheelwright, J. Hill, Y. Raste and I. Plumb (2001) 'The "Reading the Mind in the Eyes" Test Revised Version: A Study with Normal Adults, and Adults with Asperger Syndrome or High-Functioning Autism', *Journal of Child Psychology and Psychiatry*, 42, 241–52. (Reprinted with permission from Wiley.)

Figure 15.1, taken from J. Powell, S. Letson, J. Davidoff, T. Valentine and R. Greenwood (2008) 'Enhancement of Face Recognition Learning in Patients with Brain Injury Using Three Cognitive Training Procedures', *Neuropsychological Rehabilitation*, 18, 182–203. (Reprinted with permission from Taylor & Francis Ltd.)

Introduction

Faces are incredibly important stimuli that guide numerous everyday social and occupational interactions with others. Indeed, it is not only critical that we identify people we meet in both planned and spontaneous circumstances, but we also need to be able to interpret their current emotional state and intentions in order to interact with them appropriately. As such, it is not surprising that the cognitive and neural basis of face processing has received much attention over the past 30 years. Importantly, much of our knowledge about the structure and development of the healthy face-processing system has been informed by the study of individuals who present with difficulties in processing faces.

Although some of these difficulties are restricted to the recognition of facial identity, they can often involve deficits in other aspects of face perception, such as interpreting emotional expression or eye gaze direction. Interestingly, these impairments can arise from a variety of origins, and they present in acquired, neuropsychiatric and developmental disorders. Clearly, the absence of face-processing abilities can have a large impact on a person's everyday functioning, and it is of clinical importance to note that these deficits often present in conditions that are known to affect large numbers of people (e.g. autism, developmental prosopagnosia, schizophrenia and depression). Thus, research that has examined the nature of face-processing impairments in these disorders has not only had important implications in improving our understanding of the cognitive and neural basis of the conditions themselves, but has also had more practical value in highlighting behavioural abnormalities that may be used to identify those at risk of developing a particular disorder, or to monitor their response to intervention.

However, it is also clear that even clinical investigations have important theoretical implications that inform cognitive and neural models concerned with the healthy face-processing system, in addition to key debates that have prevailed in the psychological literature for decades. Indeed, many authors have contributed to the issue concerned with the specificity of the face-processing system. That is, do we have specific cognitive and neural mechanisms that are specialized only for the processing of faces, or are these systems also used to process other visual entities? Further, are we born with a pre-specified system for face processing, or does this develop in response to our visual experience with faces? Importantly, seemingly practical issues related to the assessment and treatment of face-processing deficits also have theoretical repercussions. Indeed, the cognitive neuropsychological approach can be used to guide the assessment and diagnosis of the locus of face-processing impairments within functional architectures, whereas investigations into the effectiveness of intervention techniques addresses key issues about the neural plasticity of the face-processing system. Hence, given both the theoretical and practical contributions of studies examining individuals with face-processing deficits, it is clear that assessment, diagnosis and treatment of these disorders are of critical importance to researchers and practitioners alike.

This book takes the perspective that disorders of face processing are both clinically important in terms of how they might be understood and managed by cognitive and clinical neuropsychologists, but also that even the most practical investigation might have key implications for the development and refinement of theory. Hence, the book adopts a novel, interdisciplinary approach that brings together cognitive, developmental and clinical evidence in addressing key practical and theoretical issues that are relevant to practitioners, students, and more advanced academic readers. To support the broad scope of this intended audience, the book is structured such that readers can dip in and out of chapters to meet their own requirements, and further that instructors can tailor recommended reading of the book to match the structure of their course.

The book is divided into four subsections, each containing three 'core' chapters that describe specific aspects of the literature, disorders of face processing, or practical issues. It is intended that these chapters are used to support specific lectures concerned with each topic or disorder; or they might alternatively be used by research students, practitioners or other interested readers to access information about a specific topic or disorder in isolation. To provide additional support for all readers, each chapter is presented with a list of journal articles that are recommended for further reading, often including review or critical papers that provide additional background about a particular topic. In addition, a set of guidance questions is also provided, to help the reader navigate their way through the information presented in both the chapter and additional reading, such that attention is directed to the key issues at hand.

Further, each of the four sections also contains a 'Focus Chapter' that addresses the key theoretical implications of the research discussed in the three core chapters. These focus chapters have been written for more advanced academic readers, and might also be used in a seminar or group-learning context to prompt discussion of the critical and contemporary topics that are prevalent in the psychological literature. Hence, each focus chapter is presented with recommended reading that refers the reader to original research reports and key case studies, alongside a recommended seminar or discussion activity to prompt more advanced analysis of relevant issues.

In Part I, the cognitive and neural structure of the healthy adult face-processing system is discussed. It is recommended that readers who are simply 'dipping in' to later chapters might consult this section, to gain understanding of the key models and paradigms that are typically used in face-processing research.

Indeed, the reader is cross-referenced to these chapters where appropriate throughout the book. Chapter 1 describes key behavioural work that contributes to our knowledge of face processing from a cognitive psychological viewpoint. Specifically, the dominant functional model of face processing posited by Bruce and Young (1986) is described, together with more recent refinements of the model. Further, the chapter outlines classic paradigms that demonstrate the importance of configural (or holistic) information in face processing. In Chapter 2, neuroscientific methodologies are described that have been used to inform our knowledge of the neural basis of the face-processing system, together with key findings that have contributed to the development of recent neurological models of face processing. Chapter 3 describes the social value of the face, and explores the behavioural and neurological findings that reveal the nature of non-identity processes, such as judgments of emotional expression, eye gaze direction and facial attractiveness. This section of the book culminates in a Focus Chapter (Chapter 4) that explores how research examining unimpaired adult participants contributes to the key debate concerned with the specificity of the face-processing system. Indeed, for many years this topic has been hotly debated, with some authors suggesting that specialized cognitive and neural mechanisms underpin face recognition, whereas others argue that these mechanisms are more generalized and are used to process any visual entity with which we have sufficient expertise.

Part II of the book explores acquired and neuropsychiatric disorders of face processing that affect adults. Chapter 5 describes prosopagnosia, a fascinating neurological condition where individuals lose the ability to recognize others from their face. These individuals are compared with those with delusional misidentification syndrome in Chapter 6, including the contribution of this comparison to the development of functional models of face processing. Chapter 7 describes the nature of face-processing impairments that commonly present in neuropsychiatric conditions, such as schizophrenia, depression and social anxiety disorder. Importantly, deficits in all three conditions particularly involve the processing of emotional expression, and these findings are discussed in light of evidence that suggests facial expression recognition deficits might underpin and maintain experience of these disorders. In the Focus Chapter presented in Chapter 8, the findings related to all of the above conditions are discussed and evaluated in relation to their implications for theory. Indeed, although Part I describes the theoretical contribution of studies that have examined unimpaired participants, much of the primary evidence that supports models of face processing and the face-specificity debate has come from neuropsychological 'double dissociations' involving neurological patients.

In Part III, developmental disorders of face processing are discussed. This section of the book starts in Chapter 9 with an introduction to the development of the unimpaired face-processing system. Specifically, the chapter introduces the key debate concerned with the state of the face-processing system at birth (i.e. are we born with pre-specified face-processing mechanisms, or do these only develop in response to visual experience with faces?), and additionally considers the age at which adult-like levels of face-processing ability are achieved. The subsequent two chapters describe the nature of face-processing deficits that present in developmental disorders. Specifically, Chapter 10 describes the developmental form of prosopagnosia and compares this condition to its acquired equivalent; whereas Chapter 11 considers face-processing impairments in socio-developmental disorders, such as autism, Williams syndrome and Turner's syndrome. Importantly, the varying pattern of visuo-cognitive, social and neurological deficits that present in these three conditions can greatly inform the debate concerned with the state of the face-processing system at birth. Hence, the Focus Chapter presented at the end of Part III (Chapter 12) discusses how the nature of face-processing impairments in developmental prosopagnosia and socio-developmental disorders can inform this issue.

Finally, Part IV deals with more practical issues concerned with the everyday consequences of face-processing impairments (Chapter 13), and the assessment (Chapter 14) and treatment (Chapter 15) of these deficits. Although these topics are perhaps primarily of practical importance, it should also be noted that they do not exist in a theoretical vacuum, and findings related to these issues can constantly be guided by existing theory, in addition to providing continuous evaluation and refinement of key theories and debates. Indeed, the beauty of the cognitive neuropsychological approach is that it only takes one exception to the rule to inform theory, highlighting the power of the single-case study in this theoretical framework. Thus, the final Focus Chapter of the book (Chapter 16) places these practical and clinical issues in their theoretical context.

I very much hope you enjoy reading this book, and that my intention to combine cognitive, developmental and clinical approaches to the study of face processing in a novel interdisciplinary framework has been achieved. Although the benefits of this project for the development of my own research and teaching programme have been paramount, I hope that the book goes some way, however small, towards providing readers with similar benefits in promoting their own studies, research agenda, professional practice or general interest in this topic.

PART I

The Structure and Function of the Healthy Adult Face-Processing System

1 The Cognitive Psychology of Face Recognition

The most reliable source of information that allows us to identify others comes from the internal facial features. Indeed, although the human face has evolved over thousands of years such that the basic shape and configuration of features is common to all faces (i.e., two eyes above a nose, which is above a mouth), there are still fine-grained differences between faces that allow us to identify someone we know. Fundamentally, we are able to perform this task because the presentation of a person's facial features is relatively permanent and changes little over time, making the face a reliable source of information about a person's identity.

The structure of the skull determines much of a person's facial appearance, and it is notable that forensic pathologists can accurately reconstruct a person's appearance from the skull alone. Specifically, the skull is structured such that the brain is contained within the eight plate-like bones of the cranium. Of these, the frontal bone influences facial appearance the most, by providing the structure of the forehead. Fourteen facial bones connect to the cranium and provide the framework for most of the face, including the provision of cavities for the eyes, nose, mouth and inner ear. Importantly, these include the mandible (the jaw bone), the maxilla (the upper jaw bone), the zygomatic bone (the cheek bone) and the nasal bones. Finally, cartilage and other soft tissue (including muscles, fat and skin) form shapes above this bone structure, contributing to the overall shape and spacing of the critical inner features of the face.

Thus, although we all share the same basic facial configuration, it can be seen that the shape and placement of the skull bones and the overlying facial tissue bring about differences in appearance. These differences are often subtle, yet the human brain possesses an advanced system that allows us to make fine-grained discriminations between large numbers of faces. Indeed, the processing of facial stimuli in our everyday lives is one of the most important functions of the human visual system, and is essential for successful social functioning. It is therefore not surprising that much research has examined the cognitive and neural mechanisms underpinning this process, resulting in the development of functional and neurological models of face recognition.

In this chapter, the cognitive mechanisms underpinning face processing are discussed, beginning with the dominant functional model posited by Bruce and Young (1986), and further developments of this theory. In the second part of the chapter, the visuo-cognitive processing strategies that are thought to be used in face recognition are described. It is important that you gain a good understanding of all the theories discussed in this chapter, as these concepts are repeatedly referred to throughout the book.

1.1. THE COGNITIVE ARCHITECTURE OF THE FACE-PROCESSING SYSTEM

1.1.1. The Bruce and Young (1986) functional model of face processing

The Bruce and Young (1986) model of face processing was partly developed from an earlier model posited by Hay and Young (1982). It aimed to accommodate findings that had emerged in cognitive studies of face processing using healthy participants, diary studies in which healthy participants reported the nature of everyday failures of face recognition, and neuropsychological case studies of individuals with various impairments in face processing. Importantly, Bruce and Young used these findings to identify seven different types of information that are used when we process faces, which are now described.

- *Pictorial codes.* These provide information related to the entire image that contains the face, rather than merely information about the face itself. This information can be used to aid recognition of that particular image, but is of little use when recognition of the face is tested using novel images or novel viewpoints of that individual. For this reason, researchers tend to assess memory for newly encoded faces using different images of target faces at study and test.
- *Expression codes.* These provide information about a person's affective state, and can be processed independently of face familiarity. That is, we do not need to be able to recognize a person to interpret how they are feeling from their facial expression.
- *Facial speech codes.* When we observe a person's face as they speak, we also interpret the movements of their mouth and tongue and integrate this information with what we hear. This additional visual information helps us to interpret what the person is saying.
- *Visually derived semantic codes.* These codes provide us with information about a person while simply perceiving their face: we do not need to recognize the person to derive this type of information. For instance, by mere examination of an unknown face, we can normally decide whether the person is male or

female, we can estimate their age, and we might make trait inferences about their personality or character (e.g., how trustworthy they are).

■ *Structural codes*. To recognize a face from a novel image (e.g., when the face is displayed from a different viewpoint or depicting a different expression), we need more abstract 'structural' information that is not dependent on the characteristics of a particular image. This type of information is thought to be required for recognition to occur.

■ *Identity-specific semantic codes*. This type of semantic information can only be accessed once we have recognized a particular face. For instance, you have to know that the person you bumped into in the supermarket is your brother's friend from work (but not necessarily his name) in order to recall his occupation, hobbies and favourite foods.

■ *Name codes*. These final codes provide the perceiver with the person's name. Importantly, this information is thought to be stored separately from identity-specific semantic codes, given we can recall biographical details about a person without knowledge of their name. For example, you might recall that the person you met in the supermarket works in the same office as your brother, without needing to know that his name is 'Bob' in order to access this information.

Based on the premise that these different types of information are used when we process faces, Bruce and Young proposed a cognitive model of face processing (see Figure 1.1). The model is a 'functional model' in that it adopts a box-and-arrow format that reduces each phase of processing to an independent stage that is handled separately by the brain. Specifically, the model suggests that an initial stage of processing extracts view-centred descriptions of the incoming facial stimulus. This information can be used to make a range of perceptual judgments that are not dependent on knowing a person's identity. For instance, this information can help with the discrimination of age, gender or emotional state, and can also be used to analyse facial speech or infer personality traits merely from the physical appearance of the face. Further, view-centred descriptions can be used to complete face-matching tasks, where participants are required to match simultaneously presented images of the same person, using the 'pictorial codes' described above.

However, to recognize a person from their face, a further set of processes need to be completed. In a phase termed *structural encoding*, Bruce and Young suggest the incoming facial representation is transformed from a view-centred description into a more abstract view-independent representation. Once this form of the representation has been created, it can be compared with all stored representations of known faces in the *face recognition units* (FRUs). If the incoming representation is matched to a stored representation, it can be inferred that the face belongs to a familiar individual, and the *person identity nodes* (PINs) associated with that individual are activated. This allows the perceiver to retrieve

Figure 1.1   *Bruce and Young's (1986) functional model of face processing.*

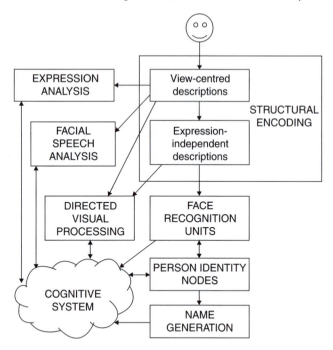

identity-specific semantic information about that person, such as their occupation and hobbies. Finally, the relevant *name information unit* is activated, such that the person's name can be retrieved independently of biographical information about that individual.

It is important to understand that functional models assume that each stage of processing occurs in a specific order, such that the overall process consists of a set of successive and hierarchical subprocesses. Further, it is not possible for a later stage of processing to occur when an earlier one has not yet been completed. The order in which Bruce and Young suggest each of the face-processing stages occurs was partly based on a diary study that reported everyday errors of face identification in healthy individuals (Young, Hay and Ellis, 1985). Specifically, participants reported that they only made certain types of error when recognizing faces, and other errors never occurred. For example, participants reported awareness that a person was familiar to them when they could not recall the context in which they knew that individual, but they did not experience the reverse pattern of impairment. Thus, this type of error suggests that semantic information can only be accessed once familiarity has been established, and therefore must occur at a later stage of processing. Another type of error that commonly occurred was when the perceiver could access biographical information about a person, yet could not recall their name. This error suggests that semantic and name information must be stored separately in the brain.

Critically, these descriptions of everyday errors in face processing received additional support from experimental studies that monitored reaction times while participants completed tasks that assessed each of the processing stages (e.g., Bruce, 1986; Young *et al.*, 1986a). Indeed, these studies found that reaction times were longer when participants were required to provide semantic or name information about a familiar face, compared with when they were asked to simply make familiarity or perceptual judgments about the target stimuli. Hence, these findings were interpreted as evidence that face processing could be separated into subprocesses that necessarily occur in a specific order.

Finally, strong evidence that supports the functional organization of the Bruce and Young model comes from neuropsychological cases studies of individuals with prosopagnosia, a selective deficit in face recognition that results from neurological trauma (Bodamer, 1947). Although individuals with prosopagnosia have a severe deficit in recognizing familiar individuals from their face, many prosopagnosics retain the ability to perform other aspects of face processing. Indeed, some individuals with prosopagnosia can make accurate perceptual judgments about faces, such as the interpretation of facial expression or the analysis of lip movements to help with speech interpretation. Importantly, such findings imply that these perceptual processes must be performed independently of face recognition.

This inference is given further weight by the existence of neuropsychological patients who present with the reverse pattern of impairment. These 'double dissociations' with prosopagnosia include patients who can recognize people from their faces but cannot interpret emotional expression (Kurucz and Feldmar, 1979) or use information from lip-reading to help with communication (Campbell, Landis and Regard, 1986). Based on these reports, the Bruce and Young model posits that certain aspects of face perception are processed independently of the face recognition pathway, such that damage to one aspect of processing does not impair other subprocesses of the model. A more thorough discussion of the contribution of prosopagnosia to the development of the Bruce and Young model can be read in Chapters 5 and 8; and the proposed functional separation of expression and identity processing is considered in more detail in Chapter 3.

In sum, the Bruce and Young model of face processing remains a dominant theory that is still widely referred to in today's literature, and has influentially directed face-processing research since its publication. As such, much work has attempted to develop the theory and clarify the workings of each subunit and its connections to other parts of the model. In particular, questions have been raised about both the model's ability to account for experimental findings of priming effects in face recognition, and differences in the processing of familiar and unfamiliar faces, and typical and distinctive faces. In the next three sections, theoretical developments of the model are discussed in reference to these issues.

1.1.2. The Interactive Activation and Competition (IAC) model

Burton, Bruce and Johnston (1990) developed an implementation of the Bruce and Young model as an IAC-type network model, based on theories that had previously been developed by McClelland and Rumelhart (1988). Specifically, the IAC model offers a computer simulation version of the face identification pathway hypothesized by Bruce and Young, with a more specific account of the manner in which the FRUs and PINs actually operate. Indeed, rather than assuming sequential completion of each stage of processing, the IAC model posits parallel activation of 'pools' of units that correspond to Bruce and Young's functional stages (i.e., the FRUs and PINs). In addition, the IAC model suggests a further stage of processing, which is represented by a pool of semantic identification units (SIUs). The model of Burton *et al.* therefore differs from that of Bruce and Young by positing that identity-specific biographical information is not stored within the PINs. Instead, the model assumes that once these units have been activated to a particular threshold, they indicate that a face is familiar. Consequently, access is provided to biographical information that is stored within the SIUs.

Further, the IAC model suggests that units within each of the pools are linked by bi-directional *inhibitory* connections (see Figure 1.2). Moreover, units that are associated with the same face but that are located within different pools are thought to be linked by bi-directional *excitatory* connections. According to the IAC model, an incoming facial representation is transformed to a view-independent representation, as suggested in Bruce and Young's model, and is compared with all stored representations within the FRUs. If a particular FRU is activated, all other FRUs stored within that pool are inhibited. The activated FRU in turn activates an associated PIN, and activation of this PIN inhibits activation of all other PINs within the pool. If that PIN activation reaches a particular threshold, familiarity is signalled, and the relevant SIUs are then activated.

In principle, the IAC model is thought to be able to account for behavioural priming effects. For instance, in *repetition priming*, a familiar face is recognized more rapidly if it has recently been seen (Bruce and Valentine, 1985). The IAC model accounts for this effect on the grounds that the initial presentation of the face will have strengthened the link between the FRU and associated PIN, such that it will take a shorter time for the PIN to be activated in successive presentations of that face. Further, the IAC model can also account for *semantic priming* effects, where a face is recognized more rapidly if the face of an associated person is presented immediately before the target face (e.g., Bruce and Valentine, 1986). For instance, an image of John Lennon's face might be recognized more rapidly after presentation of Paul McCartney's face. The IAC model can explain this effect on the assumption that the initial presentation of Paul McCartney's face activated the relevant FRU, PIN and SIUs. Because John Lennon and Paul

Figure 1.2 *The interactive activation and competition (IAC) model.*

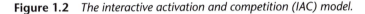

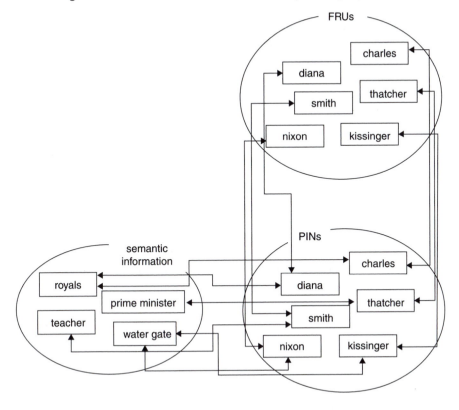

McCartney share some of the same SIUs, and links between the PINs and SIUs are bi-directional, John Lennon's PIN would also receive some activation upon presentation of his band-mate's face. Hence, when John Lennon's FRU is activated in response to presentation of his facial image, the associated PIN already has some residual activation and therefore reaches threshold for recognition at a faster rate than if the PIN had been at rest.

Finally, the IAC model has also been used to account for findings of covert (unconscious) recognition of faces in prosopagnosic participants. These findings are discussed in detail in Chapter 5.

1.1.3. Are familiar and unfamiliar faces processed in the same manner?

Cognitive studies of face recognition sometimes require participants to recognize highly familiar faces, such as those of celebrities or family members, whereas in other studies participants are asked to encode a set of faces they have never seen before for a later recognition task. Perhaps unsurprisingly, much evidence suggests that familiar and unfamiliar faces are processed in different ways. For instance, many studies have provided evidence to suggest that the inner facial features (the eyes, nose and mouth) are used to a greater extent in familiar face recognition, whereas the external features (e.g., the hair or face outline) are used to aid the recognition of newly encoded faces (Ellis, Shepherd and Davies, 1979). Further, the recognition of familiar faces is thought to be more resilient to changes in viewpoint, whereas the recognition of newly encoded faces tends to be easily disrupted when presented for recognition from a different angle (e.g., Bruce, Valentine and Baddeley, 1987).

These differences in the recognition of familiar and unfamiliar faces have been accounted for by another model that attempts to add detail to the early components of the model of Bruce and Young. Specifically, Burton and colleagues (2005) proposed the 'shape-averaging model of the FRUs', where a statistical technique known as principal components analysis creates an average representation of a particular face from multiple percepts of that person (see Figure 1.3). According to this theory, we store the average representation of a particular person in memory, and update the stored image each time we view the face. The outcome of this process is that, with increasing encounters with a face, its representation becomes richer and more robust, such that it is easier to recognize faces that we see more frequently.

According to this account, the recognition of familiar and unfamiliar faces is not a qualitatively different process; it simply differs according to the accuracy of the stored representation that is used for recognition. Further, this theory can explain why familiar face recognition uses the more stable inner features rather than the changeable external features. Indeed, the inner features tend to remain the same over time and are therefore preserved by the averaging process, whereas the external features are more likely to change (such as a person's hairstyle) and therefore are not reliable cues to identification. Burton *et al.* also suggest that the model could account for findings that familiar faces are easier to recognize across changes in viewpoint, by suggesting that more than one average representation can be created for each individual.

1.1.4. How might facial representations be organized within the FRUs?

Another prominent theory that is concerned with the nature of the FRUs is Valentine's (1991) multidimensional face space framework, which also attempts to explain how facial representations are stored in memory. Specifically, the model assumes that faces are metaphorically defined as points in a multidimensional space. That is, any characteristic that can be used to differentiate between faces is represented on an axis of face space, offering a scale along which the face can be encoded. For instance, one axis might be related to the length of the nose, whereas another might measure the distance between the eyes. The model assumes that individual faces are plotted in multidimensional face space

Figure 1.3 *An example of the 'principal components analysis' technique used by Burton and colleagues (2005).*

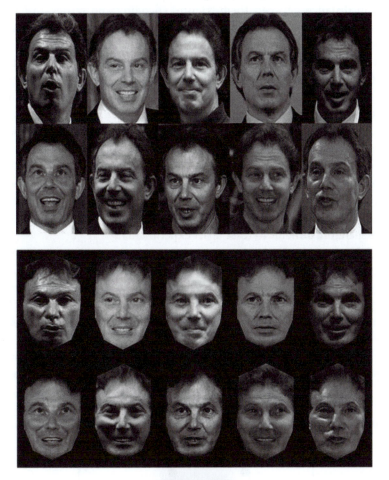

The top panel shows 10 original images of Tony Blair. In the middle panel these images have been adjusted to a standardized shape, and an average of the standardized images is displayed at the bottom of the figure.

according to their position on any number of these axes. Further, a key assumption of the model is that the similarity of two faces can be calculated as the Euclidean distance between them. Hence, encoding and retrieval of faces is influenced by the similarity of other faces stored in face space, such that nearby faces are more similar, and those that are further away are least similar.

There are two potential versions of Valentine's model (see Figure 1.4). It could be that faces are represented in terms of a deviation from a norm, such that all that is stored for each face is a vector that illustrates the direction and amount of distance from a 'prototype' or 'norm' face. On the other hand, the exemplar model suggests that each face is encoded according to its absolute value per dimension relative to other exemplars, and is therefore represented as a single point in multidimensional space without reference to a norm. Valentine posited his model as an attempt to explain the effects of distinctiveness, race and caricaturing in face recognition. As can be seen from the discussion below, the two versions of the model make very similar predictions about some of these effects, and are therefore difficult to tease apart experimentally.

First, it has been shown that it is easier to recognize more distinctive faces than more typical faces (e.g., Light, Kayra-Stuart and Hollander, 1979; Valentine and Bruce, 1986a), but that more distinctive faces are classified as 'faces' more slowly than typical faces in a face/non-face classification task (Valentine and Bruce, 1986b). Both the norm- and exemplar-based models offer similar explanations for these effects. Indeed, as most faces are typical, they cluster together in the centre of face space (either close to the norm or to other exemplars). Because there are many faces in a small area of space, it is easier to confuse typical faces

Figure 1.4   *The norm-based (a) and exemplar-based (b) versions of Valentine's (1991) Multidimensional Face Space Theory.*

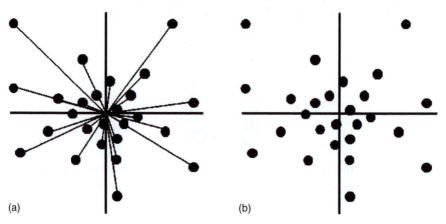

(a)   (b)

In the norm-based model, each face is plotted in relation to a norm or prototypical face. In the exemplar-based model, each face is plotted in relation to other faces.

with each other, making them harder to recognize. However, it is easier to classify these stimuli as faces given they are similar to most other faces that we
know. On the other hand, distinctive faces are scattered around the periphery
of face space in both models, with few neighbouring faces in nearby space.
Hence, it is easier to recognize a distinctive face as there are few neighbouring
faces of similar appearance. However, it is more difficult to classify these stimuli
as faces, given they are different to most faces stored in memory.

Although the two models offer similar explanations of the distinctiveness
effect, they do posit different accounts of the 'other-race effect', a robust psychological phenomenon characterized by the finding that we find it easier
to recognize faces from our own race than those from other races. Goldstein
and Chance (1980) used the norm-based model to offer an explanation of this
effect. Specifically, they suggested that the same level of dissimilarity between
two same-race faces and two other-race faces would be differently represented
in face space when placed in reference to the norm face. That is, because all
other-race faces are located further from the norm than all same-race faces, the
distance between other-race faces inevitably becomes smaller than if the same
distance was plotted closer to the norm face for same-race faces. This makes it
more difficult to distinguish between other-race faces than same-race faces. An
alternative exemplar-based account was offered by Valentine and Endo (1992),
who still found distinctiveness effects for other-race faces. The authors suggested
that other-race faces are encoded on the same axes as same-race faces, yet these
axes do not represent the characteristics that are most useful in distinguishing
between other-race faces. As such, it is very difficult to recognize other-race
faces because they vary on a completely different set of dimensions.

Finally, caricature effects have traditionally been used to support the norm-
based model. The process of caricaturing exaggerates facial features away from
the average of a prototypical face. An anti-caricature can also be produced
using the reverse procedure, making a face more similar to the prototype face.
It has been found that line-drawn caricatures are easier to recognize than the
unmanipulated face (e.g., Benson and Perrett, 1991, 1994; Rhodes, Brennan and
Carey, 1987), although smaller effects have been noted for photographic caricatures (Benson and Perrett, 1991). Norm-based models suggest the caricature
effect occurs because the exaggeration of distinctive features of a face increases
the space between that face and the norm face, while maintaining the direction
of that distance. It is thought this makes a face more distinctive while preserving the actual identity of the face.

Although it was originally thought that caricature effects could not be
explained without reference to a norm face, an exemplar-based explanation
was later offered by Lewis and Johnston (1999), based on the construction of
a Voronoi diagram (see Figure 1.5; for more information on this procedure see
Fortune, 1992). This procedure plots faces in face space in the manner described
above. Face space is then subdivided into different regions by bisecting the

Figure 1.5 *An example of a Voronoi diagram.*

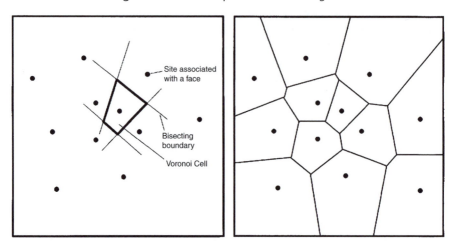

The panel on the left shows a Voronoi cell constructed in a two-dimensional space with 11 sites. Lines that bisect the space between each site and nearby sites are drawn onto the diagram, resulting in Voronoi cells. The panel on the right shows all the Voronoi cells associated with the 11 sites. Note that cells closer to the centre of the image are smaller and more frequent, and that the sites tend to be located away from the centre of their cells. It is this off-centre positioning that is thought to bring about the heightened recognition of caricatured facial images.

space between a face and its nearest neighbour, such that the region surrounding a particular face is closest to that face than to any of the neighbouring faces. This region is then stored in memory for each face, rather than the location of the face itself. The model assumes that when an incoming face is considered for recognition, the greatest activation will occur if the face can be placed in the centre of an identity region (i.e., for more distinctive faces that are located towards the periphery of face space), as neighbouring regions will receive less activation and provide less competition for recognition.

1.2. WHAT TYPE OF INFORMATION NEEDS TO BE EXTRACTED FROM A FACE FOR IT TO BE PROCESSED?

In the above discussion, the functional structure of the face-processing system was considered, with the workings and interconnections between individual components of this architecture. However, much further work has examined the nature of the information that is required by this system to process faces in an optimal manner. Together, this work has provided a rich body of evidence from a variety of paradigms, and it is generally agreed that we use a particular strategy to process faces that has been termed 'configural processing'.

This term essentially refers to our ability to put together the features of a face to process it as a whole, rather than processing each feature on an individual basis. The particular advantage of configural processing is that it takes into account the overall structure of the face, including the spatial distances between features. This provides the perceiver with more information than can be gathered from the use of featural information alone, and is thought to facilitate the recognition process.

It is important to note that two different terms are commonly used in the literature to refer to this type of processing, and these terms are often used interchangeably. Indeed, some authors refer to the strategy as 'configural processing', whereas others use the term 'holistic processing'. However, most researchers now adhere to the terminology proposed by Maurer and colleagues (Maurer, Le Grand and Mondloch, 2002), who suggested there are three types of configural processing. Specifically, the authors propose that *first-order relational processing* refers to the detection of the basic configuration of a face (i.e., two eyes above a nose above a mouth), whereas *second-order relational processing* is concerned with the processing of spatial distances between features. Finally, the authors define *holistic processing* as the interactive processing of face parts.

Much work has provided evidence for the use of configural processing in face recognition. Early evidence for the effect came from Galton (1879), who overlaid many different facial images on top of each other. Galton observed that the resulting image, although blurred, looked like a normal face rather than a combination of isolated features taken from different facial images. Indeed, given that all faces share the same common features, he interpreted this effect as evidence that faces are processed as a whole, with the spatial relationships between features providing individuating information that is crucial for recognition.

In more recent years, cognitive experiments have provided convincing evidence that configural processing is of particular use in face recognition. Given these paradigms have proven to be reliable and replicable demonstrations of the phenomenon, they have been adopted in numerous investigations that have examined whether configural processing is also impaired in individuals with face-processing deficits. Hence, it is important to gain a good understanding of the design of these experiments, as these paradigms are repeatedly considered throughout this book. The next section discusses each demonstration of configural processing in turn.

1.3. INVESTIGATIONS EXAMINING CONFIGURAL PROCESSING

1.3.1. The face inversion effect

The face inversion effect is perhaps the paradigm that has most often been used to investigate configural processing. The effect was first demonstrated by Yin (1969), who asked participants to memorize images of faces, planes, houses and stick figures. Memory of these stimuli was later tested, either from an upright or an inverted orientation. Importantly, Yin noted that inversion disrupted the recognition of faces, such that participants recognized more faces correctly from the upright rather than the inverted format. He suggested that this effect occurred because participants were no longer able to process the features of inverted faces as a whole, and instead had to rely on a suboptimal feature-by-feature strategy that resulted in a lower level of recognition performance. More recently, Goffaux and Rossion (2007) provided more specific evidence about the effects of inversion, by demonstrating that it impairs the perception of vertical distances between features.

Yin's findings were also used to draw additional conclusions about the nature of configural processing in face recognition. Specifically, although he found that inversion disrupted the recognition of all the categories of stimuli used in the study, Yin reported that the effect was much larger for faces than the other types of image. Indeed, participants were better at recognizing faces in their upright format compared with the other stimuli, but were worse at recognizing faces when they were inverted than they were for the other inverted images. Yin interpreted this finding as evidence that configural processing is more important in face recognition than in the recognition of other categories of visual stimuli. However, this conclusion is a topic of ongoing debate in the psychological literature, with some authors arguing that configural processing is only used to process faces, whereas others suggest that it is used to process all visual entities with which we have sufficient expertise. This question is considered in more detail in Chapter 4.

1.3.2. The Thatcher illusion

Another demonstration of the importance of configural processing in face recognition has been termed the 'Thatcher illusion'. Specifically, this effect was demonstrated by Thompson (1980), who modified a photographic image of Margaret Thatcher to invert the internal features of the face (the eyes, nose and mouth) while the rest of the image was retained in its upright format (see Figure 1.6). Participants were then asked to view the overall image in either an upright or inverted format, and to detect whether there were any abnormalities in the appearance of the face.

Thompson noted that participants were able to detect the unusual appearance of Margaret Thatcher in the upright image much more effectively than in the inverted image, such that the face was judged to be less 'grotesque' in the latter condition. This finding can be explained by the use of the optimal configural processing strategy for the upright but not the inverted image. Indeed, inversion is thought to reduce the perceiver's sensitivity to the spatial relations between the features and the rest of the face, and, as a result, it is much more difficult to detect minor differences that are essential for face recognition.

Figure 1.6   *The Thatcher illusion.*

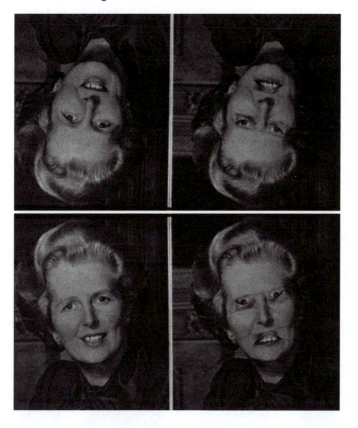

It is difficult to detect any differences between the two images when they are presented in an inverted format, whereas the 'grotesque' nature of the second image can easily be spotted in the upright format.

1.3.3. The composite effect

The importance of holistic processing in face recognition has been demonstrated using the composite effect. This paradigm was first used by Young, Hellawell and Hay (1987), who created a set of stimuli that were a combination of the upper half of one celebrity's face and the lower half of another celebrity's face. These halves were combined into one of two conditions: they were either aligned to create a whole face, or were misaligned. Further, they were presented to participants in either an upright or inverted format, and the authors asked participants to name the face shown in either the top or bottom half of the image. Interestingly, the authors found that response latencies were longer in the aligned condition, but only when the images were presented in an upright format.

The effect is explained by the automatic interference of the configural processing strategy in the upright-aligned condition. Indeed, a configural processing strategy can only be used when (a) faces are presented in an upright format, and (b) when the two halves of the face are presented in the expected facial format of the aligned condition. Hence, configural processing makes the recognition of only one half of the image more difficult in this condition, because the processing strategy essentially 'fuses' the two halves and processes them as a whole. The same effect is not noted in the inverted-aligned condition, given that inversion is known to disrupt configural processing.

After the original demonstration of the composite effect, several researchers have adapted the paradigm to investigate configural processing using novel faces. For instance Robbins and McKone (2007) presented participants with pairs of composite faces that were created using the faces of two different individuals (see Figure 1.7). In each pair the halves were either aligned or misaligned, and participants were required to decide whether one half of the face (the target half was counterbalanced across trials) was the same or different in identity. In all trials, the halves of the faces that were to-be-ignored were always of a different identity.

Figure 1.7 *Examples of composite face pairs used by Robbins and McKone (2007).*

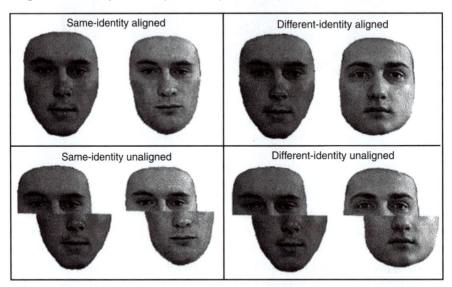

Trials where the top halves of the face are of the same identity are displayed in the panels on the left, and those that are of a different identity are on the right. The bottom halves of the faces are different in every trial. It is easier to decide whether the two top halves are the same or different in the mis-aligned (bottom row) than the aligned (top row) condition, presumably due to the automatic influence of configural processing when the two halves are aligned.

1.3.4. The part-whole effect

Another demonstration of the importance of holistic processing in upright face recognition is termed the 'part–whole effect' (Tanaka and Farah, 1993). These authors asked participants to encode images of faces and houses. In a later test phase, recall was assessed for parts of the faces or houses that were presented either in isolation (the 'part' condition), or within the original image (the 'whole' condition). As predicted by previous demonstrations of configural processing in upright faces, Tanaka and Farah found that, for facial stimuli, performance was better in the upright–whole condition compared with the other conditions. However, there was no comparable effect for houses.

1.3.5. A whole face is more than the sum of its parts

A different paradigm was used by Yovel, Paller and Levy (2005), who performed a face-matching task where faces were presented either in their whole format, or in right-half- or left-half-only conditions. The authors reasoned that, if the two halves of the face are processed independently, recognition performance for the two halves on their own should mirror accuracy in the whole condition when they are summed. If, however, the two halves are processed in an interactive manner, performance in the whole condition should be better than the combined performance in the two half conditions. As predicted, Yovel and colleagues noted the latter pattern of performance, but only for upright and not inverted faces.

1.3.6. Spacing effects

Finally, other investigations have examined second-order relational processing, or sensitivity towards the spacing of facial features. These studies suggest that we are particularly adept at detecting minor adjustments in the spacing of facial features, but only for upright and not inverted faces (e.g., Haig, 1984).

A more recent investigation of this hypothesis was performed by Freire, Lee and Symons (2000), who asked participants to judge whether two consecutively presented faces were the same or different. The authors applied two manipulations to their stimuli. First, faces were presented in either an upright or inverted orientation. Second, some of the pairs had identical features that differed in their spacing, whereas the features in other pairs were different but spaced in an identical manner. In line with previous demonstrations of configural processing, the authors observed a larger inversion effect for the pairs that differed in their spatial relations compared with those that differed in the presentation of their features. Thus, they concluded that faces are processed on the basis of information extracted about the location rather than the shape of their features.

However, the findings reported in the study of Freire *et al.* have been questioned, particularly given that the manipulations applied to the stimuli also brought about changes in image contrast and brightness, and this information could have been used to cue recognition. Indeed, later studies that did control for such effects failed to find differences in the size of the inversion effects for part and spacing conditions, suggesting they are processed by the same mechanisms. For instance, Yovel and Kanwisher (2004) found that the matching of upright faces was similar in both spacing and part conditions, but there was no such correlation for inverted faces or upright and inverted houses. Hence, the authors concluded that face-processing mechanisms extract information about both spacing and parts, but the two types of information are processed independently, perhaps by more general object processing mechanisms.

1.4. THE DUAL-ROUTE HYPOTHESIS

As illustrated by the above discussion, the importance of configural information in face processing has been well documented. However, it is also evident that although configural processing seems to be the optimal strategy used to process faces, recognition can still proceed when this strategy is not available to the perceiver. That is, we can still recognize faces on the basis of featural information alone, although performance might be less efficient. This pattern of findings has been interpreted as evidence that there are in fact two routes that are used in face recognition: the optimal configural processing route, and a suboptimal featural pathway.

Evidence that supports this dual-route hypothesis comes from a study that was performed by Collishaw and Hole (2000). These authors applied a series of manipulations to faces that were presented to participants in a face recognition test. Specifically, the authors disrupted configural processing by either inverting or scrambling the faces. Although the effects of inversion have already been discussed, it is thought that scrambling facial features preserves featural information but prevents the perceiver from putting these features together to process the overall configuration of the face. Further, the authors blurred some of their facial stimuli, preserving configural information but removing the more detailed featural information. Collishaw and Hole reasoned that, if there really are two routes to recognition, recognition should still be possible when either configural (i.e., the inverted and scrambled conditions) or featural (i.e., the blurred condition) information is removed from the stimuli. Their findings supported this hypothesis, and additionally revealed that, when faces were both blurred and inverted or scrambled (presumably removing both configural and featural information), participants were merely guessing when they attempted to recognize the faces.

Further evidence supporting the dual-route hypothesis comes from neuropsychological studies of individuals with prosopagnosia. Indeed, several studies have failed to find evidence of a face inversion effect in their prosopagnosic participants, suggesting that the impairment might be attributable to a failure in configural processing (see Chapter 5 for a more thorough discussion of these findings). Further, some authors have reported an 'inverted inversion effect', where individuals with prosopagnosia perform at a lower level than control participants in the recognition of upright faces, but outperform controls in recognizing inverted faces. An explanation for this pattern of findings that is compatible with the dual-route hypothesis has been offered by de Gelder and Rouw (2000b). These authors suggest that configural processing might only be partly impaired in individuals with prosopagnosia, such that a damaged configural processing mechanism still attempts to process upright faces, but fails to do so effectively. However, for inverted faces, all perceivers have to use the featural processing route. Importantly, this route is not only preserved in individuals with prosopagnosia, but they are also more accustomed to using this strategy than control participants, accounting for their superior recognition of inverted faces.

CHAPTER SUMMARY

■ Bruce and Young (1986) proposed a functional model of face processing based on evidence from diary-studies and cognitive experiments using healthy participants, and neuropsychological case studies. The model suggests that face processing can be reduced to a sequential and hierarchical set of subprocesses.

■ Other researchers have further developed the Bruce and Young model since its original conception, to provide more detail about the workings of its subprocesses and their inter-relations. For example, the IAC model (Burton, Bruce and Johnston, 1990) provides a computer simulation version of the identification pathway, to account for behavioural priming effects observed in experimental investigations. Further, the shape-averaging model of the FRUs of Burton *et al.* (2005) attempts to account for differences in the processing of familiar and unfamiliar faces; and Valentine's (1991) multidimensional face space framework provides a hypothesis of how facial representations might be organized in the FRUs.

■ Other studies have examined the nature of the information that is required by the face-processing system, and identified three different types of configural information. Specifically, these refer to the processing of first- and second-order relational information, and holistic processing (Maurer, Le Grand and Mondloch, 2002).

■ There have been many experimental demonstrations that support the importance of configural processing in face recognition. However, it seems that a suboptimal featural strategy can also be used to process faces (the dual-route hypothesis: Collishaw and Hole, 2000), which is supported by both experimental evidence and reports of an 'inverted inversion effect' in some individuals with prosopagnosia.

FURTHER READING

Bruce, V. and Young, A. (1986) 'Understanding Face Recognition', *British Journal of Psychology,* 77, 305–27.

Burton, A. M., Bruce, V. and Johnston, R. A. (1990) 'Understanding Face Recognition with an Interactive Activation Model', *British Journal of Psychology,* 81, 361–80.

Burton, A. M., Jenkins, R., Hancock, P. B. J. and White, D. (2005) 'Robust Representations for Face Recognition', *Cognitive Psychology,* 51, 256–84.

De Gelder, B. and Rouw, R. (2000) 'Paradoxical Configuration Effects for Faces and Objects in Prosopagnosia', *Neuropsychologia,* 38, 1271–9.

Maurer, D., Le Grand, R. and Mondloch, C. J. (2002) 'The Many Faces of Configural Processing', *Trends in Cognitive Science,* 6, 255–60.

Valentine, T. (1991) 'A Unified Account of the Effects of Distinctiveness, Inversion and Race in Face Recognition', *Quarterly Journal of Experimental Psychology,* 43A, 161–204.

GUIDANCE QUESTIONS

Use the following questions to guide your reading of this chapter and the recommended papers.

1. What are the characteristics of a 'functional model' in cognitive neuropsychology? Discuss with reference to Bruce and Young's model of face processing.
2. Although Bruce and Young's model proved to have a lasting impact on the course of face-processing research, are there any weaknesses associated with it? Have more recent models overcome these issues?
3. What are the different types of configural processing, how have they been demonstrated and how are they used in face recognition?
4. What is the 'inverted inversion effect' and how has this finding contributed to our knowledge about the processing strategies used in face recognition?

2 The Cognitive Neuroscience of Face Processing

In the last chapter, behavioural investigations that have informed our understanding of the workings of the face-processing system were discussed. Although this evidence has been invaluable in developing our knowledge about how we recognize faces, more recent studies have used a range of neuroscientific techniques to further our understanding about the neural systems that underpin these effects. In the current chapter, each of these methodologies is discussed in turn, together with key findings that are thought to explain how the neurological face-processing system operates. The chapter culminates with the description of a recent neurological model of face processing, which pulls together the evidence reported in neuroscientific investigations.

2.1. NEUROSCIENTIFIC METHODOLOGIES USED TO INVESTIGATE FACE PROCESSING

2.1.1. Single-cell recording

Early studies used a procedure termed 'single-cell recording' to examine the neurological basis of face processing. This methodology measures the electrophysiological responses of a single neuron, and the resultant data can be used to provide an insight into the topographical mapping of the human cortex. Such studies were used to explore the neurological basis of face processing in monkeys in the 1970s and 1980s (for a review see Gross, 2005), and reported the existence of cells in the superior temporal sulcus (STS) and inferior temporal cortex that mostly only responded to facial stimuli (e.g., Gross, Rocha-Miranda and Bender, 1972). These findings were interpreted as early evidence supporting the existence of a face-specific neural system. Later studies investigated whether specific cells in these regions only respond to certain facial images. Interestingly, Perrett and his colleagues found that some cells responded to facial images of all sizes and viewpoints (e.g., Perrett, Rolls and Caan, 1982), whereas others only responded to faces presented from particular viewpoints (e.g., Perrett *et al.*, 1992).

2.1.2. Event-related potentials (ERPs)

ERPs measure a scalp electrical response that is time-locked to a given stimulus. This electrical activity is generated when neurons within certain brain areas are communicating with each other by the transmission of electrical signals. These signals can be recorded using a series of electrodes that are placed on the scalp, and it has been found that when we process faces, activity occurs in certain neural areas at specific time intervals after stimulus onset. These activations are referred to as 'responses' or 'components', and have been used to tell us (a) how rapidly brain activity occurs in response to a stimulus, (b) how much activity there is and (c) roughly where in the brain this occurs. Thus, ERPs are named according to the direction of the potential (positive or negative), and the time in milliseconds (ms) at which the activity peaks after stimulus presentation.

Three ERP components have been identified that are particularly important in face processing, and the order in which these components have been found to occur provides supporting evidence for Bruce and Young's (1986) sequential model of face processing. Specifically, the N170 component is thought to represent processing at the level of structural encoding, the N250 corresponds to the actual identification of a face and the N400 is thought to reflect the access of semantic or biographical information about a familiar person.

By far, most research has examined the N170, and many studies investigating individuals with disorders of face processing have examined whether this response is present or absent in neuropsychological participants. In part, this is because many studies have provided evidence of the existence of the N170, and hence it is a reliable and robust finding. For instance, much evidence has suggested that the N170 only occurs in response to facial stimuli (Bentin *et al.*, 1996; Eimer, 2000), and several studies have shown that the component is larger and occurs slightly later when a face is inverted (e.g., Jacques, d'Arripe and Rossion, 2007).

Early evidence suggested that the N170 reflects the structural encoding of a face, given it does not differ according to either familiarity or gender (e.g., Bentin and Deouell, 2000). Indeed, according to Bruce and Young's sequential model, these processes only occur after structural encoding is complete. However, there is some evidence against this hypothesis. For example, Tanaka and Porterfield (2002) found an increase in the N170 when participants view their own face, suggesting some information related to facial identity might be processed at this stage. Further, other studies have found a reduction in the N170 for repeated presentations of the same face (e.g., Itier and Taylor, 2004; Jacques and Rossion, 2004), although a similar effect was not found by Yovel and colleagues (2003). However, these findings suggest that, under some circumstances, identity information can be processed as rapidly as 170 ms after stimulus onset.

2.1.3. Magnetoencephalography (MEG)

MEG provides a similar measure to ERPs, but measures the magnetic fields produced by electrical activity in the brain, and provides more information about the location of these effects. Interestingly, MEG studies provide evidence that supports the existence of the N170, by finding a similar face-selective negative component that also appears 170 ms after stimulus onset, and that is delayed for inverted faces (Liu *et al.*, 2000). This component has been termed the 'M170'.

In line with some findings reported in ERP experiments, investigations using MEG have also found that information about facial identity might be processed at this early stage. For example, it has been found that the M170 is larger for personally familiar than unfamiliar faces, particularly over the right hemisphere (e.g., Harris and Aguirre, 2008); and another study reported a strong positive correlation between performance in a face recognition test and the amplitude of the M170 response (Tanskanen *et al.*, 2007).

Further evidence supporting an early influence of facial identification was provided in a study reported by Liu, Harris and Kanwisher (2002). These authors examined whether performance on a face recognition test correlated with the amplitude of the M170 and the M100, another early component that is thought to represent the behavioural detection of a facial stimulus. Interestingly, although the M100 was not found to be sensitive to performance on the face recognition task, this measure was found to modulate the size of the M170.

However, some differences have been noted between the N170 and M170. For example, the delayed M170 that Liu *et al.* (2000) noted in response to inverted faces did not differ in amplitude to that observed for upright faces, whereas this has been reported for the N170 in ERP studies. Further, it has also been found that the amplitude of the M170 is similar over both the right and left hemispheres, whereas several groups of authors have noted that the N170 is larger over the right hemisphere (e.g., Henson *et al.*, 2002; Yovel *et al.*, 2003). Thus, although there appear to be some similarities in the nature of the N170 and M170 responses, there are also key differences between them.

2.1.4. Functional magnetic resonance imaging (fMRI)

fMRI is a neuroimaging technique that assesses the level of activation in different areas of the brain, by measuring the 'blood oxygenation level dependent' (BOLD) effect. The BOLD effect refers to changes in blood flow and oxygen consumption in a particular region of the brain, in response to a need for more oxygen following localized activation of neurons. Participants taking part in an fMRI study normally complete a computerized cognitive test while they lie within a scanner. Studies that have examined the neural regions used in face processing have consistently reported activation in three main areas of the brain (see Figure 2.1): a lateral occipital region known as the occipital face area (OFA), an area in the temporal lobes known as the 'fusiform face area' (FFA) and

Figure 2.1   *Brain areas that are implicated in face perception.*

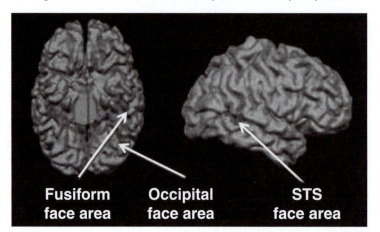

The left-hand image displays the brain from underneath, and the locations of the FFA and OFA are indicated in the right hemisphere. The image on the right shows the right hemisphere from the side view, and indicates the location of the face-responsive region in posterior STS.

a region in the posterior STS. Findings that relate to each of these three areas are now discussed in turn.

OFA. Although fewer investigations have examined the role of the OFA in face processing, it seems that the region might be responsible for the early processing of facial stimuli, perhaps corresponding to the structural encoding stage of Bruce and Young's functional model. Indeed, several studies have suggested that the OFA represents face parts before subsequent processing of more complex aspects of the face, and before configural processing occurs (Pitcher, Walsh and Duchaine, 2011). For example, Liu and colleagues performed a study where participants viewed stimuli in which face parts were either present or absent, and were presented with a normal or scrambled configuration. The authors found that the size of the BOLD response in the OFA was larger for stimuli that contained face parts compared with those that did not, but the effect did not differ between the scrambled and normal stimuli (Liu, Harris and Kanwisher, 2010). Hence, the OFA appears to be sensitive to the parts of a face rather the spacing of those parts, and seems to preferentially represent the physical structure and components of facial stimuli.

FFA. The FFA is a neural region within the temporal lobes that appears to respond specifically to faces (Kanwisher, McDermott and Chun, 1997; McCarthy *et al.*, 1997). For example, Kanwisher, McDermott and Chun (1997) monitored brain activity while participants viewed upright faces, upright faces displayed in profile, scrambled faces, hands, objects and houses. The authors noted regions in the fusiform gyrus that were only activated in response to faces, and they interpreted this finding as evidence for a specialized neural area dedicated to face processing. In another study, Yovel and Kanwisher (2005) compared activation levels in the FFA between pairs of images that depicted faces of the same or different individuals. Interestingly, these authors noted an increased response in the FFA to pairs of different faces, suggesting the region might specifically be responsible for processing face familiarity. In addition, further studies have provided evidence that the FFA is also selectively activated in response to the visual imagery of faces, but not other categories of objects (e.g., O'Craven and Kanwisher, 2000; Cox, Meyers and Sinha, 2004).

It is also of interest that other studies suggest configural processing might also be underpinned by the FFA. For example, the region shows increased activation for upright compared with inverted faces, whereas neural areas thought to be responsible for object processing show the reverse effect (e.g., Yovel and Kanwisher, 2005; Schiltz and Rossion, 2006). Further studies have examined neural activation in the FFA while participants complete the composite face task (see Chapter 1), and report greater activation for aligned than misaligned upright faces, suggesting the FFA might also be responsible for holistic processing mechanisms.

STS. Several studies have suggested that, although the FFA appears to be responsible for the processing of facial identity, the STS is responsible for processing other aspects of faces, such as gaze direction and emotional expression. For instance, Hoffman and Haxby (2000) reported evidence that suggests a dissociation between the STS and FFA. Specifically, they noted greater activation in the FFA when participants processed faces according to their familiarity rather than their gaze direction, but the reverse pattern of findings in the STS. Converging findings were reported by Grill-Spector, Knouf and Kanwisher (2004), who found that face recognition performance did not correlate with activation levels in the STS. These findings led Haxby and colleagues to suggest that the FFA might be responsible for processing those aspects of faces that are non-changeable, such as identity and gender, whereas the STS might process changeable aspects of faces, such as expression and the direction of eye gaze (Haxby, Hoffman and Gobbini, 2000).

In sum, these three face-selective regions appear to have different roles in the processing of facial stimuli. Further, it has been suggested that the three regions represent the core components of the neural face-processing system, and have been encompassed in a recent neurological model of face processing that was first proposed by Haxby *et al.* (2000) and later modified by Gobbini and Haxby (2007). Before this model is described in the final section of the chapter, recent findings from an alternative methodology that provide collaborating evidence for neuroimaging findings are discussed.

2.1.5. Transcranial magnetic stimulation (TMS)

Recent studies have used TMS to investigate the neural regions implicated in face processing. Specifically TMS has been used with healthy participants to induce a 'virtual' lesion to a particular area of the brain, by the deliverance of an electromagnetic pulse through that cortical region. The experimenter produces this pulse by generating an electrical current through a metal coil. The current rapidly changes its magnetic field, and when the coil is placed on a participant's scalp, it causes cell membranes to depolarize, raising the resting membrane potential of some neurons. After neural disruption, experimenters commonly ask participants to complete processing tasks using standard measures of reaction time and accuracy to assess any changes in performance. One particular advantage of this method is that participants can act as their own controls by taking part in the same test without TMS involvement.

A further advantage of TMS is that, similar to studies of patients, it can demonstrate that a particular region is *necessary* for face processing, whereas other neuroscientific methods can only provide information about the location of face-processing areas in the brain, and the timing of their involvement. Further, TMS avoids the limiting factors that present in patient studies by removing potential confounds such as individual differences in premorbid abilities, and the effect of any cortical remapping that might have occurred following the injury.

Unfortunately, not all face-selective regions that have been identified in fMRI studies can be accessed by TMS, including the FFA. Further, little work has examined the influence of TMS on the STS. In one study, however, TMS to the right STS was found to disrupt the perception of eye gaze direction but not emotional expression (Pourtois *et al.*, 2004), supporting the suggestion that the STS is implicated in gaze processing (Haxby *et al.*, 2000).

More studies have used TMS to disrupt processing in the OFA. For instance, Pitcher *et al.* (2009) reported that delivery of TMS over the right OFA disrupted the discrimination of faces but not objects or bodies, providing further evidence that this neural region is face-selective. Pitcher *et al.* (2007) performed a further study where participants were required to discriminate between faces that differed according either their face parts (i.e., specific features) or in the spacing between features; and houses were also used as control stimuli under the same manipulation. The authors found that, when TMS was delivered over the right OFA, discrimination of only the faces in the part condition was disrupted. In a second experiment, Pitcher and colleagues asked participants to perform the same task, but delivered TMS in six different time windows after stimulus onset: 20–60 ms, 60–100 ms, 100–140 ms, 130–170 ms, 170–210 ms and 210–250 ms. These windows were selected so that the TMS pulses coincided with the M100 and N170/M170, as identified in the ERP and MEG studies described above. Interestingly, participants only became impaired at the task when the pulse was delivered in the 60–100 ms window, supporting previous evidence that the OFA processes face parts at an early stage of the recognition process.

2.2. A NEUROLOGICAL MODEL OF FACE PROCESSING

Gobbini and Haxby's (2007) neurological model subdivides face processing into two systems (see Figure 2.2). First, the authors suggest there is a core system, containing the FFA, STS and OFA, that is responsible for the visual analysis of faces. Based on the evidence described above, it is suggested that the OFA is responsible for early visual processing and the encoding of the basic visual appearance of the face. Subsequently, the FFA processes non-changeable aspects of the face such as identity and gender, whereas the STS processes changeable aspects of the face such as expression and eye gaze direction. Thus, the model has a branching structure that distinguishes between the processing of identity and the perception of changeable aspects of the face that facilitate social communication.

Second, Gobbini and Haxby suggest there is an extended system that interacts with the core system. Specifically, neural structures that access person-specific semantic and biographical knowledge are thought to interact with the FFA in further processing facial identity. These structures include the anterior paracingulate and the posterior STS/temporal parietal junction; and the precuneus is thought to be involved in the retrieval of episodic memories. Further, the amygdala, insula and striatum have been associated with the representation of different emotions, and activation within these areas has been shown to be

Figure 2.2   *Gobbini and Haxby's (2007) distributed model of face processing.*

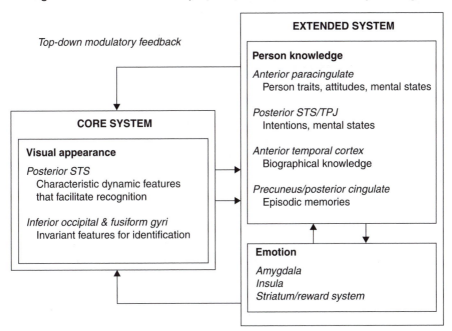

modulated by face familiarity (e.g., Gobbini *et al.*, 2004). Gobbini and Haxby suggest these areas process our emotional response to a familiar individual, including their current affective state.

Although this model appears at first sight to provide a tight neurological basis to Bruce and Young's functional model of face processing, it is important to note that there are some critical differences in its assumptions. First, Gobbini and Haxby's model suggests a more general system is responsible for processing all changeable aspects of a face (e.g., expression, eye gaze and lip speech), whereas Bruce and Young posit independent systems for each of these processes. Second, the neurological model assumes that face processing is an interactive process that integrates information from neural regions that process the physical configuration of faces with those that process the meaning of that configuration. For example, the model suggests that the STS processes the arrangement of the facial features to extract the expression displayed on a face, whereas the extended emotion system processes the actual meaning of that expression.

Hence, the functional roles related to a particular cognitive process are not reduced to single 'boxes' as in the Bruce and Young model; rather, they involve the concerted activity of a variety of neural areas that all contribute to that function. In addition, these regions can participate in more than one cognitive process by interacting with other systems within the model. For example, intraparietal regions have been shown to be involved in the perception of eye gaze direction, but also direct spatial attention according to other non-visual cues. Thus, Gobbini and Haxby's distributed model of face processing posits an interactive system, as opposed to the functionally disparate system proposed by Bruce and Young.

CHAPTER SUMMARY

■ Several different methodologies have been used to investigate the neural underpinnings of the face-processing system, and converging evidence has been produced by these different types of investigation.

■ Studies that have used ERPs or MEG differ in whether they measure electrical or magnetic responses produced by the human brain, but both methods have consistently revealed the existence of the N170 (Bentin *et al.*, 1996; Eimer, 2000) or M170 (Liu *et al.*, 2000) component that appears to reflect the structural encoding stage of face processing. There is conflicting evidence, however, about whether identity information influences this early stage of processing (e.g., Liu, Harris and Kanwisher, 2002; Tanaka and Porterfield, 2002).

■ fMRI studies have revealed three key areas in the brain that participate in face processing. The OFA appears to be involved in the very early visual analysis of a face that encodes part-based information (Pitcher, Walsh and Duchaine, 2011), whereas the FFA is responsible for processing facial identity (Kanwisher *et al.*, 1997). Finally, much evidence suggests the STS processes the social aspects of faces, such as emotional expression and eye gaze direction (Hoffman and Haxby, 2000).

■ Recent TMS studies have investigated processing in the OFA, and provide converging evidence that this region encodes part-based information at an early stage of processing (Pitcher *et al.*, 2007, 2009). Unfortunately, the FFA is unavailable to TMS, and little work so far has investigated the STS using this method.

■ Gobbini and Haxby (2007) posited a distributed model of face processing that represents these three areas as players in a 'core system' responsible for the visual analysis of facial stimuli. This system interacts with an extended system that provides biographical information about familiar people, and processes the social and emotional meaning of the physical information extracted from a face.

FURTHER READING

Eimer, M. (2000) 'The Face-Specific N170 Component Reflects Late Stages in the Structural Encoding of Faces', *Neuroreport,* 11, 2319–24.

Gobbini, M. I. and Haxby, J. V. (2007) 'Neural Systems for Recognition of Familiar Faces', *Neuropsychologia,* 45, 32–41.

Gobbini, M. I., Leibenluft, E., Santiago, N. and Haxby, J. V. (2004) 'Social and Emotional Attachment in the Neural Representation of Faces', *NeuroImage,* 22, 1628–35.

Gross, C. G. (2005) 'Processing the Facial Image: A Brief History', *American Psychologist,* 60, 755–63.

Kanwisher, N., McDermott, J. and Chun, M. (1997) 'The Fusiform Face Area: A Module in Human Extrastriate Cortex Specialized for Face Perception', *Journal of Neuroscience,* 17, 4302–11.

Pitcher, D., Walsh, V. and Duchaine, B. (2011). 'The Role of the Occipital Face Area in the Cortical Face Perception Network', *Experimental Brain Research,* 209, 481–93.

GUIDANCE QUESTIONS

Use the following questions to guide your reading of this chapter and the recommended papers.

1. What are the key features of each of the neuroscientific methods that have been used to investigate the neurological structure of the face-processing system?

2. What is the N170 response, and what is the evidence to suggest that this ERP component reflects processing at the 'structural encoding' level of Bruce and Young's model?
3. Which areas of the brain have been revealed by fMRI studies to be particularly involved in face processing?
4. What are the main features of Gobbini and Haxby's neurological model of face processing? To what extent is this model an extension of Bruce and Young's functional model?

3 The Social Value of the Face

In the previous chapter, the neurological model of face processing proposed by Gobbini and Haxby (2007) was discussed. Importantly, in addition to accounting for face identification, this model encompasses mechanisms that are responsible for processing social aspects of the face, including emotional expression and eye gaze direction. Clearly these are important sources of social information that guide our interactions with other people. In this chapter, the literature surrounding these aspects of face perception is reviewed, culminating in a discussion about how this information might be integrated with our perceptions of facial attractiveness to provide us with an ongoing complex assessment of the intentions and wishes of those people around us.

3.1. EMOTIONAL EXPRESSION

Interpreting the emotional expression displayed on the face of others is critical for successful social interaction. Perhaps because this process is such a fundamental part of our everyday lives, it has received much attention in the literature over the past few decades. In this section, two key issues that have been hotly debated in the psychological literature are discussed. First, the cultural universality of emotional expression recognition is considered, followed by a discussion concerned with the proposed independence of facial expression and facial identity recognition, as hypothesized in the functional model posited by Bruce and Young (1986).

3.1.1. Is the processing of emotional expression universal?

A key question that has been examined in the literature on emotional expression asks whether the processing of facial expression is universal across all cultures, or whether individuals from different cultures produce and interpret particular expressions in a varying manner. Indeed, if the same expressions can be interpreted by individuals from a wide range of cultures, the process may be innate and common to all human beings. Alternatively, if there are marked differences between cultures, the expression and perception of facial emotion may be a learned process.

This issue has been extensively examined by Ekman and his colleagues. In an early study, Ekman, Sorenson and Friesen (1969) tested participants from five literate cultures (the USA, Japan, Brazil, Chile and Argentina) on their ability to recognize six different expressions: anger, disgust, fear, happiness, sadness and surprise (see Figure 3.1). The authors hypothesized that the processing of facial expression might be universal, and this could be attributed to the relationship between distinctive patterns of the movement of facial muscles and particular emotional expressions. As predicted, Ekman *et al.* reported a high level of accuracy across all the participants, indicating that the processing of emotional expression might indeed be universal. However, this study was limited because it only examined the process in participants from literate, well-developed cultures, and thus it was perhaps unsurprising that a high level of agreement was reached across participants.

In a later study, Ekman and Friesen (1971) tested participants from the Fore tribe in New Guinea, a preliterate isolated culture that had very little contact with people from other cultures. However, the authors used a different methodology to assess the processing of facial expression in these participants. Specifically,

Figure 3.1   *Images of the six basic emotional expressions (anger, disgust, fear, happiness, sadness and surprise) identified by Ekman and colleagues.*

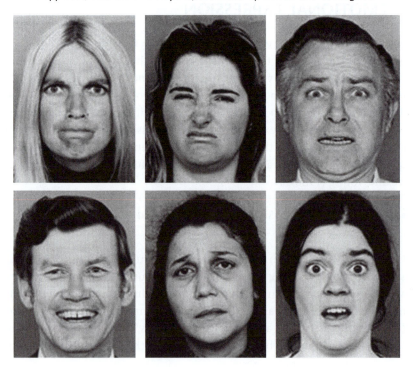

they read the participants a short passage that described a particular emotional situation, such as, 'His friends have come and he is happy', or 'His child has died and he feels very sad'. Participants were then asked to express the emotion that they thought was appropriate for that situation, and these expressions were video-taped by the authors. In further support of their hypothesis for universal processing of facial expression, Ekman and Friesen found that the expressions displayed by the New Guinean participants were very similar to those displayed by American participants in response to the same situations. Further, the American participants were also able to identify correctly the expressions displayed by the New Guinean participants.

Further evidence that the processing of emotional expression might be universal comes from studies that have examined the process in other species. For example, Da Costa and colleagues (2004) presented sheep with pairs of stimuli that displayed either two human faces or two sheep faces, and one face in each pair displayed a positive expression and the other a negative expression. The authors found that the sheep preferred to look at the positive faces in 80 per cent of the trials, and this effect did not differ between the human and sheep pairs. They interpreted this finding as evidence that there is at least some degree of universality in the processing of facial expression.

Additional support for the universality hypothesis comes from a recent meta-analysis that considered data from 97 investigations (Elfenbein and Ambady, 2002). In support of the work by Ekman and colleagues, the authors found strong evidence for the universality of emotional expression processing, with only three per cent of studies providing evidence of below-chance recognition of a particular emotional expression. Interestingly, the review also reported some evidence for an own-group advantage in the recognition of emotional expressions, such that participants tended to be more accurate when interpreting facial expressions displayed by individuals from their own culture as opposed to those from other cultures. A similar advantage has also been reported for cat-lovers and basketball players, who are more accurate than control participants at recognizing the expressions displayed by cats or basketball players, respectively (e.g., Thibault, Bougeois and Hess, 2006). Hence, these findings suggest that the same basic emotions may be common to all cultures, yet we seem to be more accurate at recognizing these expressions when they are displayed by individuals from our own culture.

It has been suggested that this in-group advantage in expression recognition can be attributed to either language differences between cultures, or to cultural variations in the 'display' or 'decoding' rules that provide conscious management of the production of universal facial expressions (Ekman, 1971). Indeed, these 'social norms' might intensify, diminish, neutralize or mask the display of particular expressions that would otherwise be produced automatically. However, carefully balanced experimental designs have countered such claims, as have findings such as those described by Thibault *et al.* (2006). Indeed, these authors found inter-group differences in the recognition of facial expressions between individuals from the same culture, suggest decoding-rule explanations are unlikely to account for the effect.

An alternative explanation for in-group differences in the recognition of emotional expressions suggests the bias might be attributed to 'non-verbal accents': subtle differences in the expression of emotions between groups and cultures that go beyond display-rules (Elfenbein and Ambady, 2003b). For instance, Elfenbein and colleagues (2007) reported that individuals from Canada and those from the west–central African country of Gabon used different facial muscles to pose the same expression. Further, the same authors provided evidence that the accuracy of emotion recognition across nations appears to be related to the distance between the country of the perceiver and that of the individual displaying the expression (Elfenbein and Ambady, 2003a). Specifically, accuracy was greater when there was a short distance between the nation of the perceiver and the expresser, but reduced as this distance increased.

Finally, although there appears to be strong evidence supporting the claim that the processing of facial expression is universal to all cultures, there are some methodological limitations with studies that have investigated this issue. Specifically, Russell (1994) raised the concern that accuracy in emotional expression recognition reduces when participants are asked to recognize spontaneous rather than posed expressions, and early experimental work supports this hypothesis (e.g., Motley and Camden, 1988). Further findings supporting the concern were provided in a more recent study, where American participants were asked to interpret the spontaneously produced facial expressions displayed by New Guinean participants (see Naab and Russell, 2007). These authors found that, although overall performance on the task was above chance, it was inaccurate for more than half of the expressions. Hence, there may be less universality in the recognition of spontaneously produced expressions than the posed expressions that have been used in most studies.

3.1.2. Are expression and identity processing truly independent?

A second topic that has prompted much debate in the literature on emotional expression concerns the proposed independence of the identity and expression pathways, as hypothesized in Bruce and Young's (1986) functional model of face processing (see Chapter 1). Bruce and Young proposed this functional separation of the two processes on the basis of experimental findings using healthy participants. For example, familiarity and repetition priming appears to facilitate the processing of identity but not expression (Young et al., 1986b; Ellis, Young and Flude, 1990), and participants are able to selectively attend to either identity or emotion without much interference from the irrelevant stimulus dimension (Etcoff, 1984). Further, the ability to recognize an emotional expression is not influenced by the familiarity of a face, and vice versa (e.g., Campbell *et al.*, 1996).

Other evidence for independent processing streams comes from studies using event-related potentials (ERPs). For example, Bobes and colleagues (2000) recorded ERPs while participants matched faces according to their identity or their emotional expression. ERPs to mismatched trials in both tasks elicited a negativity around 400 ms that was similar in latency and amplitude, yet differed in scalp topography. In another study, Caharel *et al.* (2005) measured ERPs while participants performed familiarity or expression judgments. The authors found that neural responses in both tasks were observable at an early stage in processing, but they did not interact. Converging evidence was reported by Sergent and colleagues (1994). These authors also found evidence of segregated processing of identity and expression, with identity judgments being performed in the ventro-medial region of the right hemisphere, and expression judgments in the latter part of the right hemisphere and the dorsal region of the limbic system. Finally, studies that used single-cell recordings report specialized neurons for the processing of identity and expression, and further work suggests these neurons may be located in different cortical regions (Hasselmo, Rolls and Bayliss, 1986, 1989).

Despite the large body of evidence that appears to support independent processing of identity and expression, some authors have questioned the reliability of this evidence. For instance, Calder and Young (2005) question the neuroanatomical evidence thought to support independent processing streams. Indeed, although there is increasing evidence for independent mechanisms for the processing of identity and expression (the former is thought to occur in the face-processing area of the fusiform gyrus, the latter in the superior temporal sulcus (STS)), neuroimaging studies also suggest bi-directional interactions between neural systems encoding identity and expression. Indeed, several reports have noted increased activation of the fusiform gyrus (responsible for identification) in the processing of emotional compared with neutral faces (e.g., Critchley, Daly, Phillips *et al.*, 2000). On the other hand, the level of familiarity of a face can modulate affective responses in the amygdala, a neural region that is responsible for processing affective significance (Gobbini *et al.*, 2004).

More in-depth analysis of the neurophysiological evidence that is thought to support the independence hypothesis also questions these findings. For example, Sergent *et al.* (1994) provided evidence that separable cerebral regions are activated in identity and expression processing. Yet, other regions simultaneously responded to both dimensions, suggesting less cortical specialization for the two processes than previously envisaged. A similar pattern was observed in the studies reported by Hasselmo and colleagues (1986, 1989), as neurons were also found that responded either to both types of information, or that showed an interaction between expression and identity processing.

Further evidence for a closer relationship between identity and expression processing comes from behavioural studies. For example, Schyns and

Oliva (1999) demonstrated that identity classifications influenced the visual information used in an expression classification task. In another study, Kottoor (1989) found faces encoded with a happy expression were remembered more accurately than those encoded with neutral or pout expressions. Converging evidence came from Foa *et al.* (2000), who found better memory for faces encoded with emotional (happy, angry or disgust) expressions than neutral expressions, and D'Argembeau and Van der Linden (2007) found better memory for faces encoded with happy compared with angry expressions. Other studies have also reported facilitatory influences of positive emotional expressions in the recognition of famous faces (e.g., Kaufmann and Schweinberger, 2004; Gallegos and Tranel, 2005). Further, Endo *et al.* (1992) reported findings that indicate the degree of familiarity with a face influences the effect of expression on recognition. Although famous faces were more easily recognized when they displayed a happy compared with a neutral expression, the reverse finding emerged for personally familiar faces. Interestingly, Bate, Haslam and Hodgson (2009) used eye movement indicators of recognition to provide additional evidence of a bi-directional influence of emotional expression in face recognition. Specifically, although happy expressions facilitated the processing of famous faces, the authors noted that angry expressions facilitated the processing of novel faces.

A final set of studies have explored how emotional expression influences feelings of familiarity. Specifically, Baudouin and colleagues (2000) reported higher ratings of familiarity for both famous and unknown faces when they displayed happy compared with neutral expressions. Interestingly, two other studies have replicated this finding, and additionally reported a decrease in familiarity ratings for faces displaying angry compared with happy and neutral expressions (Lander and Metcalfe, 2007; Dobel *et al.*, 2008).

Although considerable evidence has therefore demonstrated that there may be a closer relationship between expression and identity processing than previously envisaged by Bruce and Young (1986), Calder and Young (2005) conclude that existing evidence nevertheless suggests that at least some aspects of facial identity and expression recognition involve the same visual route. Hence, more work is required before firm conclusions can be drawn on the precise relationship between expression and identity processing. You can read more about this issue in Chapter 8, where the contribution of evidence from neuropsychological case studies is considered.

3.2. EYE GAZE DIRECTION

Although much research has examined the processing of emotional expression, in recent years increasing attention has been directed towards other aspects of facial perception, particularly the processing of eye gaze direction. Gathering information about where others are looking is perhaps as valuable as processing their facial expression, given that people tend to look at things they plan to act upon, and determining this information allows the perceiver to infer the intentions of others. Evidence from the developmental literature has illustrated the importance of this process, and suggests it might have a biological basis that underpins the development of more sophisticated social functions (for a recent review see Striano and Reid, 2006). Indeed, a preference for looking at the eye region of other faces has been observed immediately after birth (Batki *et al.*, 2000), and making eye contact with others is thought to be important for the development of empathy and 'Theory of Mind' (Baron-Cohen, 1995).

This section begins with a brief description of the visuo-cognitive and neural mechanisms underpinning the perception of eye gaze direction, before discussing evidence that suggests our attention is particularly orientated towards the eyes of others. Finally, evidence is considered that suggests information about eye gaze direction plays an important role in interpreting the facial expression of people in our social environment.

3.2.1. How do we know where others are looking?

To detect where other people are looking, we examine the position of their pupils within their eyes. This process is facilitated by the fact that the pupil and iris form a relatively small dark region in the eye, with large regions of white sclera on each side. This contrast in the colouring of the different components of the eye makes it easier for humans to infer eye gaze direction than other primates. However, the geometry of the human eye also appears to facilitate this process. Indeed, Ando (2002) noted that gaze direction can also be successfully determined in stimuli where no luminance information is available, and the eye is only represented by the outline of an oval and a circle. Further, Ando went on to suggest that, although both luminance and geometry may be important in determining the eye gaze direction of others, information from luminance may be used for a more rapid representation of gaze direction, as a geometric analysis is more time-consuming and vulnerable to interference from other dimensions.

In the previous chapter, we discussed the neural mechanisms that might underpin the processing of gaze direction, as summarized within Gobbini and Haxby's (2007) neurological model of face processing. This model suggests that the anterior STS might compute gaze direction in others, and this information is then used to infer the mental state and emotions of others, and to inform the perceiver's attention system about potential targets in the surrounding environment. Although the affective state of the perceiver might be processed in an interactive manner by the posterior STS (Puce *et al.*, 1998), amygdala (Hooker *et al.*, 2003) and medial prefrontal cortex (Calder *et al.*, 2002), regions of the inferior parietal cortex seem to underpin the shifting of attention in the perceiver (Pelphrey *et al.*, 2003). This latter process has been the subject of many decades of behavioural research, and these findings are summarized in the next section.

3.2.2. Are eyes prioritized by the attention system?

Given the large amount of perceptual information that constantly enters our visual system, it is very important that our attention is directed towards relevant input that contributes to our current behavioural goals. This redirection of our attention towards salient visual information is termed 'orienting of attention', and it has traditionally been investigated using a variation of the spatial cueing paradigm (Posner, 1980). Such computerized experiments present participants with a large number of trials, where an arrow is displayed in the centre of the screen, pointing to either the left or the right (see Figure 3.2). A target (such as a small circle) then appears on either side of the display, and its location is normally unrelated to the direction of the arrow. The participant is instructed to press a key corresponding to the location of the target, while ignoring the arrow completely. A difference in reaction times and/or accuracy levels is usually noted between congruent (those where the direction of the arrow matches the location of the target) and incongruent trials. This difference in performance is termed the 'cueing effect', and is thought to reflect attention shifts to the cued location.

This paradigm has been adopted to investigate shifts of attention that occur in response to eye gaze direction, by replacing the arrows with a facial stimulus in which the eyes point to either the left or right of the screen, or, in some instances, straight ahead. Such studies have replicated the cueing effect using eyes instead of arrows as the cueing stimuli (e.g., Friesen and Kingstone, 1998; Driver *et al.*, 1999). Further, some studies have presented the eyes within the context of a whole face to cue attention, whereas others only present the eye region in isolation. Nevertheless, nearly all studies using eyes rather than arrows as the cueing stimuli have demonstrated faster reaction times to targets appearing in the cued rather than the uncued direction.

Figure 3.2 *The visual cueing paradigm.*

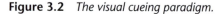

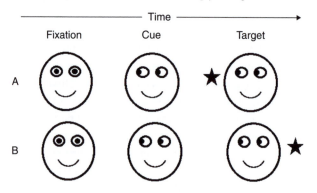

Participants are required to respond to the location of the target while ignoring the direction eye gaze. Panel A shows a congruent condition and Panel B an incongruent condition.

A further set of studies examined whether the cueing effect is of the same magnitude when measured in response to arrows as opposed to eyes. These studies aimed to examine whether the eyes are more salient to the perceiver than arrows, given their social importance. If this is the case, we would expect eyes to have a greater cueing effect than arrows, as they should direct attention more effectively. However, it has consistently been reported that eyes and arrows bring about similar cueing effects in healthy participants (see, for example, Tipples, 2002), even when arrows are embedded in the place of eyes in a facial context (Bayliss and Tipper, 2005).

Despite these findings, other research has noted small effects that might reflect the increased social salience of gaze as opposed to arrow cues. For instance, Friesen *et al.* (2004) reported that participants find it easier to orient in the opposite direction of an arrow than an eye cue, and Bayliss, di Pellegrino and Tipper (2004) found a smaller emotional response was evoked in a perceiver following an arrow compared with an eye cue. Further work examining patients with split brains indicates that different neural mechanisms might underpin gaze cueing (Kingstone, Friesen and Gazzaniga, 2000) and arrow cueing (Ristic, Friesen and Kingstone, 2002). Finally, Birmingham and colleagues used an alternative paradigm to examine whether eyes and arrows are equivalent social stimuli. Indeed, the authors suggested that the cueing task may fail to measure some of the ways that eyes are special, and instead monitored participants' eye movements as they viewed real-world scenes containing both eyes and arrows. Interestingly, they found that participants preferred to look at people and their eyes, and they rarely attended to arrows. Hence, Birmingham and colleagues concluded that eyes may be important social stimuli that are prioritized above arrows by the attention system (Birmingham, Bischof and Kingstone, 2009).

3.2.3. How is eye gaze direction integrated with other cues to attentional direction?

Often, other cues to the locus of attention may provide contradictory information to that gleaned from eye gaze direction. For instance, the direction of a person's head can sometimes provide conflicting information about the direction of a person's attention, particularly if they are looking at something out of the corner of their eye. Interestingly, Perrett *et al.* (1992) found that different cells in the macaque STS coded head as opposed to gaze direction, but the cells that coded gaze direction were dominant in determining the neural response. This finding suggests that, when both types of cue are available, we determine a person's direction of attention primarily using their eye gaze and suppress the contradictory information received from head direction. In addition, further evidence has suggested that the direction of the body can also inform the perceiver about a person's direction of attention, and hence this information might also need to be compared and integrated with head and eye orientation.

Based on these findings, Perrett and colleagues hypothesized a neural mechanism termed the 'direction-of-attention detector'. The authors suggested that this mechanism integrates information from a person's eye gaze direction, head orientation and body posture to infer the locus of their attention. Importantly, the authors suggested that these three detectors have a hierarchical arrangement, because they differ in the accuracy with which they can be used to determine the focus of a person's attention. Indeed, Perrett *et al.* suggested that information gleaned from eye gaze direction is prioritized over the other two detectors, and information from body posture is given the least priority. Hence, if contradictory information about a person's attention is gleaned from detectors lower down in the hierarchy, this information is suppressed by inhibitory connections in order that the most informative detector is prioritized.

However, several studies have provided evidence against the model of Perrett *et al.* model, by suggesting that contradictory information that is gleaned from head direction is difficult to suppress and can influence the perception of eye gaze direction (e.g., Cline, 1967; Anstis, Mayhew and Morley, 1969). For instance, study the image displayed in Figure 3.3. This figure presents an example of the 'Wollaston illusion' (Wollaston, 1824), in which the eyes of the two faces appear to be staring in different directions. However, the eye gaze of each face is actually identical, and it is the slight difference in head angle that brings about the illusion. Hence, the Wollaston illusion suggests that head direction can also influence judgments of attention direction.

Further evidence supporting this conclusion came from a more recent experimental investigation. Specifically, Langton, Watt and Bruce (2000) asked participants to view a series of faces where eye gaze direction was either congruent or incongruent with head direction. Participants were asked to judge the direction of attention for each face using only one of the cues and ignoring the other.

Figure 3.3   *The Wollaston illusion.*

The direction of eye gaze is identical in the two images, but the differing head orientation brings about the illusion that they are gazing in different directions.

Contrary to the predictions of the model of Perrett *et al.*, reaction times were quicker in the congruent compared with the incongruent condition, regardless of whether participants were focusing on eye gaze or head direction. Hence, both dimensions appear to provide important information about the focus of a person's attention, and both streams of information seem to be processed in an interactive manner rather than being prioritized according to a hierarchical arrangement.

3.2.4. How is eye gaze direction integrated with emotional expression?

Finally, some work has suggested that eye gaze direction can have important consequences for our interpretation of facial expressions of emotion. Indeed, both dimensions tell us about the mental states and likely future behaviour of others, and rapid interpretation of these cues is vital for successful social interaction. Further, although we are able to process either expression or eye gaze direction independently of the other dimension, we can only completely interpret a particular expression if we know the locus of that person's attention. For instance, if a person is displaying a fearful expression, it makes evolutionary sense for us to locate the source of the threat in the surrounding environment. Hence, it seems logical to assume that information gleaned from facial expression and eye gaze direction must be combined to place that expression in its social context.

This hypothesis is supported by Gobbini and Haxby's (2007) neurological model of face processing, where the STS and amygdala are thought to be involved in the processing of both eye gaze direction and emotional expression. The authors base this hypothesis on neuroimaging studies that report activation of these areas while participants make facial judgments on each dimension (Haxby *et al.*, 2000; Vuilleumier *et al.*, 2001), and neuropsychological investigations that report deficits in judgments of both gaze direction and facial expressions following amygdala lesions (Aggleton, 1993; Young *et al.*, 1995).

Further evidence that implicates interactive processing of eye gaze direction and facial expression comes from a neuroimaging study reported by Adams *et al.* (2003). These authors found a difference in amygdala activation according to both facial expression and eye gaze direction. Specifically, reduced amygdala activity was observed in response to fearful faces with averted gaze or angry faces with direct gaze, as opposed to the converse conditions. The authors suggested that the former two conditions might represent a threat to the perceiver, either from a source within the environment or the person being viewed; whereas the converse conditions require additional interpretation. As such, Adams *et al.* proposed that the amygdala might be particularly involved in resolving ambiguity about threatening faces, and gaze direction might provide important information to help with this process.

Such a suggestion is in line with hypotheses that basic approach and avoidance behaviours are processed by separate neural systems (e.g., Cacioppo and Gardner, 1999). Indeed, Adams and Kleck (2005) performed a further study that investigated the influence of gaze direction on other approach (joy and anger) and avoidance (sadness and fear) emotional expressions. Interestingly, the authors noted that faces with averted gaze were judged to represent avoidance expressions more than those with direct gaze. Hence, contrary to the idea that direct eye gaze facilitates face perception (e.g., Mason, Hood and Macrae, 2004), for avoidance expressions, perception seems to be enhanced by averted as opposed to direct gaze. However, Bindemann, Burton and Langton (2008) reported a series of studies that failed to replicate this finding, suggesting less interaction between the perception of eye gaze direction and emotional expression than previously envisaged.

Finally, Bayliss and colleagues (2006, 2007) reported a further interaction of gaze direction and emotional expression in a task where participants were required to provide evaluative judgments of objects. Specifically, the authors found that participants preferred objects that were viewed by happy as opposed to disgusted faces, but this effect only occurred when the objects were the subject of the person's eye gaze.

Although most evidence suggests that gaze direction influences judgments of facial expression, there is much less evidence to support the reverse pattern, particularly when healthy participants are investigated (e.g., Hietanen and Leppänen, 2003). However, some evidence to suggest that emotional expression can influence visual cueing has been noted in highly anxious participants. For instance, Mathews *et al.* (2003) found stronger cueing effects when the eyes of fearful as opposed to neutral faces were used to shift attention. However, it is unclear whether this finding can be attributed to the visual properties of the eyes rather than their social significance. Indeed, Tipples (2005) presented evidence that suggests simply widening the eyes of the gaze stimulus can enhance the cueing effect, and as fearful eyes are wider than neutral eyes, this might explain the effect reported by Mathews and colleagues. Hence, although much evidence suggests that eye gaze direction can modulate the analysis of facial expression, there is less evidence to support the reverse effect.

3.3. INTERACTION OF EMOTIONAL EXPRESSION, EYE GAZE DIRECTION AND FACIAL ATTRACTIVENESS

Physical attractiveness influences many different aspects of human social interaction. Indeed, people prefer to date, employ and vote for physically attractive individuals (see Hosoda, Stone-Romero and Coats, 2003; Langlois *et al.*, 2000), and tend to attribute positive personality traits to unfamiliar attractive faces (Dion, Berscheid and Walster, 1972).

Although we have already noted that eye gaze direction can influence our interpretations of other people's facial expressions, further research has reported that both emotional expression and eye gaze direction can also influence our judgments of facial attractiveness. For instance, neuroimaging evidence has revealed increased activation in the brain's reward centres (i.e., medial orbitofrontal cortex, ventral thalamus) when we view attractive compared with unattractive faces (Aharon *et al.*, 2001). Interestingly, this effect is modulated by both facial expression and eye gaze direction (Kampe *et al.*, 2001; O'Doherty *et al.*, 2003). Specifically, attractive faces seem to be more rewarding when they display happy as opposed to neutral expressions, and when their eyes look directly at the perceiver.

A more recent behavioural study examined the three-way interaction between expression, eye gaze direction and facial attractiveness. Indeed, Jones *et al.* (2006) asked participants to choose between attractive and unattractive versions of female faces, that were presented with either a happy or neutral expression and with direct or averted gaze. The authors found that when eye gaze was direct, participants preferred the attractive faces that were smiling. However, when faces were displayed with averted gaze, participants preferred the attractive faces with neutral expressions. These findings were interpreted as evidence that attraction is also influenced by the degree to which a person is interested in the perceiver (i.e., that they are smiling at you as opposed to someone else), as this minimizes the chance of rejection in social interactions. Hence, the perceiver can identify the most attractive individual who is most open to interaction and likely to reciprocate interest.

In sum, these findings indicate that out brain is adept at integrating many different cues when reading faces. This is important because the interpretation of facial expressions can differ depending on whether they are directed towards or away from us, and can influence decisions about the people we choose to interact with in social situations, and potentially even about those we choose to mate with. Thus, our brain's ability to integrate information about gaze direction, emotional expression and facial attractiveness demonstrates the sophistication of the processing system that underpins face perception in social contexts.

CHAPTER SUMMARY

■ Ekman and colleagues proposed the existence of six basic emotional expressions that are common to all cultures: anger, disgust, fear, happiness, sadness and surprise (Ekman, Soresnson and Friesen, 1969; Ekman and Friesen, 1971).

■ Further work suggests that although these expressions might be universal, we interpret the expressions displayed by individuals in our in-group more accurately than those from our out-group (Elfenbein and Ambady, 2002). This effect may be explained by non-verbal accents, which are subtle differences in the expression of emotions between groups (Elfenbein and Ambady, 2003b).

■ Far fewer studies have examined the recognition of spontaneously produced expressions, but evidence suggests less universality in the recognition of these expressions as opposed to posed expressions (Russell, 1994).

■ It has traditionally been thought that identity and expression are processed by independent mechanisms (Bruce and Young, 1986). However, recent evidence has called this hypothesis into question, and suggests there may be a closer relationship between the two processes than previously envisaged (Calder and Young, 2005).

■ Processing the gaze direction of another person is an important social cue, as it provides us with rich information about the surrounding environment and the mental state of the gazer. Hence, it is unsurprising that we are highly sensitive from infancy to other people's gaze direction (Batki *et al.*, 2000).

■ Research has demonstrated that averted gaze cues trigger an automatic shift of attention, even when the observer tries to ignore the cue (Posner, 1980). There is some evidence to suggest that our attention is more effectively shifted in response to eye as opposed to arrow cues (Friesen *et al.*, 2004).

■ We detect the gaze direction of others using the visual details of the eyes, head direction and body posture. Although Perrett and colleagues (1992) suggested this information is processed in a hierarchical manner, there is evidence to suggest that head direction in particular can influence our perception of gaze direction (Langton, Watt and Bruce, 2000).

■ Much evidence suggests that eye gaze can influence the interpretation of emotional expression (Adams *et al.*, 2003), although there is less evidence to support the reverse effect.

■ Both facial expression and eye gaze direction influence our judgments of facial attractiveness, such that we prefer smiling faces that are looking directly at us (Jones *et al.*, 2006). This finding is thought to reflect our desire to identify the most attractive person who might be interested in interacting with us, and demonstrates the complexity of the face perception system.

FURTHER READING

Calder, A. J. and Young, A. W. (2005) 'Understanding Facial Identity and Facial Expression Recognition', *Nature Neuroscience Reviews*, 6, 641–53.

Elfenbein, H. A., and Ambady, N. (2003) 'Universals and Cultural Differences in Recognizing Emotions', *Current Directions in Psychological Science*, 12, 159–64.

Frischen, A., Bayliss, A. P. and Tipper, S. P. (2007). 'Gaze Cueing of Attention: Visual Attention, Social Cognition, and Individual Differences', *Psychological Bulletin*, 133, 694–724.

Itier, R. J. and Batty, M. (2009) 'Neural Bases of Eye and Gaze Processing: The Core of Social Cognition', *Neuroscience and Biobehavioral Reviews,* 33, 843–63.

Jones, B. C., DeBruine, L. M., Little, A. C., Conway, C. A., and Feinberg, D. R. (2006) 'Integrating Gaze Direction and Expression in Preferences for Attractive Faces', *Psychological Science,* 17, 588–91.

GUIDANCE QUESTIONS

Use the following questions to guide your reading of this chapter and the recommended papers.

1. Does cross-cultural evidence support the existence of the six basic emotional expressions?
2. Does emotional expression influence identity recognition?
3. What is the evidence to suggest that we are highly sensitive to other people's gaze direction?
4. Does existing evidence support independent processing of different aspects of social face perception, or is there a more dynamic relationship between these sources of information?

4 Focus Chapter: Are Faces Special?

4.1. DOMAIN-SPECIFICITY AND DOMAIN-GENERAL HYPOTHESES

It is clear from the first three chapters of this book that faces are exceptionally important social stimuli that help us to function in our everyday lives. As such, it is not surprising that both behavioural and neuroimaging studies have revealed specific processing strategies and neural regions that are implicated in face recognition. Indeed, in Chapter 1 it was noted that we use an optimal configural processing strategy to recognize faces. Further, in Chapter 2, Gobbini and Haxby's (2007) neurological model of face processing was described. Although this model hypothesizes that all aspects of faces are processed within a distributed and overlapping neural network, it also posits that face identification occurs within the 'fusiform face area' (FFA), an area of cortex that seems to be particularly activated in response to faces. Thus, both behavioural and neuroimaging evidence suggests that humans might have specific cognitive and neural mechanisms that are reserved for the processing of facial stimuli.

However, this issue has been the subject of much debate in the psychological literature. Indeed, although some authors argue that face recognition is 'special' in that it involves face-specific cognitive and neural processes (the 'domain specificity' argument), others suggest that the processing of faces only seems to be special because we have more experience in processing this category of visual stimuli than we do in others (the 'expertise hypothesis'). Further, the expertise hypothesis posits that, if we gain sufficient expertise with any non-facial visual category, we use the same cognitive and neural mechanisms to process those stimuli as we do for faces.

In the current chapter, an overview of the evidence supporting each side of this debate is presented, focusing on studies that use healthy adults as participants. This evidence is examined in relation to cognitive experiments that illustrate the importance of configural processing in face recognition (see Chapter 1), and the various neuroscientific techniques that were described in Chapter 2.

4.2. EVIDENCE FROM COGNITIVE EXPERIMENTS

The notion that upright faces receive special processing has been supported by several cognitive experiments that demonstrate the existence of processing strategies that are only used for facial stimuli. Indeed, these studies suggest that faces are processed in a 'holistic' or 'configural' manner that takes account of the overall representation, including the spaces between features. On the other hand, objects and inverted faces are thought to be processed in a qualitatively different manner, using a feature-by-feature strategy.

Several classic paradigms have been used to demonstrate that different strategies are used to process faces and objects (see Chapter 1). Perhaps the most well-known paradigm to demonstrate the importance of configural information in face but not object processing is the face inversion effect. Indeed, Yin (1969) demonstrated that the cost of inverting faces is more severe in the recognition of faces compared with other categories of objects, such as houses. This effect was explained by the notion that upright faces benefit from the use of an optimal configural strategy that processes the face as a whole, but this strategy cannot be used for upright objects. Further, the optimal configural strategy cannot be used to process inverted faces or objects, and recognition performance declines in these conditions. Hence, there is a greater difference in recognition performance between upright and inverted faces than the difference between the same conditions for objects, presumably reflecting specialized processing mechanisms for upright faces.

In a more recent study, Yovel and Kanwisher (2004) reported further evidence that suggests spatial relations between features are not processed in objects. They presented participants with images of faces that were manipulated to differ according to the spacing between features (configural condition), or by holding spatial relations constant and replacing the features themselves (featural condition). Further, participants also viewed images of houses that differed according to the spacing between the windows and doors, or in the actual appearance of these components. Participants completed a sequential matching task in which they had to decide whether two successively presented images differed or not, and some trials were presented in an upright manner and others were inverted. In further support of the domain specificity argument, the authors only observed an inversion effect in both the spacing and parts condition for faces and not for houses.

Further demonstrations of the importance of configural processing for faces but not other categories of objects comes from the composite (Young, Hellawell and Hay, 1987) and part–whole (Tanaka and Farah, 1993) effects. In the composite face task, participants are presented with facial images that are composed from two half faces of different individuals, and the halves are presented in either aligned or misaligned conditions. The effect is characterized by the finding that participants find it more difficult to make perceptual judgments about one face half in the aligned compared with the misaligned condition, presumably because of the automatic influence of configural processing for aligned stimuli. The part–whole effect refers to the finding that participants recognize a part of a face more accurately when they view it in the context of a whole face than when they view it alone. Critically, although these effects have been observed in numerous studies for facial stimuli, they tend to be absent or reduced for non-facial stimuli (Tanaka and Farah, 1993). Hence, the configural processing strategy seems to be reserved only for the processing of faces, supporting the domain specificity viewpoint.

However, other evidence has been reported that supports the expertise hypothesis, suggesting that configural processing mechanisms are also used for non-facial visual entities with which we have sufficient expertise. Indeed, Diamond and Carey (1986) presented the seminal finding that dog-show judges displayed face-sized inversion effects for the breed they had expertise in. Later evidence supporting the expertise hypothesis was presented in a series of laboratory studies reported by Gauthier and colleagues (Gauthier and Tarr, 1997a; Gauthier *et al.*, 1998; Gauthier and Tarr, 2002). These researchers created a set of computer-generated objects termed 'Greebles', which were designed to be of a similar visual complexity to faces (see Figure 4.1). In approximately eight training sessions, participants encoded the appearance of individual Greebles, in addition to information about their name, gender and familial status. In later

Figure 4.1 *Examples of Greebles used by Gauthier and colleagues.*

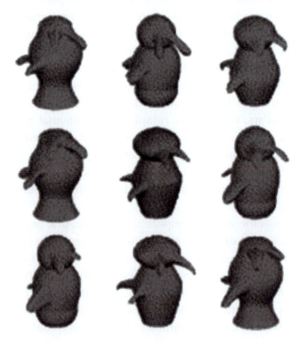

recognition tasks, the authors reported behavioural evidence that implicated the use of configural processing mechanisms, using the classic paradigms described above. Further reports indicated that experience with Greebles resulted in the activation of face-related neural areas during later recognition tasks (Gauthier *et al.*, 2000; Tarr and Gauthier, 2000; Rossion *et al.*, 2002).

However, other evidence has questioned the findings reported in studies that seem to support the expertise hypothesis. For instance McKone and colleagues (McKone and Kanwisher, 2005; McKone, Kanwisher and Duchaine, 2007) point out that no study using real-world experts has replicated the findings reported by Diamond and Carey (1986). Indeed, Robbins and McKone (2007) attempted to directly replicate the study by examining the recognition of dogs in experts compared with novices, and failed to find any evidence supporting the use of configural processing using the inversion, part–whole and composite tasks. McKone and colleagues also state that the size of the effects noted in the recognition of Greebles do not match those that have been observed for faces; and Robbins and McKone (2003) failed to note any influence of configural processing in the recognition of inverted faces after 10 hours of training. Finally, Busey and Vanderkolk (2005) investigated whether inversion influenced the processing of fingerprints in individuals who were expert in this domain. The authors did not note a face-sized inversion effect in this study, although recognition accuracy in recognizing the two halves of the stimuli did not additively match that achieved in the whole condition. That is, presentation of the whole face resulted in superior performance compared with the sum of performance in the two half conditions (see Chapter 1), suggesting some involvement of configural processing mechanisms.

Hence, there are some limitations in studies that provide data in support of the expertise hypothesis. However, other investigations have provided evidence of a face-sized inversion effect in the recognition of human bodies. For instance, Reed *et al.* (2003) presented participants with a perceptual matching task using upright and inverted faces, houses and bodies. The authors noted inversion effects that were similar in size for faces and bodies, but no such effect for houses. In a later study, Reed *et al.* (2006) found that inversion influenced the recognition of whole bodies compared with whole houses, but not the recognition of body or house parts. Further, a second experiment found a similar-sized inversion effect for the recognition of bodies and faces. Hence, these studies suggest that bodies may be one class of stimuli that is processed in a similar manner to faces.

However, neuroimaging findings do not support the behavioural findings discussed above. Indeed, Schwarzlose, Baker and Kanwisher (2005) found distinctive regions in the fusiform gyrus were activated in response to face and body stimuli. Further, investigations into the development of these processes indicate that the preference for upright faces is present from birth (e.g., Cassia, Turati and Simion, 2004), whereas intact and scrambled body stimuli cannot be differentiated until 2 years of age (Slaughter, Heron and Sim, 2002). In sum, these latter findings indicate that bodies and faces are not processed by the same neural mechanisms, even if it is the case that configural processing is also used to recognize bodies.

4.3. EVIDENCE FROM SINGLE-CELL RECORDING

The bulk of evidence from single-cell recordings supports the face-specificity hypothesis. Indeed, many studies have found face-selective responses in single neurons in the temporal lobes of macaques (e.g., Desimone *et al.*, 1984; Tsao *et al.*, 2003). Further, a recent study that combined fMRI and single-cell recording in monkeys provided striking evidence that supports the existence of face-specific processing mechanisms. Indeed, Tsao *et al.* (2006) took recordings from single cells while monkeys viewed a set of faces and objects. The authors found that 97 per cent of visually responsive cells responded more to faces than they did to objects. Further, although responses to nearly all objects did not differ from baseline measures, those that did elicit responses tended to have similar shapes to faces. These findings suggest that face-selective cells are densely packed in cortex and are only used in the processing of faces. Finally, Foldiak *et al.* (2004) used rapid serial visual presentation to demonstrate the existence of face-specific cells. Specifically, the authors presented macaques with over 1000 natural images, and found that the 70 strongest responses that were produced by some cells were all for facial stimuli.

4.4. EVIDENCE FROM EVENT-RELATED POTENTIAL (ERP)/MAGNETOENCEPHALOGRAPHY STUDIES

Some studies have provided evidence that the face-selective N170 event-related potential (ERP) response can be noted in experts viewing stimuli from non-facial visual entities (see, for example, Tanaka and Curran, 2001; Rossion *et al.*, 2002; Gauthier *et al.*, 2003). Further, the study reported by Busey and Vanderkolk (2005) using fingerprint experts also monitored the N170 in their participants, and found that the response was delayed for inverted compared with upright fingerprints. This pattern of findings is similar to that observed for upright and inverted faces (see Chapter 2), indicating some similarity between the processing of the two categories. However, other work has demonstrated that the N170 can also be delayed when non-experts view inverted objects (see, for example, Rossion, Joyce *et al.*, 2003), indicating that the finding is not necessarily indicative of face-like processing.

Although these studies provide some support for the expertise hypothesis, McKone and Kanwisher (2005) point out that no study has demonstrated the basic result that would provide more convincing evidence. That is, no study has reported an enhanced N170 for both faces and objects of expertise compared with control objects. In addition, other studies have failed to note face-like N170/M170 responses for objects of expertise. For instance, Xu, Liu and Kanwisher (2005) used magnetoencephalography to investigate the recognition of cars in expert participants. The authors did not observe an increased M170 response for cars compared with other stimuli, and found that the amplitude of the response did not correlate with recognition performance. Hence, there is little evidence from this methodology to support the expertise hypothesis.

4.5. EVIDENCE FROM NEUROIMAGING EXPERIMENTS

As discussed in Chapter 2, fMRI studies have identified regions of cortex that are implicated in face processing both in monkeys (see Tsao et al., 2003; Pinsk et al., 2005; Zangenehpour and Chaudhuri, 2005) and human participants (see Kanwisher et al., 1997; McCarthy et al., 1997). The main region that appears to be particularly involved in face processing is the FFA, located in the ventral occipitotemporal cortex. According to Gobbini and Haxby's (2007) neurological model of face processing, the FFA is responsible for face recognition processes, although two other regions are also thought to be involved in the 'core' system for face processing. These last two regions (the occipital face area and superior temporal sulcus) also appear to be face-selective, but are not detectable in all participants and seem to perform different functions to the FFA (Kanwisher and Yovel, 2006). Hence, in the current discussion, only evidence about the FFA is considered.

Importantly, much evidence suggests that the FFA responds preferentially to faces, supporting the domain-specificity viewpoint. Indeed, several neuroimaging studies have found much larger activation in this area in response to faces as opposed to non-facial objects such as houses and other human body parts such as hands (e.g., Kanwisher et al., 1997). Further, two of the classic behavioural markers of face processing appear to be associated with activity in the FFA: greater sensitivity to differences between upright compared with inverted faces (Yovel and Kanwisher, 2005), and holistic processing (Schiltz and Rossion, 2006).

Such findings are clearly in opposition to the expertise hypothesis, which predicts that the FFA should also be activated by objects of expertise to a greater extent than by control objects. However, some evidence supporting the expertise hypothesis has been presented. For instance, Gauthier et al. (2000) reported evidence demonstrating increased FFA activation when bird and car experts viewed stimuli from their categories of expertise. Converging evidence that replicated this finding was presented in a later study (Xu, Liu and Kanwisher, 2005); but Rhodes et al. (2004) only found small increases in FFA activation in expert perceivers, and Grill-Spector, Knouf and Kanwisher (2004) failed to find any effect at all. Further, in a review of all fMRI studies that have investigated the expertise hypothesis, McKone *et al.* (2007) conclude that, when real-world expertise effects are found in the FFA, the response to faces is still twice as high as that observed in response to objects of expertise.

Other studies have also provided evidence in support of the expertise hypothesis by training participants to become experts in the perception of computer-generated non-facial stimuli. For instance, Gauthier *et al.* (1999) noted increased FFA activation in response to Greebles after several hours of training. However, three recent studies (Moore, Cohen and Ranganath, 2006; Op de Beeck *et al.*, 2006; Yue, Tjan and Biederman, 2006) trained participants to make fine discriminations between non-facial stimuli, and did not find an increased response in the FFA for trained compared with untrained objects. Yet, all three studies did find increased activation in the lateral occipital complex for trained objects, a region that appears to be involved in the processing of general object shape. In addition, further studies have also found larger effects of expertise outside the FFA than within it (e.g., Gauthier *et al.*, 2000; Rhodes *et al.*, 2004). Hence, several studies suggest that expertise with objects increases responses in object-selective but not face-selective areas, supporting the face-specificity viewpoint.

In response to these findings, Kanwisher and Yovel (2006) suggest that the increased activation that has been noted in the FFA for objects of expertise does not necessarily reflect a special role for the region in processing these stimuli. Rather, they suggest that such activation may simply reflect an overall pattern of increased attention towards stimuli with which a viewer has much experience. For instance, a fingerprint expert will be drawn towards fingerprints to a greater extent than non-expert viewers, bringing about increased activation in response to these stimuli in many neural regions, including the FFA. Converging evidence that supports this attentional explanation comes from reports that suggest the level of FFA activation in response to objects of expertise correlates with behavioural performance in location-discrimination but not identity-discrimination tasks (e.g., Grill-Spector, Knouf and Kanwisher, 2004; Gauthier *et al.*, 2000).

In sum, it appears that neural activation in the FFA is smaller in response to objects of expertise than it is for faces, and any increases that are noted in the FFA appear to be uncorrelated with behavioural performance on recognition tests. Further, neural activation is not restricted to this area when objects of expertise are perceived. Thus, these findings may be explained by the hypothesis that viewers simply pay more attention to objects with which they have expertise, bringing about increased activation in multiple extrastriate regions.

CHAPTER SUMMARY

■ A long-standing debate in cognitive neuroscience is concerned with the extent to which particular neural regions are specified to process only one visual entity (domain-specificity) as opposed to several types of visual stimuli (domain-generality).

- This debate has particularly been applied to face processing, where some authors believe we have specialized cognitive and neural mechanisms that only process faces, whereas others suggest these mechanisms are used to process any category of object with which we have sufficient visual expertise.
- Many behavioural studies using classic paradigms have suggested we use configural processing mechanisms only to process upright faces (Yin, 1969; Young, Hellawell and Hay, 1987; Tanaka and Farah, 1993). However, other evidence from both real-world (Diamond and Carey, 1986) and laboratory-based studies (e.g., Gauthier *et al.*, 2000) suggests similar effects can be noted for non-facial categories, although several investigations have failed to replicate these findings (e.g., Robbins and McKone, 2007).
- Neuroscientific studies have reported convincing evidence that suggests particular regions of cortex (notably the FFA) are specialized for the processing of faces (see, for example, Kanwisher *et al.*, 1997), although other evidence suggests these areas can also be activated in response to objects with which participants have particular expertise (e.g., Gauthier *et al.*, 2000).
- An alternative explanation for these effects is based on findings that FFA activation in response to non-facial objects of expertise is not as large as it is for faces, and other regions of cortex are simultaneously activated (Kanwisher and Yovel, 2006). Specifically, this hypothesis suggests that expert viewers simply pay more attention to objects with which they have expertise, resulting in a general increase in neural activation.

FURTHER READING

Bukach, C. M., Gauthier, I. and Tarr, M. J. (2006) 'Beyond Faces and Modularity: The Power of an Expertise Framework', *Trends in Cognitive Science,* 10, 159–66.

Diamond, R. and Carey, S. (1986) 'Why Faces are and are not Special: An Effect of Expertise', *Journal of Experimental Psychology: General,* 115, 107–17.

Gauthier, I., Skudlarksi, P., Gore, J. C. and Anderson, A. W. (2000) 'Expertise for Cars and Birds Recruit Brain Areas Involved in Face Recognition', *Nature Neuroscience,* 3, 191–7.

Gauthier, I., Williams, P. C., Tarr, M. J. and Tanaka, J. W. (1998) 'Training "Greeble" Experts: A Framework for Studying Expert Object Recognition Processes', *Vision Research,* 38, 2401–28.

Kanwisher, N., McDermott, J. and Chun, M. (1997) 'The Fusiform Face Area: A Module in Human Extrastriate Cortex Specialized for Face Perception', *Journal of Neuroscience,* 17, 4302–11.

Kanwisher, N. and Yovel, G. (2006) 'The Fusiform Face Area: A Cortical Region Specialized for the Perception of Faces', *Philosophical Transactions of the Royal Society B*, 361, 2109–28.

DISCUSSION QUESTIONS

1. Are faces special? Based on the current evidence, can we make a firm conclusion in either direction?
2. Are findings from behavioural studies as convincing as those from neuroscientific studies in support of your conclusion to the above question?
3. What further experimental or neuroscientific work might be carried out further to inform the debate?
4. How might studies of neuropsychological patients inform this debate? This issue is discussed in later Focus Chapters (Chapters 8 and 12); however, before reading these chapters, can you think of any particular patterns of impairment that might support either side of the argument?

PART II

Acquired and Neuropsychiatric Disorders of Face Processing

5 Acquired Prosopagnosia

Prosopagnosia is a cognitive disorder characterized by a severe deficit in face recognition, which cannot be attributed to lower-level visual problems, higher-level semantic impairments or cognitive alterations such as mental confusion or amnesia. Prosopagnosics can normally recognize that a particular visual stimulus is a face, but they cannot discriminate between different faces, and hence cannot recognize the faces of familiar people. This impairment is severe, and includes not only the faces of close friends and acquaintances, but also family members, siblings, spouses and, in some cases, even their own face. However, prosopagnosics can often identify familiar people using alternative cues to recognition, such as hairstyle, clothing, voice or gait. Importantly, this indicates that prosopagnosia is essentially a disorder of visual perception, and general semantic knowledge about familiar people remains intact and accessible from other modalities.

Broadly speaking, two types of prosopagnosia have been reported in the literature. First, there are a limited number of descriptions of individuals who *acquired* the disorder after a neurological injury or illness. These people had normal face-processing abilities before onset of the condition, and case reports of such individuals extend back to the mid-nineteenth century. However, more recently there have been increasing reports of people who have *developmental* prosopagnosia, which describes a lifelong face recognition impairment in the absence of neurological injury. In the current chapter, only the acquired form of the disorder is discussed. You can read more about developmental prosopagnosia in Chapter 10.

5.1. A BRIEF HISTORY OF ACQUIRED PROSOPAGNOSIA

Wigan (1844) offered the first report of acquired prosopagnosia (AP) that appeared in the neurological literature, and this was soon followed by other case descriptions in the late nineteenth century (e.g., Charcot, 1883; Jackson, 1876; Quaglino and Borelli, 1867; Wilbrand, 1887) and throughout the twentieth century (for a review see Grüsser and Landis, 1991). However, prosopagnosia was originally considered to be part of a generalized visual agnosia that affected objects as well as faces, until a landmark paper by Hoff and Pötzl appeared in 1937. These authors reported the case of a patient who was impaired at recognizing familiar faces, but retained the ability to recognize other categories of objects. Hence, Hoff and Pöltz suggested that face-processing skills can be selectively disrupted after neurological trauma. However, the term 'prosopagnosia' was not coined for another ten years, when Bodamer (1947) described three patients who had suffered brain damage in the Second World War. Specifically, Bodamer described the cases of three wounded soldiers who had acquired various patterns of face-processing deficits as a result of neurological injury. In his paper, he referred to this disorder as 'prosopagnosia', combining the Greek word for 'face' ('prospon') with the word 'agnosia', meaning 'non-knowledge'.

5.2. PREVALENCE

In the years since Bodamer first coined the term 'prosopagnosia', over 100 cases of the acquired form of the disorder have been reported in the literature (for reviews see Farah, 1990; Grüsser and Landis, 1991). Despite this, it is clear that AP is rare, and hence there have been few estimates of its prevalence. Indeed, it is thought that the prevalence of 'pure' AP is very low. For instance, Zihl and von Cramon (1986) examined 258 patients with posterior lesions of various origins (e.g., closed head injury, encephalitis, tumours, cerebral infarcts), and found that none suffered from isolated prosopagnosia. Further, Gloning, Gloning and Hoff (1967) reported that only one of 241 patients with lesions to occipital or nearby regions experienced prosopagnosia in the absence of other cognitive deficits.

However, if an impairment in face recognition is viewed as a 'symptom' rather than a disorder in its own right, the prevalence does increase. For example, Hécaen and Angelergues (1962, 1963) reported prosopagnosia among other deficits in six per cent of 382 patients with posterior cerebral lesions of various origins. In a more recent study, Valentine *et al.* (2006) screened 91 patients who had suffered brain damage at least six months before testing. The researchers performed a battery of cognitive and perceptual tests, and also asked patients and caregivers to rate each individual's everyday face recognition abilities. Objective measures of face recognition ability indicated that 77 per cent of the patients achieved a low score on Warrington's Recognition Memory for Faces Test (Warrington, 1984), and 50 per cent of the patients reported everyday difficulties in face recognition. Thus, although many of these patients were likely to have higher-level problems such as generalized memory impairments, this study suggests that face recognition difficulties are much more commonly observed than earlier studies suggest, albeit in the context of a more generalized pattern of cognitive and perceptual impairments.

5.3. AETIOLOGY

Many causes of the lesions that bring about AP have been reported, including stroke, carbon monoxide poisoning, temporal lobectomy, encephalitis, neoplasm (tumour) and head trauma. Further, recent reports have described cases of AP alongside degenerative conditions such as frontotemporal and semantic dementia (Josephs *et al.*, 2009), and after temporal lobe atrophy (Chan *et al.*, 2009; Joubert *et al.*, 2003). Some recent detailed analyses indicate that the primary site of damage in most cases is to posterior regions of the brain (e.g.,, Arnott *et al.*, 2008). However, damage to more anterior regions has been reported to bring about 'prosopamnesia', a condition in which patients retain the ability to recognize faces that they knew before the neurological accident, but cannot create stable representations of new faces in memory (Crane and Milner, 2002; Tippett, Miller and Farah, 2000; Williams, Berberovic and Mattingley, 2007).

There has been some debate about the hemispheric lateralization of damage that brings about AP. Indeed, it was traditionally thought that the condition results from unilateral damage to the right hemisphere, particularly the right occipitotemporal area. In line with this hypothesis, de Renzi *et al.* (1994) reported unilateral occipitotemporal lesions in three cases of AP, and cited 27 previously reported cases that presented with similar damage. However, other authors have argued that AP can also result from bilateral lesions. For example, Damasio, Damasio and Van Hoesen (1982) re-examined eight cases that were originally thought to be underpinned by unilateral damage to the right hemisphere, and found that all had symmetrical damage in bilateral areas. Further, several more recent reports have also described AP in the context of bilateral damage (e.g., Barton *et al.*, 2002; Boutsen and Humphreys, 2002); and some reports suggest the disorder can also result from unilateral left hemisphere lesions (Barton, 2008; Mattson, Levin and Grafman, 2000; McNeil and Warrington, 1993; Wright *et al.*, 2006). Importantly, such evidence suggests that the left hemisphere might also play a fundamental role in face processing. However, de Renzi, Zambolin and Crisi (1987) suggested that prosopagnosia resulting from left hemisphere lesions can result in a more variable pattern of symptoms.

Alternatively, others have suggested that unilateral lesions (regardless of hemisphere) bring about more selective impairments in face processing, whereas bilateral lesions cause more extensive disruption (Boeri and Salmaggi, 1994; Warrington and James, 1967). This latter suggestion seems logical, given that, when only one hemisphere is affected, it is plausible that neural areas in the undamaged hemisphere might compensate for lost abilities at least to some degree; whereas no such compensation can occur in patients with damage to both sides of the brain.

5.4. CO-MORBID IMPAIRMENTS

As described above, AP can often result from extensive bilateral lesions, and therefore other visual impairments often accompany the disorder. Indeed, lower-level visual impairments are occasionally observed in AP cases, and can include difficulties in discriminating luminance, spatial resolution, curvature, line orientation or contrast at low spatial frequencies. However, these deficits are unlikely to underpin the prosopagnosia itself, and instead merely present alongside the disorder (Barton, Cherkasova, Press *et al.*, 2004). It is relatively more common to observe participants with AP with poor contrast sensitivity at higher frequencies, and it is possible that such difficulties may more directly contribute to the face-processing impairment by affecting the ability to extract fine-grained information (Barton, Cherkasova, Press *et al.*, 2004; Caldara *et al.*, 2005). Further, many participants with AP have visual field defects, particularly affecting the left side of space. Indeed, one study surveyed 69 individuals with AP, and found that only 12 per cent of the sample had no such deficits (Bouvier and Engel, 2006). The same study also revealed that 52 per cent of the AP cases suffered from a co-morbid impairment in colour perception (achromatopsia), often associated with unilateral or bilateral damage in the temporo-occipital junction (Meadows, 1974).

It has also been reported that individuals with AP experience navigational difficulties (topographagnosia), which can affect vectorial orientation (difficulties in processing angle and distance) or memory for places and landmarks (Landis, 2004). Such difficulties have been observed in many AP cases. For instance, Hécaen and Angelergues (1962) found that 38 per cent of their sample of patients with AP with unilateral lesions also suffered from topographagnosia, whereas 77 per cent of patients with topographagnosia had difficulties with face recognition. In another study, Landis and colleagues tested the face recognition ability of 16 patients with topographic deficits, and found impairments in seven of the cases (Landis, Cummings, Benson *et al.*, 1986).

Further, most participants with AP also have problems recognizing shapes and objects, usually resulting from larger lesions in bilateral posterior regions. In some cases, the deficit concerns categories for which the patient developed a visual expertise before acquiring the lesion. For example, Assal, Favre and Anderes (1984) described a prosopagnosic farmer who also experienced difficulties in recognizing his cows. Such reports have been used to support the 'expertise hypothesis' (see Chapters 4 and 8), and have been interpreted as evidence that we do not have specialized neural systems for face processing. Indeed, given that most participants with AP seem to experience co-morbid deficits in object processing, this evidence certainly seems to suggest that faces are not special. However, there are some isolated cases of AP who have normal object recognition abilities, providing support for the other side of the argument. The theoretical implications of these cases are discussed in more detail in Chapter 8.

Finally, co-morbid difficulties in non-identification aspects of face processing are also noted in some participants with AP. These can include difficulties in extracting other information from a face, such as gender or age. Alternatively, the impairments can affect the patient's ability to make social judgments about a person, including interpretation of their emotional state by facial expression analysis, or in judging the attractiveness or trustworthiness of that person based on their facial characteristics. Importantly, the presence of such additional deficits in some (but not all) participants with AP has been used as evidence to suggest that different subtypes of the disorder exist. These subtypes are theoretically important, as they can be accommodated within Bruce and Young's (1986) dominant theory of face processing, and have been used to predict other aspects of the neurocognitive profile that is associated with each subtype. These subtypes are considered in the next section.

5.5. SUBTYPES OF PROSOPAGNOSIA

Previous work has suggested a basic dichotomy that has been useful in distinguishing between subtypes of visuo-cognitive disorders (Lissauer, 1890). Indeed, neuropsychological investigations have described cases that are representative of either visual *apperceptive* agnosia, or visual *associative* agnosia. Whereas apperceptive agnosics present with visual deficits that prevent them from creating a correct percept of an in-coming stimulus, associative agnosics are thought to be able to construct a normal visual percept, but cannot adequately associate that percept with visual representations of objects stored in memory. This basic dichotomy has also been applied to AP, and the two subtypes are broadly distinguished by the presence or absence of an accompanying deficit in facial perception. Specifically, apperceptive prosopagnosics are thought to be unable to create a correct percept of a face, whereas it is thought that face perception is largely intact in associative prosopagnosia, but these individuals are unable to give any meaning to a correctly elaborated visual representation of a face (De Renzi *et al.*, 1991).

These two subtypes have been mapped onto functional models of face processing (e.g., Bruce and Young, 1986; see Figure 1.1), such that apperceptive prosopagnosia is thought to represent an impairment at the level of structural encoding, whereas the lesion in associative prosopagnosia is believed to be located either within the face recognition units (FRUs), or in the link between the FRUs and the person identity nodes (PINs). The ability to complete face matching tasks that place no demands on face memory have traditionally been used to partition AP. Indeed, apperceptive prosopagnosics should not be able to complete this task as they are unable to create an intact representation of a face, whereas associative prosopagnosics should perform well on such tests given their face perception is intact and the deficit is thought to be higher-order.

Although this basic dichotomy has been widely applied to cases of AP reported in the literature, it is important to note that some authors disagree that such a broad distinction can be applied to all cases of visual agnosia. For instance, Farah (1990) reviewed 99 cases of associative visual agnosia and reported that all of them in fact presented with some degree of perceptual impairment. She therefore concluded that the perceptual and mnesic representations involved in object recognition are not clearly distinct. Farah's account is based on the observation that very few of the patients who have been described as associative agnosics have been adequately tested for perceptual abnormalities. Further, in the rare cases where particularly demanding visual tasks have been presented to associative agnosic patients, their results have suggested some critical deficits in high-level visual processing. Thus, Farah's concerns imply that it may be more accurate to distinguish between apperceptive and associative prosopagnosia based on the extent of perceptual impairment, rather than its simple presence or absence.

Despite some debate in the literature about the precise nature of the apperceptive/associative distinction, it is generally agreed that the dichotomy is of particular theoretical relevance in AP, given evidence of a relationship between visual impairment and covert recognition. The term 'covert recognition' is used to refer to the finding that, despite loss of the ability to consciously recognize a face, some participants with AP nevertheless show evidence of face recognition at an unconscious or implicit level.

Indeed, different types of covert face recognition can be observed in AP. Specifically, *behavioural* covert recognition can be detected on a variety of computerized face recognition tasks, using basic measures of accuracy or response time. For example, in a *name-relearning task*, a famous face is presented alongside two names, one of which is the celebrity's correct name, and the other is incorrect. The participant is required to learn to associate one of the two names with the face. Covert recognition is demonstrated when participants remember more of the correct name-face pairings than the incorrect ones. Another behavioural assessment of covert recognition is the *face interference task*. In this test, a face and name are presented simultaneously, and the participant is asked to make a rapid category decision for the pairing (e.g., 'Is this the face of an actress or not?'). Covert recognition is thought to be present when the participant makes more rapid responses for face-name pairings that are from the same category than for those that are not. A final behavioural test of covert recognition is the *face-name priming task*. In this paradigm, the participant views a face followed by a name, and is asked to decide quickly whether the name belongs to a famous person or not. When the participant's response times are found to be quicker for famous names that are presented after an image of that person's face, it is believed that covert recognition is observed.

Importantly, behavioural covert recognition has not been demonstrated in all patients with AP, and this evidence has been used to reinforce the apperceptive/

associative distinction. Specifically, behavioural covert recognition has been noted in many patients with an associative impairment, but in few with an apperceptive impairment, and this pattern of findings can be accommodated within the model of Bruce and Young (1986). Indeed, as described earlier in this chapter, patients with apperceptive prosopagnosia are thought to have a deficit at the level of structural encoding. Hence, because these patients are unable to create an intact percept of a face, it makes sense that no recognition can be supported by the face-processing system in these individuals, whether at a conscious or unconscious level.

On the other hand, patients with associative prosopagnosia are thought to have a higher-order impairment that affects their actual memory for facial representations. Indeed, these patients are thought to be able to perceive faces in essentially a normal manner, allowing at least some structural information to feed into the face identification system. Hence, some residual processing within the face recognition system might be able to support covert but not overt recognition. Several authors have proposed theories about how this process might occur. For instance, Farah et al. (1993) suggest that covert face recognition is supported by the identity pathway attempting to work in the normal manner. However, the facial representations stored within the FRUs have become degraded or damaged, and hence do not provide enough information to support full overt recognition but do allow covert face processing to proceed. Other theories provide 'disconnection' accounts of covert face processing. For example, de Haan, Bauer and Greve (1992) suggest that the face-processing system itself remains relatively intact in AP, but becomes disconnected from a higher cognitive system responsible for conscious awareness. Alternatively, Burton et al. (1991) suggest that certain components of the face-processing system become disconnected from each other. This explanation fits neatly with the more recent neural-network implementations of the model of Bruce and Young, that more explicitly account for covert recognition (e.g., Burton et al., 1990: see Chapter 1).

Other forms of covert face recognition use physiological rather than behavioural measures. Perhaps the most well-known method of monitoring physiological covert face recognition involves the recording of a person's skin conductance response. Specifically, this technique records changes in the electrical conductivity of a person's skin, usually by connecting small electrodes to two fingers on the non-dominant hand. These electrodes are then used to measure changes in the participant's arousal levels, by measuring the amount of sweat that is in the skin's sweat ducts while the participant views familiar and novel faces. Sweat is produced in greater quantities when we are aroused, and is also a good conductor of electricity. Hence, given we experience greater arousal in response to familiar faces than novel faces, this technique can be used to indicate covert face recognition when greater levels of skin conductance are observed for familiar than for novel faces.

It is important to realize that physiological evidence of covert recognition cannot be accommodated within the models of face recognition that we have discussed so far. Indeed, although both Bruce and Young's (1986) model and Burton *et al.*'s (1990) interactive activation and competition (IAC) model can accommodate evidence of behavioural covert recognition, neither can explain how increased levels of arousal might occur in face processing. Hence, a modification of the functional model of face processing was proposed by Bauer (1984), in response to findings of an intact skin conductance response in prosopagnosic participants. Specifically, Bauer suggested that there are two independent routes to face recognition (see Figure 5.1). The first processes facial identity, and corresponds to the main face recognition pathway in the functional model of Bruce and Young. In neuroanatomical terms, Bauer suggested that this pathway follows a ventral route, involving neural structures such as the longitudinal fasciculus. Bauer termed the second pathway the 'dorsal' route, and suggested that this is where the emotional significance of a face is processed, as measured by the skin conductance response. He suggested that this latter route passes

Figure 5.1 *Bauer's (1984) diagram demonstrating the ventral visual–limbic pathway and the dorsal visual–limbic pathway in the human brain.*

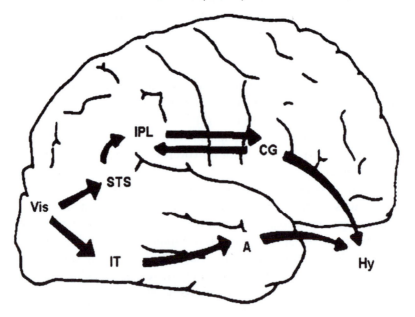

The visual association cortex (VIS), superior temporal sulcus (STS), inferior parietal lobe (IPL), cingulate gyrus (CG) and hypothalamus (Hy) are located within the dorsal visual–limbic pathway; whereas the ventral visual–limbic pathway contains the visual association cortex (VIS), the inferior temporal lobe (IT), the amygdala (A), and the hypothalamus (Hy).

from visual cortex through the superior temporal sulcus, inferior parietal lobe and cingulate gyrus to the limbic system, including the amygdala. In the next chapter, Bauer's dual-route model of face processing is further discussed with reference to another disorder of face processing, the Capgras delusion.

Finally, other researchers have used alternative techniques to provide evidence of covert face recognition in their cases of AP. Importantly, research has demonstrated that different patterns of brain activity are associated with the viewing of familiar and novel faces, and these have been used to indicate covert recognition in AP. For example, Bobes *et al.* (2003) used this methodology to provide evidence of covert face recognition in their prosopagnosic patient, FE. Specifically, FE was asked to view pairs of unfamiliar faces, and he was required to decide whether each pair contained images of the same person or of two different people. FE performed poorly in this task, yet the researchers still recorded an enhanced N300 response when he viewed same-face compared with different-face pairings. Bobes and colleagues interpreted this as evidence of covert recognition in patient FE.

5.6. CAN AP BE ATTRIBUTED TO A DEFICIT IN CONFIGURAL PROCESSING?

In Chapter 1, the importance of configural information in face processing was discussed. Indeed, although both configural and featural information seems to be used to recognize faces, the process fundamentally relies on the optimal configural processing strategy. It is therefore of note that several studies have reported impaired configural processing in their participants with AP, and it is possible that this difficulty might contribute to face-processing deficits in the disorder.

The ability to use the optimal configural processing strategy in face recognition has commonly been investigated using the face inversion effect (see Chapter 1). This phenomenon is characterized by the finding that unimpaired participants are better at recognizing faces presented in an upright rather than an inverted orientation, and the difference in performance between the two conditions is disproportionately larger than that noted for other classes of objects (Yin, 1969). This finding has been interpreted as evidence that the processing of upright faces relies on configural processing, a strategy that is not available to perceivers when faces are viewed upside down, forcing a reliance on the suboptimal featural processing strategy. Several studies have failed to find evidence of the inversion effect in their participants with AP, suggesting these individuals use a featural processing strategy for upright as well as inverted faces (e.g., Boutsen and Humphreys, 2002; de Gelder and Rouw, 2000b; Delvenne *et al.*, 2004).

Further studies have reported evidence of an 'inverted inversion effect', where patients with AP display superior performance in the inverted compared with the upright condition (de Gelder, Bachoud-Lévi and Degos, 1998; Boutsen and Humphreys, 2002). Although at first sight it appears to be difficult to explain this finding, researchers have suggested that it can be accommodated by the interference caused by residual configural processing abilities. According to this explanation, the ability to process faces configurally is not entirely absent in AP, and the strategy is still automatically initiated in response to upright faces, interfering with the featural processing strategy. This brings about poorer performance in the recognition of upright faces as opposed to inverted faces, where featural processing can proceed in the normal manner. Further, because patients with AP are more accustomed to using featural processing than unimpaired participants, they perform at a higher level in the inverted condition than controls.

Further evidence that configural processing might be impaired in AP has been presented from eye movement studies. Caldara *et al.* (2005) demonstrated an abnormal pattern of feature exploration in their participant with AP, who preferred to look at the mouth and external features of a face in a recognition task. This was in contrast to control participants, who focused on all of the internal features and particularly the eye region of the face. The authors suggested this pattern of findings indicated impaired configural processing in their participant with AP. This hypothesis fits well with the findings of other eye-tracking studies that also report aberrant patterns of feature exploration in participants with AP. Specifically, Lê, Raufaste and Démonet (2003) reported that patient SB preferentially attended to the hair and hairline of the face. Further, in face detection tasks, control participants fixated fewer areas of interest than SB, a finding that was again attributed to SB's inability to engage configural–holistic processes. In another study, Stephan and Caine (2009) also found that their patient with AP (SC) preferred to look at peripheral regions (hair, forehead) of the face rather than the inner features. The authors interpreted the results as evidence that SC's face recognition deficit could be linked to an inability to assemble an accurate and unified face percept. However, not all eye movement studies have reported unusual scanpaths in participants with AP. For instance, Rizzo, Hurtig and Damasio (1987) found no deviation in the eye movement pattern elicited to faces in two participants with AP compared with controls.

5.7. FUNCTIONAL MAGNETIC RESONANCE IMAGING (FMRI) STUDIES

Although many studies have used structural neuroimaging to examine the lesion site in AP, fewer studies have used functional magnetic resonance imaging (fMRI) to examine the neural underpinnings of face processing in these individuals. However, some interesting findings have been reported. For example, Marotta, Genovese and Behrmann (2001) showed that, compared with control participants, patients with AP have reduced activation in the right hemisphere (and particularly the fusiform face area), but increased activation in the posterior left hemisphere when viewing facial stimuli. The authors suggest this pattern of findings fit well with those noted in behavioural studies that suggest configural processing is impaired in AP. Indeed, it is thought that configural processing is supported by mechanisms in the right hemisphere, whereas featural processing occurs in the left hemisphere.

In contrast, however, normal activation of the fusiform face area has been observed in a patient with AP (PS), who suffered tissue loss in the right inferior lateral occipital lobe and left medial temporal lobe (Schiltz *et al.*, 2006; Sorger *et al.*, 2007). Further, Steeves *et al.* (2006) reported a similar finding in their prosopagnosic patient, DF. Finally, other studies have used fMRI to examine whether face-selective processing can still be noted in individuals with AP. In some cases, researchers have failed to find evidence of preserved selective activation for faces compared with other categories of objects (e.g., Hadjikhani and de Gelder, 2002). On the other hand, Steeves *et al.* (2009) reported two cases of AP who had normal face-selective activation in all unaffected areas of the face-processing network.

Hence, it can be seen that few neuroimaging studies have investigated face processing in AP, and discrepant findings have emerged between existing studies. As with behavioural work, this is likely to reflect the complexity of the disorder and the varied pattern of lesions that present in different cases.

CHAPTER SUMMARY

■ Acquired prosopagnosia is a rare disorder that tends to result from neurological trauma to the occipitotemporal region of the right hemisphere (de Renzi *et al.*, 1994), or bilateral lesions affecting both hemispheres (Damasio, Damasio and Van Hoesen, 1982). The latter type of injury tends to result in a more severe problem affecting other cognitive processes (Warrington and James, 1967).

■ Although 'pure' prosopagnosia is very rare, face recognition problems more commonly occur alongside other cognitive deficits (Valentine *et al.*, 2006).

■ Often, a range of other visual processes are also affected (e.g., visual field defects and achromatopsia), and many prosopagnosics suffer from topographagnosia (Hécaen and Angelergues (1962).

■ Most prosopagnosics have problems recognizing objects, and often other aspects of face processing are also disrupted (e.g., Assal, Favre and Anderes, 1984).

■ Prosopagnosia can be subdivided into two functional subtypes: apperceptive prosopagnosics have problems creating a visual percept of a face, whereas associative prosopagnosics can perceive faces normally and are thought to have a higher-level disorder (De Renzi *et al.*, 1991). 'Covert' or 'unconscious' face recognition can be observed in most associative prosopagnosics, but few apperceptive prosopagnosics.

■ Much evidence suggests many prosopagnosics have a deficit in configural processing (see, for example, Boutsen and Humphreys, 2002; de Gelder and Rouw, 2000b; Delvenne *et al.*, 2004).

■ Little fMRI work has been performed so far, and a varied pattern of findings have been noted.

FURTHER READING

Bauer, R. M. (1984) 'Autonomic Recognition of Names and Faces in Prosopagnosia: A Neuropsychological Application of the Guilty Knowledge Test', *Neuropsychologia, 22*, 457–69.

Caldara, R., Schyns, P., Mayer, E., Smith, M. Z., Gosselin, F. and Rossion, B. (2005) 'Does Prosopagnosia Take the Eyes out of Face Representations? Evidence for a Defect in Representing Diagnostic Facial Information Following Brain Damage', *Journal of Cognitive Neuroscience, 17*, 1652–66.

De Renzi, E., Faglioni, P., Grossi, D. and Nichelli, P. (1991) 'Apperceptive and Associative Forms of Prosopagnosia', *Cortex, 27*, 213–21.

Farah, M. J., O'Reilly, R. C. and Vecera, S. P. (1993). 'Dissociated Overt and Covert Recognition as an Emergent Property of a Lesioned Neural Network', *Psychological Review, 100*, 571–88.

Valentine, T., Powell, J., Davidoff, F., Letson, S. and Greenwood, R. (2006) 'Prevalence and Correlates of Face Recognition Impairments after Acquired Brain Injury', *Neuropsychological Rehabilitation, 16*, 272–97.

GUIDANCE QUESTIONS

Use the following questions to guide your reading of this chapter and the recommended papers.

1. How common is acquired prosopagnosia, and how can the disorder originate?
2. To what extent does evidence support the existence of different subtypes of prosopagnosia?
3. How have structural and functional neuroimaging studies contributed to our understanding of prosopagnosia?

6 Delusional Misidentification Syndrome

Delusional misidentification syndrome (DMS) refers to a group of conditions in which a person consistently misidentifies people, places, objects or events. Given this book is only concerned with disorders of person recognition, only delusions affecting this entity will be discussed. According to Ellis, Whitley and Luauté (1994), there are four main delusional misidentification disorders that affect person recognition: Capgras delusion, Fregoli syndrome, intermetamorphosis and subjective doubles. Christodoulou (1978) suggested that these four disorders can be further divided into two broad subtypes: those that involve hypo- or under-identification of a well-known person (i.e., Capgras syndrome), and those that involve hyper- or over-identification of a person not known well to the patient (i.e., Fregoli syndrome, intermetamorphosis and subjective doubles). This chapter begins with an introduction to each of these disorders, followed by discussion of the aetiological and functional basis of DMS.

6.1. TYPES OF DMS

6.1.1. Capgras delusion

The Capgras delusion is the most common form of DMS, and was named after Joseph Capgras, a French psychiatrist who first described the disorder (Capgras and Reboul-Lachaux, 1923). Specifically, Capgras reported the case of a French woman who complained that her husband and other people she knew had been replaced by 'doubles'. Indeed, the Capgras delusion is characterized by the mistaken belief that a person who is close to the patient has been replaced by a double or imposter. It is important to understand that the patient recognizes that the physical appearance of the imposter is identical to the misidentified person, but they are psychologically different. Thus, the Capgras delusion differs from prosopagnosia, given the person accurately recognizes the face of the misidentified person, but believes the person inside that body has been replaced.

6.1.2. Fregoli delusion

The Fregoli delusion is named after the Italian actor Leopoldo Fregoli, who became famous for his ability to change his appearance quickly during live shows. The condition itself is therefore characterized by the delusional belief that several different people are actually the same person but in disguise. Further, the patient often additionally experiences a paranoid belief that this person is persecuting them. The disorder was first described by Courbon and Fail (1927), who reported a 27-year-old woman who believed she was being persecuted by two actors that she often saw at the theatre. She believed these people pursued her closely, taking the form of other people who she knew or met.

6.1.3. Intermetamorphosis

Courbon and Tusques (1932) described a variant of Fregoli syndrome, which they termed 'intermetamorphosis'. In this form of the disorder, the patient believes that certain individuals interchange with one another, taking on both psychological and physical similarities (rather than being in disguise). A recent case of intermetamorphosis was described by Assal and Mendez (2003), who reported a man with Alzheimer's disease who mistook his wife for his deceased mother and for his sister. Whenever he was asked to account for this delusional misidentification, he stated that he had never been married or that his wife had left him. The patient also experienced further delusions at a later point in time, mistaking his son for his brother and his daughter for another sister.

6.1.4. Subjective doubles

A final form of DMS that commonly co-occurs alongside the Capgras delusion was reported by Christodoulou in 1978. Specifically, the delusion of 'subjective doubles' refers to a patient's mistaken belief that he or she has a double or 'Doppelgänger' with the same physical appearance. However, the patient usually believes that their double has a different personality, and is going about the world leading a life of their own. Further, the patient can believe that all or some part of his or her personality has been transplanted into the double's head. For example, Silva and Leong (1991) reported a man who became depersonalized after an operation, and was convinced his brain had been transplanted into someone else's head. He later claimed that he met and recognized his double.

6.2. COMMON FEATURES OF DMS

Having described the four main types of DMS that affect person recognition, it should be clear that the concept of the 'double' is evident in all four disorders.

However, these disorders also share other characteristics that distinguish them from more general conditions (Feinberg and Roane, 2005), as follows.

- As the patient consistently misidentifies the same aspect of a person, the disorder is unlikely to be caused by a general impairment in memory or perception.
- The patient is usually unaware of their delusion, either due to psychological denial or anosognosia (unawareness of their condition owing to physiological damage in the brain).
- The misidentification is also resilient against correction, and represents a fixed (false) belief that is a 'true' delusion. Thus, patients defend their belief even when they are repeatedly and persistently confronted with its illogical nature. Importantly, this characteristic of DMS distinguishes it from other forms of confabulation (e.g., amnestic confabulation), and from general unawareness.
- Finally, DMS is often characterized by abnormalities in the right hemisphere of the brain. The aetiology of DMS in discussed in more detail below.

6.3. PREVALENCE

DMS is most frequently encountered alongside neuropsychiatric disorders such as schizophrenia or mood disorders, and more rarely after brain injury or neurodegenerative conditions such as Alzheimer's disease, Parkinson's disease and dementia. The most common types of DMS are Capgras delusion and Fregoli syndrome, but all types of DMS can co-occur or present in isolation. DMS is uncommon (but perhaps not rare given delusions are a key feature of schizophrenia), and is thought to affect less than one per cent of the general population. Indeed, Dohn and Crews (1986) observed Capgras delusion in 15 per cent of their sample of schizophrenic patients, corresponding to 0.12 per cent of the general population. Other studies have examined the prevalence of DMS among patients who have Alzheimer's disease, and presented rather discrepant prevalence rates that indicate between two and 30 per cent of these individuals suffer from the condition (Harwood *et al.*, 1999; Silva *et al.*, 2001).

6.4. AETIOLOGY

There is strong evidence that dysfunction in the right hemisphere underpins DMS, particularly involving the frontal lobe. For example, Förstl, Almeida *et al.* (1991) reviewed a diverse group of DMS cases and found right-sided abnormalities in 19 of their 20 patients with focal lesions. In another study, Fleminger and Burns (1993) reported that their sample of patients with DMS also had greater damage to the right hemisphere, principally affecting the frontal, temporal and parietal lobes. Further, a more recent study examined 29 cases of DMS, and found that although 15 had bilateral lesions, the remaining 14 cases all had lesions restricted to the right hemisphere, and no cases had only left hemisphere lesions (Feinberg *et al.*, 2005). In addition, these authors also found a relationship between frontal lobe damage and DMS. Specifically, lesions that only affected the frontal lobe were found in 34.5 per cent of the cases, and in no case did parietal or temporal damage alone produce DMS. Finally, a similar pattern of findings was noted in a study that examined DMS in patients with Alzheimer's disease. Specifically, Förstl and colleagues found greater atrophy in the right frontal lobe in their patients who had Alzheimer's disease and DMS, compared with control participants with dementia but no DMS (Förstl, Burns *et al.*, 1991).

The studies described above provide convincing evidence that the right frontal lobe might play an important role in contributing to DMS. Some authors have provided more specific hypotheses regarding the link between right frontal lobe damage and DMS. Indeed, Alexander, Stuss and Benton (1979) suggested that a deep right frontal lesion could functionally disconnect the structure from temporal and limbic regions. As a result, inaccurate familiarity information might be accessed about certain individuals, and frontal lobe damage could bring about a further inability to resolve any arising cognitive conflict experienced by the perceiver.

Another group of authors hypothesized that DMS might involve disruption to the hippocampus, a structure located within the temporal lobe that is thought to play a fundamental role in memory consolidation. Specifically, Staton, Brunback and Wilson (1982) suggested that the hippocampus might become disconnected from other parts of the brain that are also important for memory storage, preventing new information from becoming associated with existing information. The authors suggested that this disconnection might bring about reduplicative forms of DMS.

Similar hypotheses suggest that abnormalities within the temporal lobe (including the face-processing system) might underpin DMS. Indeed, some neuroimaging studies have provided evidence that the fusiform gyrus itself might be impaired. For example, Hudson and Grace (2000) reported a patient who had Fregoli delusion, and consistently misidentified her husband as her deceased sister. The researchers used magnetic resonance imaging to identify that the patient had suffered damage to a small area in the anterior right fusiform gyrus, a small area in the anterior middle and inferior temporal gyri, and had associated parahippocampal and hippocampal atrophy. The authors suggested that the fusiform face area might have become disconnected from the anterior inferior part of the temporal lobe where long-term visual memories are stored.

Such attempts to account for DMS within the face-processing system fit well with theories that have attempted to accommodate the disorder within functional models of face processing. These models are discussed and evaluated in the next section.

6.5. CAN DMS BE ACCOUNTED FOR WITHIN FUNCTIONAL MODELS OF FACE PROCESSING?

Importantly, some researchers have suggested that delusional misidentification disorders might be accommodated within Bruce and Young's (1986) model of face processing (see Chapter 1). For example, Ellis and Young (1990) suggested that the model can account for intermetamorphosis in instances where the threshold for face recognition unit (FRU) activation is abnormally low. More specifically, if the FRUs for particular individuals can be falsely activated in response to unknown or incorrect facial representations, that individual might be incorrectly recognized as someone else. Further, the authors suggested that dysfunction at the level of the person identity nodes (PINs) might account for Fregoli syndrome. Indeed, excessive activation of the PIN system and consequential activation of an incorrect PIN in response to a correctly activated FRU could explain the false belief that a familiar person is disguised as someone else.

However, it is much more difficult to explain Capgras delusion within Bruce and Young's model; as a result, some authors have extended the model to account for this disorder. In Chapter 5, the 'dual-route' model of face processing was discussed. This model was first introduced by Bauer (1984), to account for the finding that several individuals with acquired prosopagnosia still demonstrate a preserved skin conductance response (SCR) when they view familiar faces. To recap, Bauer suggested that the facial identity pathway follows a ventral route, involving neural structures such as the longitudinal fasciculus. On the other hand, Bauer suggested that a second 'dorsal' pathway processes the emotional significance of a face, as measured by the SCR. He suggested that this latter route passes from visual cortex through the superior temporal sulcus, inferior parietal lobe and cingulate gyrus to the limbic system, including the amygdala.

Importantly, Bauer's dual-route model was later adopted by Ellis and Young (1990) to explain Capgras delusion. These authors suggested that the face-processing deficit observed in individuals with Capgras delusion is the double dissociation or reverse pattern to that seen in prosopagnosia. Indeed, it had been demonstrated that prosopagnosics still show an intact SCR for familiar faces, despite not being able to overtly recognize these faces. Hence, the face recognition pathway is thought to be impaired in these individuals, but the second affective route is intact. Conversely, Ellis and Young suggest that the main identity pathway remains intact in Capgras delusion (given these individuals can still recognize familiar faces), but it is the affective route that is impaired. Indeed, individuals with Capgras delusion appear to have an incorrect emotional response to certain familiar individuals, indicating dysfunction in this pathway. If this hypothesis is correct, Ellis and Young reasoned that Capgras patients should not demonstrate an intact SCR for familiar faces. This prediction was tested by Ellis *et al.* (1997), who examined five patients with Capgras syndrome. In line with Ellis and Young's hypothesis, most of the patients were able to recognize the faces just as well as unimpaired control participants, but all failed to show a heightened SCR when viewing familiar faces.

More recently, Breen, Caine and Coltheart (2000) criticized Bauer's dual-route model on the basis that the model posits the existence of two distinct face-processing systems, one processing identity and the other affective significance. Instead, Breen and colleagues argued that it is unlikely that the dorsal (affective) route is capable of any form of face processing, given evidence suggests the neural structures in this route primarily underpin the processing of visually guided actions. Hence, the authors offer the more parsimonious suggestion that both facial identity and our affective response to familiar faces are processed within the same ventral pathway. Indeed, Breen *et al.* suggest that facial familiarity is initially computed, and affective analysis can then proceed in ventral limbic structures, particularly the amygdala.

In functional terms, the authors suggest that, once initial familiarity has been computed, the face recognition pathway bifurcates at the level of the FRUs, such that face identification and affective analysis occur in parallel (see Figure 6.1). Hence, the face recognition impairment in prosopagnosia can be accounted for by a disruption within the FRUs or a disconnection between the FRUs and the PINs, whereas the autonomic response to familiar faces is intact. On the other hand, face identification can proceed uninterrupted in the Capgras delusion, allowing the patient to correctly identify a face, but a disruption in the connection between the FRUs and the affective response module (or within this module itself) could bring about a reduced or absent autonomic response to familiar faces. Hence, according to Breen *et al.*, the absence of an emotional response to a familiar face is thought to bring about the delusion.

However, Ellis and Lewis (2001) proposed a further extension to the dual-route model, citing evidence that the loss of emotional responsiveness alone cannot underpin the Capgras delusion. Indeed, the authors point out that many brain-injured patients lose the ability to have appropriate emotional responses to faces, but do not go on to experience the Capgras delusion (e.g., Tranel, Damasio and Damasio, 1995). Thus, Ellis and Lewis suggested that, although the lost affective response might be essential for the disorder to develop, an additional anomaly must also be present. They suggest that this might take the form of an 'integrative device' (see Figure 6.1) that compares the outputs of the identification and affective routes. The Capgras delusion is then experienced when the integrative device does not receive the expected emotional response to a particular face, bringing about an attribution that results in the delusional belief. Although the integrative device is displayed within the dual-route model in Figure 6.1, it should be noted that Ellis and Lewis acknowledge that the device might operate outside of the face-processing system.

As a final note, Breen, Coltheart and Caine (2001) disagree with Ellis and Lewis' hypothesis, arguing that the integrative device is not required. Instead, the authors suggest that a double-headed arrow placed between the PINs and

Figure 6.1   *An adaptation of the dual-route model of face processing (and related functions that occur outside of the face processing system) proposed by Breen et al. (2000) and later modified by Ellis and Lewis (2001).*

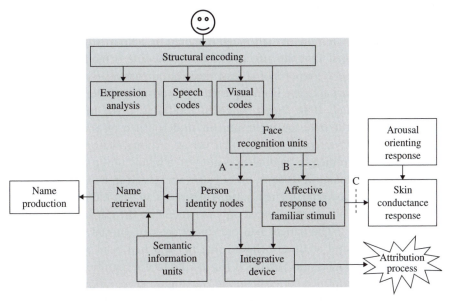

A lesion at the location marked 'A' would bring about prosopagnosia, whereas a lesion at location 'B' would cause Capgras delusion, given the integrative device would receive conflicting information from the two pathways. The delusion would not result from a lesion at the 'C' location, as the integrative device would not suffer from such a confliction. Note that Breen *et al.* proposed that the PINs and affective response modules are directly connected (not represented in the figure), and that the integrative device is not needed.

affective response module would allow for the same integrative and misattribution process. In response, Lewis and Ellis (2001) argued that the presence of such an arrow would allow damage to be circumvented, and hence the additional device is necessary. Thus, although the Breen *et al.* model offers a more parsimonious account of the Capgras delusion than earlier dual-route models, some of the finer details of the model are still under debate.

6.6. NON-FACE-SPECIFIC ACCOUNTS OF DMS

The modified dual-route models of face processing that have been offered by Breen *et al.* (2000) and Ellis and Lewis (2001) have been well-received by researchers within the face-processing field. However, other authors have highlighted concerns that DMS might not originate from an impairment in the face-processing system itself. For example, many patients with DMS not only misidentify people, but also objects, places and events; and it is currently unclear how the dual-route model might explain the co-occurrence of these different types of DMS.

Further, it has also been shown that many cases of Capgras delusion are not limited to the visual modality (although it should be acknowledged that Breen *et al.* do not suggest that the affective response module is modality-specific). For instance, there are reports of at least three blind patients who believe that familiar people or pets have been replaced by imposters (see Reid, Young and Hellawell; Rojo *et al.*, 1991; Signer, Van Ness and Davis, 1990). In these cases of 'blind Capgras', the delusion is presumably underpinned by the absence of a heightened affective response to familiar voices, although autonomic processing of the misidentified individuals was not tested in any of the cases.

However, physiological recognition of voices was tested in a case reported by Lewis and Sherwood (2001). These authors describe a 59-year-old female patient, HL, who was not blind but appeared only to experience the Capgras delusion in response to voices. The patient had previously been diagnosed with schizoaffective disorder, and at times believed that her son had been replaced by an imposter. When Lewis and Sherwood tested HL's face recognition ability, they found that she performed perfectly on the Warrington Recognition Test for Faces (Warrington, 1984), and that she showed differential SCRs for familiar and unfamiliar faces. Hence, both the identification and affective pathways within the face-processing system appeared to be intact. However, the authors found no evidence of a heightened SCR when HL listened to familiar voices, despite noting the predicted pattern of performance in control participants. Thus, this study implies that both familiar voices and familiar faces normally trigger a heightened affective response in healthy adults, presumably by accessing the same affective response module. Yet, the pattern of performance observed in patient HL provides initial evidence that the module can be accessed by separate modality-specific pathways, and these pathways can become selectively impaired. Future work is clearly needed to determine which aspects of the affective processing pathway are modality-specific and which are restricted to the face-processing system.

Finally, as discussed at the beginning of this chapter, there is much aetiological evidence to suggest that the frontal lobes must be involved in the disorder, and these structures are not part of the core face-processing system. However, Coltheart, Langdon and McKay (2007) suggest a 'two-process' theory that neatly brings together these different lines of evidence, in addition to encompassing ideas from the dual-route models. Specifically, the authors propose that two different abnormalities are required for the disorder to occur. They suggest that the first abnormality prompts the delusional belief and is responsible for the content of the delusion, and this abnormality is different for each type of delusion. For example, Coltheart and colleagues agree with Breen *et al.* that the Capgras delusion is caused by the failure of the patient to have the expected autonomic response to a familiar face. As pointed out by Ellis and Lewis (2001), this abnormality must be present for the disorder to occur, but is not sufficient on its own. Hence, a second abnormality is required, and Coltheart and colleagues suggest this dysfunction is common to all delusions. Specifically, the authors propose that this latter abnormality arises from damage to a belief evaluation system that might operate in the right frontal cortex, and prevents the patient from rejecting the delusion despite the strong evidence against it.

Thus, Coltheart *et al.*'s model appears to bring together both anatomical and behavioural evidence in providing a coherent account of DMS, and it is of interest that Young (2008) recently advocated an interactionist model that successfully endorses the two-process theory.

CHAPTER SUMMARY

- There are four main delusional misidentification disorders that affect person recognition: Capgras delusion, Fregoli delusion, intermetamorphosis and subjective doubles. These disorders have the common theme of 'doubles'.
- DMS is frequently encountered in neuropsychiatric settings (Dohn and Crews, 1986), and more rarely after brain injury and in neurodegenerative disorders (Silva *et al.*, 2001).
- Imaging studies implicate the right hemisphere in DMS, particularly the right frontal lobe (Feinberg *et al.*, 2005; Förstl, Almeida, *et al.*, 1991). There is also some aetiological evidence that suggests there may be abnormalities in the fusiform gyrus (Hudson and Grace, 2000).
- Capgras delusion has traditionally been explained within the dual-route model of face processing, and is seen as the double dissociation to prosopagnosia (Ellis and Young, 1990; Breen *et al.*, 2000; Ellis and Lewis, 2001).
- The two-process theory proposed by Coltheart *et al.* (2007) offers an account of DMS that requires impairments both within the affective pathway to recognition and in a belief evaluation device that is located within the right frontal lobe.

FURTHER READING

Breen, N., Caine, D. and Coltheart, M. (2000) 'Models of Face Recognition and Delusional Misidentification: A Critical Review', *Cognitive Neuropsychology*, 17 (1/2/3), 55–71.

Christodoulou, G. N., Margariti, M., Kontaxakis, V. P. and Christodoulou, N. G. (2009) 'The Delusional Misidentification Syndromes: Strange, Fascinating, and Instructive', *Current Psychiatry Reports*, 11, 185–9.

Coltheart, M., Langdon, R. and McKay, R. (2007). 'Schizophrenia and Monothematic Delusions', *Schizophrenia Bulletin*, 33, 642–7.

Ellis, H. D. and Lewis, M. B. (2001) 'Capgras Delusion: A Window on Face Recognition', *Trends in Cognitive Sciences*, 5 (4), 149–56.

Feinberg, T. E. and Roane, D. M. (2005) 'Delusional Misidentification', *Psychiatric Clinics of North America*, 28, 665–83.

GUIDANCE QUESTIONS

Use the following questions to guide your reading of this chapter and the recommended papers.

1. What are the main characteristics of each of the four main delusional misidentification disorders that affect person recognition?
2. How consistent is the aetiological evidence that suggests an abnormality in the right frontal lobe might underpin DMS?
3. Can DMS be accommodated within functional models of face processing?
4. To what extent does the two-process theory of Coltheart *et al.* (2007) reconcile the available evidence on DMS?

7 Face-Processing Deficits in Neuropsychiatric Disorders

Individuals with major psychiatric illnesses such as schizophrenia and mood disorders commonly suffer from deficits in social perception, and particularly display abnormal processing of facial expressions of emotion. Importantly, emotional expressions signal our own affective state and allow us to interpret those of others, and many researchers believe that these processes influence and regulate our own affective feelings and mood. Hence, it is unsurprising that some theories suggest that impaired perception of facial expression might underpin the socio-communicative problems commonly observed in individuals with major psychiatric illnesses. In the current chapter, the nature of face-processing impairments in three major neuropsychiatric disorders is discussed. Before you begin this chapter, you may find it useful to read Chapter 3, where the social aspects of face perception in unimpaired participants are described.

7.1. SCHIZOPHRENIA

Schizophrenia is a chronic neuropsychiatric disorder that is most common in late adolescence and early adulthood, and affects 0.3–0.7 per cent of the population (McGrath *et al.*, 2008). There are many models of the aetiology of schizophrenia, but generally it is thought to arise from a combination of genetics and environmental factors, including living environment (those who live in an urban environment are twice as likely to develop the disorder (Krabbendam and van Os, 2005)), social isolation, family dysfunction, unemployment, poor housing conditions, a history of childhood abuse or trauma, and drug use (e.g., cannabis, cocaine, amphetamines).

Schizophrenia is characterized by two classes of symptoms (van Os and Kapur, 2009). Positive symptoms are those that are present, such as hallucinations, delusions, and disorganized thinking and speech. Negative symptoms are those that are absent, such as a lack of social skills, motivation and emotional responsiveness. It is therefore not surprising that individuals with schizophrenia usually suffer from dysfunctional social interactions. For this reason, much research has examined the face-processing abilities of this group. In particular, there has been a surge of interest in the finding that many schizophrenics are impaired at identifying emotions from facial expressions.

7.1.1. Deficits in recognizing facial expressions of emotion

Some researchers have examined whether the recognition of negative emotional expressions is more impaired than the recognition of positive expressions in participants with schizophrenia. For example, Brune (2005) showed participants faces displaying either positive or negative expressions, and asked them to identify the emotion depicted on each face. They found that schizophrenics were more impaired at recognizing the negative expressions than the positive expressions. Other researchers have suggested the impairment is even more specific, and that the recognition of certain negative emotions is more impaired than that of other negative expressions. Several studies have provided evidence to support this hypothesis, although different researchers have found that different negative expressions are selectively impaired. For example, it has been found that the recognition of fear (e.g., Evangeli and Broks, 2000; Hall *et al.*, 2008), disgust (Mandal, 1987) and sadness (Silver *et al.*, 2002) can be selectively disrupted in individuals with the disorder.

However, it might be claimed that positive expressions are simply less complex than negative expressions, and any difficulties in processing these stimuli might therefore be obscured by ceiling effects and reduced task demands. This issue was addressed by Kohler *et al.* (2003), who increased task difficulty by presenting participants with faces displaying high- and low-intensity emotional expressions. Results indicated that the schizophrenic group did not receive any benefit from an increase in the intensity of the emotional expression, and this effect was particularly pronounced for expressions of fear. Hence, this study indicates that individuals with schizophrenia are poorer at recognizing all facial expressions than control participants, but the recognition of fear is particularly disrupted. Further, it is of note that the authors found that their schizophrenic participants also tended to misclassify neutral expressions as disgust. Interestingly, findings from another study suggest that schizophrenics might also misclassify happy faces as displaying fear or sadness (Tsoi *et al.*, 2008).

Further, there is evidence to suggest that the ability to recognize facial expressions also varies according to the particular presentation of the disorder. Indeed, some studies have shown that impairments in recognizing emotional expressions might be associated with the occurrence of cognitive impairment (Bozikas *et al.*, 2004) or negative symptoms (Schneider *et al.*, 1995). For example, the ability to recognize fear has been found to be poorer in individuals who display negative symptoms (see Van't Wout and van Dijke et al., 2007), whereas individuals who suffer from paranoia or persecutory delusions (positive symptoms) seem to misattribute emotional significance to neutral (see Kohler et al., 2003) or ambiguous (Combs and Gouvier, 2004) information. Hence, the occurrence of delusions in schizophrenia might be underpinned by the false attribution of affective significance to neutral stimuli in the environment (Kapur, 2003).

There is also some evidence to suggest that the difficulty in interpreting emotional expressions might be linked to illness progression (Mueser et al., 1997). Indeed, some studies report greater deficits in chronic compared with acute phases of schizophrenia (e.g., Kucharska-Pietura et al., 2005), whereas other evidence suggests that the impairment can be present either before (Baum and Walker, 1995) or from onset (Edwards et al., 2001) of the disorder. Although more research is required to test these hypotheses, it is possible that impairments in emotional expression recognition might predate the onset of schizophrenia and worsen as the disorder progresses. Hence, monitoring the ability to interpret facial expressions of emotion might be a useful tool to identify illness progression in both individuals with diagnoses of schizophrenia and those who might be at risk of developing the disorder.

7.1.2. How specific is the impairment in recognizing emotional expressions?

Although it is clear that individuals with schizophrenia suffer from impairments in interpreting emotional expressions, an ongoing debate in the literature questions whether the impairment can be attributed to a more generalized cognitive impairment, a problem in processing all aspects of faces or a specific problem in recognizing facial expressions of emotion. In the discussion below, each of these hypotheses is considered in turn.

Some authors have suggested that the deficit in recognizing emotional expressions can be attributed to a more general cognitive impairment, given evidence that individuals with schizophrenia display poor levels of performance on almost all cognitive tasks (Chapman and Chapman, 1973). This finding is thought to reflect the fact that schizophrenia is often accompanied by at least some degree of general intellectual impairment (McKenna, 2007). In particular, it has been suggested that generalized deficits in memory and attention might underpin the expression recognition deficit, given several studies have provided evidence of improved performance when simpler experimental designs are used, such as matching faces that are displayed from the same viewpoint (Hooker and Park, 2002).

A detailed assessment of more generalized mechanisms that might underpin the expression recognition deficit in schizophrenia was performed by Chen et al. (2009). Participants were asked to complete three tasks: a visual detection task where they were required to detect a briefly presented face from basic configural information, a perceptual discrimination task where they had to discriminate between faces of varying similarity, and a working memory task with the same format as the perceptual discrimination task, but with a time lag of three or ten seconds between the two images. The authors found that participants with schizophrenia were severely impaired at both the visual detection and working memory tasks, and moderately impaired at the perceptual discrimination task. They interpreted their findings as evidence of generalized impairments in schizophrenia, given the tasks did not require actual interpretation of facial identity or expression.

Other authors have suggested the impairment in recognizing emotional expressions can be attributed to a generalized visuo-spatial deficit. For example, Whittaker, Deakin and Tomenson (2001) tested schizophrenic participants on a range of tests that assessed face-processing ability and non-facial visuo-spatial processing. Interestingly, they observed that performance on the two types of test was correlated, suggesting that the impairment in recognizing facial expressions might be explained by deficits in lower-level visual processing. Converging evidence was provided by Norton *et al.* (2009), who tested participants with schizophrenia on their ability to interpret emotional expressions, recognize facial identity and to detect visual contrast on non-facial stimuli. The researchers found that the schizophrenic participants were poor at recognizing both positive and negative emotional expressions. Importantly, performance at recognizing fearful expressions was predicted by performance on both the facial identification and the contrast detection tasks, suggesting that the expression recognition impairment is at least partly explained by a lower-level perceptual impairment.

Finally, other researchers have posited alternative hypotheses that suggest the deficit in recognizing facial expressions might be grounded in non-facial processing mechanisms. For example, Silver *et al.* (2006) suggested that a generalized problem in monitoring errors might underpin the impairment, whereas other authors suggest that individuals with schizophrenia might find faces more fear-evoking and therefore avoid looking at them. Indeed, Mandal, Pandey and Prasad (1998) provided evidence that schizophrenic participants prefer to stand further away from emotional faces than controls, particularly when they display happy or sad expressions. The authors account for the finding by suggesting that faces (and particularly the eye region of faces) make schizophrenics feel anxious, causing them to interpret all faces as fearful or anxiety-producing.

Other evidence suggests that the deficit specifically lies within the face-processing system, although it is unclear whether the problem is restricted to the processing of emotional expression, or if it extends to all aspects of face processing. Indeed, several researchers have only found deficits in the recognition of emotional expressions in their schizophrenic participants, and conclude that the impairment does not extend to the recognition of identity, age or gender.

For example, Walker, McGuire and Bettes (1984) found that participants with schizophrenia performed poorly on tests of expression recognition, but within the normal range on the Benton Facial Recognition Test that requires participants to match faces according to identity (Benton and Van Allen, 1968). A similar finding was reported by Hall *et al.* (2004), who found that individuals with schizophrenia were poor at recognizing all facial expressions, but performed as well as controls in identity recognition tasks.

Despite these findings, other evidence suggests that individuals with schizophrenia have an impairment in processing all aspects of faces, which happens to include the recognition of different facial expressions. Hence, this viewpoint suggests the impairment resides within the face-processing system itself, but is not specific to the processing of facial expression. Evidence supporting this viewpoint comes from studies that observed poor performance in both expression recognition tasks and control tasks that assess the ability to recognize facial identity. For example, Feinberg *et al.* (1986) found that participants with schizophrenia performed poorly in tasks that required them to match or label facial expressions of emotion, as well as tasks requiring them to assess facial identity. Impaired performance on both expression and identity recognition tasks has also been demonstrated in other studies where the identification task used a face-matching paradigm (e.g., Kucharska-Pictura *et al.*, 2005; Penn *et al.*, 2000), in tasks where participants are asked to learn new faces with both immediate and delayed recall (Whittaker *et al.*, 2001), and in face recognition tasks using familiar faces (e.g., Sachs *et al.*, 2004). Finally, other studies have examined other aspects of facial processing by using the visual comparison task. For instance, Kohler *et al.* (2000) found that their schizophrenic participants demonstrated impaired performance compared with controls on tasks requiring judgements of emotional expression and age perception.

Studies of event-related potentials have also provided evidence supporting the hypothesis that individuals with schizophrenia have a more widespread problem in facial processing. For example, Wynn *et al.* (2001) compared the P100, N170 and N250 responses while participants either judged the emotional expression or the gender of a series of faces. Although the P100 and N170 were found to be similar for schizophrenic participants and controls, the N250 was smaller for the schizophrenic group, regardless of the type of task the participants were performing. This finding suggests that early aspects of face processing are preserved in schizophrenia, and it is the later stages of processing that are affected by the disorder. However, other studies have reported reduced or absent N170 responses in schizophrenic participants while viewing affective faces (Lynn and Salisbury, 2008; Onitsuka *et al.*, 2006). Finally, Turetsky *et al.* (2007) reported an interesting pattern of findings that might account for these differences across studies. These authors found that the N170 response did differ between control and schizophrenic participant groups, but that the size of this difference was modulated by the nature of the illness. Specifically, participants who reported fewer delusions had a larger N170 and performed more in line with control participants. This pattern of findings suggests that the severity of the schizophrenia might predict the magnitude of the expression recognition impairment.

In sum, considerable evidence has been reported that supports all sides of the debate, and no conclusion has yet been reached. However, it is notable that Edwards *et al.* (2002) conducted a systematic review of studies performed between 1987 and 1998 and found few studies included adequate control tasks that mirrored the expression recognition tasks. Indeed, several studies used the Benton Facial Recognition Test as a test of the ability to process facial identity, and this test has received criticism in recent years, given findings that non-facial cues can be used to aid performance (e.g., Duchaine and Weidenfeld, 2003; Duchaine and Nakayama, 2004; see Chapter 14). Hence, this question remains a hotly debated topic in the psychological literature.

7.1.3. Is there a deficit in configural processing in schizophrenia?

Recall from Chapter 1 that face processing is believed to rely on the use of configural information, and it has been suggested that deficits in this strategy might underpin impaired face recognition in individuals with acquired prosopagnosia. In a similar vein, it has been suggested that configural processing might also be impaired in individuals with schizophrenia, and this deficit might account for their problems in face processing.

Several studies have provided support for this hypothesis, demonstrating an over-reliance on featural rather than configural information when schizophrenic participants process facial stimuli. Indeed, this finding has been demonstrated using the face inversion effect (Shin *et al.*, 2008), and studies that have manipulated the spacing of facial features (e.g., Baudouin, Vernet and Franck, 2008). A recent study investigated the use of configural and featural processing strategies in 26 individuals with schizophrenia using a fractured face task (Joshua and Rossel, 2009). In this study, participants were presented with a set of famous faces for recognition, either in their normal 'whole' form or in a fractured format. Specifically, fractured faces were presented in five or six segments, such that featural information was preserved but configural information was disrupted. The authors noted a similar pattern of performance for control participants and schizophrenic participants for whole faces, but interestingly the schizophrenic group performed better than controls in the fractured condition.

Converging evidence has also been reported in studies that monitored participants' eye movements as they inspect faces (for a review see Marsh and Williams, 2006). For example, Loughland, Williams and Gordon (2002) noted that schizophrenic participants avoided fixating on the facial features, and demonstrated more restricted scanpaths than control participants. Interestingly, this effect was particularly pronounced for faces displaying positive or neutral emotional expressions. Such studies provide additional evidence for abnormal visual processing of faces by individuals with schizophrenia, and suggest that configural processing might be disrupted in the disorder.

Further evidence that indicates configural processing is impaired in schizophrenia comes from a neuroimaging study reported by Fakra *et al.* (2008). These authors asked participants to complete a face-matching task and an expression recognition task while brain activation was monitored. Although no differences were noted between schizophrenic and control participants in the recognition task, an interesting pattern of findings emerged in the matching task. Specifically, Fakra *et al.* found that, compared with controls, schizophrenic participants demonstrated lower levels of activation in the area of the brain typically associated with configural processing (the fusiform face area (FFA)) but greater activation in neural areas associated with featural processing (inferior parietal cortex, left middle temporal lobe, right precuneus).

However, some conflicting data have been reported. For instance, Schwarz *et al.* (2002) noted a normal face inversion effect in their schizophrenic participants, and a similar pattern of findings was reported by Chambon *et al.* (2006). Although these studies suggest that configural processing is not impaired in individuals with schizophrenia, it is of note that Chambon *et al.* did find that their participants with more severe symptoms demonstrated a weaker face inversion effect, indicating that configural processing was more impaired in these individuals.

7.1.4. Neuroimaging evidence

Several neuroimaging studies have investigated whether schizophrenic participants present with either structural or functional neural abnormalities that might underpin their problems in processing faces. In particular, these studies have examined processing in the critical face area of the brain (the FFA), and the main structure known to process emotion (the amygdala). Given that individuals with schizophrenia seem to be particularly impaired at recognizing fearful facial expressions, it is of note that the amygdala is especially activated when healthy participants view the eye region of fearful faces (see, for example, Adams *et al.*, 2003), and that bilateral damage to the amygdala results in a greater impairment in recognizing fearful expressions than other expressions (Calder *et al.*, 1996). Hence, these findings raise the possibility that deficits in recognizing facial expressions of recognition in schizophrenia may result from an underlying problem with the amygdala (Perlman *et al.*, 2004).

First, several studies have reported structural abnormalities in either the FFA or the amygdala. Indeed, investigations using magnetic resonance imaging (MRI) have indicated that the FFA seems to be significantly smaller in some patients with schizophrenia (see, for example, Lee *et al.*, 2002), and other works suggests that the magnitude of the face-processing impairment is associated with the reduction in volume of the FFA (Onitsuka *et al.*, 2006). A similar finding has been reported for the amygdala. Specifically, Namiki *et al.* (2007) found the volume of the amygdala was also smaller than that of controls in their participants with schizophrenia, and again the reduction in size was associated with the magnitude of the patients' deficit in processing facial expression. Together, these findings suggest that neuroanatomical dysfunction might underpin the impairments in face processing in individuals with schizophrenia.

Second, other studies have used functional magnetic resonance imaging (fMRI) to assess activation in both the FFA and amygdala in face-processing tasks. A handful of studies have examined activation in the FFA with mixed findings. Indeed, some investigations have noted differences between schizophrenic and control participants in levels of FFA activation in face-processing tasks. For instance, Walther *et al.* (2009) found that FFA activation increased in their control participants when they were learning a set of new faces, but the same finding did not emerge in their schizophrenic group. Conversely, other studies have found no differences between controls and schizophrenic participants in levels of FFA activation. For example, although Anilkumar *et al.* (2008) found behavioural differences in face recognition performance between schizophrenic and control groups, there was no difference between the participant groups in levels of brain activity. A similar effect was also reported by Yoon *et al.* (2006), who also found no difference in FFA activation between control and patient groups when viewing faces.

Several fMRI studies have also demonstrated abnormal reductions in amygdala activity in schizophrenic compared with control participants when viewing facial expressions of emotion (see, for example, Gur *et al.*, 2002, 2007; Habel *et al.*, 2004). Further, Fakra *et al.* (2008) found an abnormal pattern of amygdala–prefrontal cortical functional connectivity in an expression matching task in their schizophrenic participants, whereas other studies have reported reduced activity in the hippocampus as well as the amygdala (Gur *et al.*, 2002, Hempel *et al.*, 2003).

Some studies have specifically examined amygdala activation in response to fearful facial expressions, and found reduced levels of activity (Gur *et al.*, 2002; Michalopoulou *et al.*, 2008). Further, Gur *et al.* (2007) found increased amygdala activity in schizophrenic relative to control participants when fearful faces were incorrectly identified, but the reverse finding when fearful faces were correctly identified. This pattern of findings suggests that uncertainty about the emotion expressed in a face may lead to increased amygdala activity in individuals with schizophrenia.

Findings from a study reported by Holt, Kunkel and Weiss (2006) suggest that, in addition to amygdala activation being modulated by ambiguous expressions, the decrease in amygdala activity that has been observed when schizophrenic participants view fearful faces might actually be explained by abnormally increased amygdala activation in response to neutral faces. Specifically, the authors found that schizophrenic participants displayed greater amygdala activation in response to both neutral and fearful faces compared with a baseline condition. Further, a similar paradigm was used by Hall *et al.* (2008), who found that the increase in amygdala activation in their schizophrenic participants was slightly greater in response to neutral compared with fearful faces, when compared with a baseline condition. Converging evidence comes from Williams *et al.* (2004), who monitored the skin conductance response in their schizophrenic participants, and reported greater autonomic responses when participants viewed both neutral and fearful facial expressions compared with controls. Together, these studies raise the possibility that the apparent deficit in amygdala activation to fearful faces may in fact be explained by atypical neural processing of neutral faces.

Finally, several neuroimaging studies suggest a relationship between levels of amygdala activation and symptomatology in schizophrenia. For example, some studies have shown schizophrenics with positive psychotic symptoms demonstrate a reduction in amygdala activation when viewing fearful expressions compared with both non-paranoid patients (see Williams *et al.*, 2004) and healthy individuals (see Phillips *et al.*, 1999; Williams *et al.*, 2004). However, as noted above, this effect could be underpinned by increased amygdala activation in response to neutral faces rather than reduced activation in response to fearful faces. Consistent with this interpretation, Surguladze *et al.* (2006) reported a positive correlation between the magnitude of parahippocampal gyral activity in response to neutral expressions and severity of psychosis. A similar association has also been reported between amygdala activation in response to fearful facial expressions of decreasing intensity and levels of positive psychotic symptoms (Russell *et al.*, 2007). These studies provide further evidence that abnormal amygdala activity in schizophrenia might occur in response to neutral or ambiguous facial expressions, and that the extent of this effect might be linked to the severity of the psychosis.

In sum, the studies described above suggest positive psychotic symptoms in schizophrenia might be linked to functional abnormalities in medial temporal cortical structures, including the amygdala, hippocampus and parahippocampal gyrus. However, it should be noted that it is possible that the varied amygdala activation noted in these studies might simply be attributed to an increased emotional response to all facial stimuli. Indeed, evidence suggests that individuals with schizophrenia find faces more aversive than control participants, suggesting that increased amygdala activity might represent heightened anxiety or fear in response to any face.

As a final note, there is also some evidence to suggest neural abnormalities in other areas might be linked to the severity of negative symptoms of schizophrenia. For instance, Michalopoulou *et al.* (2008) failed to find any differences in neural activation according to the extent of positive symptoms in their schizophrenic participants, but they did find reduced activation in the left superior temporal gyrus in patients with more negative symptoms. This finding makes sense as negative symptoms are associated with reduced emotional responses and social interaction, indicating a relationship between these symptoms and reduced neural activation.

7.1.5. Summary of schizophrenia

■ Much evidence suggests that individuals with schizophrenia are impaired at recognizing facial expressions of emotion, particularly fear (Kohler *et al.*, 2003; Tsoi *et al.*, 2008).

■ An ongoing debate in the literature questions whether the impairment can be attributed to a more generalized cognitive impairment (Chapman and Chapman, 1973), a problem in processing all aspects of faces (Feinberg *et al.*, 1986) or a specific problem in recognizing facial expressions of emotion (Hall *et al.*, 2004). Owing to methodological issues with some studies, this debate has not yet been resolved.

■ There is strong behavioural and eye movement evidence to suggest that individuals with schizophrenia are unable to process faces configurally (see Shin *et al.*, 2008; Lougland, Williams and Gordon, 2002).

■ Neuroimaging studies indicate there may be structural abnormalities in both the FFA (Lee *et al.*, 2002; Onitsuka *et al.*, 2006) and the amygdala (Namiki *et al.*, 2007).

■ fMRI investigations suggest positive symptoms of schizophrenia might be underpinned by abnormal functional relationships between the amygdala, hippocampus and parahippocampal gyrus, leading to abnormal assignment of emotional salience to ambiguous, potentially threatening facial stimuli (e.g., Russell *et al.*, 2007).

7.2. DEPRESSION

Major depressive disorder is associated with repetitive episodes of severe low mood, low self-esteem and a loss of interest in everyday activities (anhedonia). It has been estimated that depression has a prevalence of between eight and 12 per cent in most countries (Andrade *et al.*, 2003), making it one of the most frequently occurring clinical disorders. Many models of the aetiology of depression have been suggested, encompassing biological, psychological and social factors that might bring about and maintain the disorder. Further, cognitive theories of depression implicate biases in the processing of emotional stimuli, and suggest these biases play a role in the onset, maintenance and recurrence of depressive episodes (Beck, 1976; Ingram, 1984). Importantly, facial expressions of emotion are particularly salient emotional cues in our social environment, and investigation of the processing of facial expression in depressed participants is therefore likely to improve our understanding of the disorder significantly (Gotlib and

Hammen, 1992). Hence, much work has examined the processing of emotional expression in this patient group, and these findings are discussed below.

7.2.1. Behavioural deficits in emotional expression recognition

Several studies have investigated the ability of depressed participants to recognize and label basic emotional expressions. Interestingly, some studies have reported that individuals with depression have a particular deficit in recognizing neutral facial expressions, and tend to attribute emotional significance falsely to these stimuli. For instance, Leppänen *et al.* (2004) found no difference in the recognition of happy and sad faces in their depressed participant group compared with controls, yet depressed participants were slower at recognizing neutral faces and tended to mistakenly classify them as emotive (either happy or sad). In another study, Gur *et al.* (1992) reported a similar pattern of findings. Specifically, the authors found that depressed participants tended to classify neutral faces as sad and happy faces as neutral, although their overall performance was not impaired compared with controls. However, other studies have failed to find significant impairments in the recognition of the basic emotions in their depressed participants (see, for example, Kan *et al.*, 2004; Weniger *et al.*, 2004).

Other studies have investigated the recognition of less intense emotional expressions, by using morphed facial stimuli. For example, Surguladze *et al.* (2004) investigated the ability of depressed participants to recognize more subtle emotional expressions by using stimuli that had been morphed to express only 50 per cent of the emotional intensity displayed in standard images. The authors found that depressed participants were less likely than control participants to label the 50 per cent happy faces correctly, suggesting they had difficulty identifying mildly happy expressions.

Converging evidence was provided by Joorman and Gotlib (2006), who presented depressed participants with facial images on morph continua that slowly changed from neutral to full-intensity expressions. In line with the findings of Surguladze *et al.*, the researchers found that the depressed participants needed to see happy expressions at a higher intensity than both controls and participants with social anxiety disorder to categorize them correctly as happy. Interestingly, the depressed patients were able to recognize expressions of both sadness and anger at lower levels of intensity. It therefore seems that individuals with depression may be particularly impaired at recognizing mildly happy expressions, and may be more likely to misinterpret the positive emotion associated with these stimuli.

Finally, some studies using depressed participants have provided evidence that suggests the impaired recognition of facial expressions occurs even when the processing of expression is irrelevant to the task in hand. For example,

Ridout *et al.* (2009) showed participants neutral, sad and happy faces and asked them to judge the gender of each face. They found that depressed participants took a longer time to make this decision when faces displayed a happy expression compared with the other two conditions. In another study, Gilboa-Schechtman *et al.* (2004) asked depressed participants to view a set of faces displaying different emotional expressions, and participants were asked to judge the expression while ignoring the gender of the face, or vice versa. The authors found that the depressed participants found it difficult to ignore the emotional expression displayed on the face, even when it was irrelevant to task demands. Hence, these findings suggest that the abnormal processing of facial expression in individuals with depression might occur at a fundamental level and be an automated process.

7.2.2. Is the impairment face-specific?

Although much evidence supports the view that the processing of facial expression is atypical in individuals with depression, little research has examined whether this is a face-specific deficit or whether it is simply the result of more generalized cognitive impairments. However, a recent study did examine this issue in women with depression. Specifically, Langenecker *et al.* (2005) asked their depressed and control participants to complete a wide range of cognitive tasks, and noted the depressed women were significantly poorer than controls at expression recognition, inhibitory control and executive function tasks. Interestingly, these latter processes stop people from responding in an inappropriate manner to environmental stimuli, suggesting that individuals with depression might not only interpret emotional faces incorrectly, but they might also respond inappropriately to these stimuli.

7.2.3. Neuroimaging evidence

Some structural investigations have used MRI to demonstrate abnormal amygdala volumes in individuals with depression, and interestingly a different pattern of performance has emerged for adults compared with children and adolescents with the disorder. Specifically, although adults with recent-onset depression have been found to have enlarged amygdalae (Lange and Irle, 2004), children and adolescents appear to have decreased amygdala volumes (Rosso *et al.*, 2005).

Findings from fMRI investigations have also revealed insightful findings in participants with depression. In a recent study, Surguladze *et al.* (2005) found that depressed participants failed to show a linear increase in activation in bilateral fusiform gyri and ventral striatum in response to happy faces that increased in intensity. Further, the depressed patients did show a linear increase in activity in the right fusiform gyrus, ventral striatum and left parahippocampal gyrus in response to sad faces of increasing intensity, a finding that was noted in control participants. A similar pattern of findings was noted in another study. Indeed, Fu *et al.* (2004) reported that, compared with healthy controls, depressed participants showed greater levels of activation in the ventral striatum and amygdala in response to sad faces. This pattern of findings suggests that the cognitive bias towards interpreting events in a negative manner might be accounted for by hypo-activation (under-activation) in critical neural areas when depressed individuals view positive faces, and hyper-activation (over-activation) of these areas in response to negative faces.

It has been suggested that the increased activity in response to negative faces might occur as a result of reduced connectivity between cortical and limbic brain areas, which might bring about a failure to modulate and inhibit inappropriate emotional reactions to environmental stimuli. This hypothesis was tested by Anand, Li and Wang (2005), who monitored activity in anterior cingulate cortex and limbic brain regions (i.e., the amygdala, pallidostriatum and medial thalamus), in addition to the connectivity between them. Not only did depressed participants show increased activity in the amygdala, pallidostriatum, insula, anterior cingulate cortex and anteromedial prefrontal cortex in response to negative pictures, but they also showed decreased connectivity between anterior cingulate cortex and limbic regions during emotional stimulation. Hence, the study by Anand *et al.* provides evidence to support the view that inappropriate emotional reactions to facial stimuli by depressed individuals might be attributed to reduced connectivity between cortical and limbic structures.

Other fMRI studies have provided evidence that suggests a potential biological mechanism underpinning anhedonia in depression. Indeed, Keedwell *et al.* (2005a, 2005b) examined neural activity while depressed participants viewed happy faces during a period of happy mood induction. They found increased activity in dorsomedial prefrontal cortex that positively correlated with the severity of the anhedonia, whereas activity within the striatum decreased according to anhedonia severity. Hence, these findings suggest that emotional responses to positive stimuli are also not regulated appropriately in individuals with depression, and this dysfunction might underpin the loss of interest in everyday pleasurable activities that is often noted in the disorder.

Several studies have examined whether these atypical neural activation patterns are remedied after intervention, and evidence suggests that neural functioning returns to more normal patterns in response to treatment. Such findings have been reported after cognitive behavioural therapy (Costafreda *et al.*, 2009; Fu *et al.*, 2008) and psychopharmacological intervention. Indeed, Fu *et al.* (2007) found that the reduced activation in the limbic and extrastriate visual regions of the brain when viewing happy faces became less severe after eight weeks of treatment with fluoxetine (Prozac); and Keedwell *et al.* (2009) found that subgenual cingulate activity to happy facial expressions also increased after antidepressant treatment. Further, Sheline *et al.* (2001) noted that heightened levels of activation in the left amygdala in response to fearful faces was reduced after eight weeks treatment with sertraline (a selective serotonin-reuptake inhibitor).

Finally, intervention has also been found to improve functional connectivity between neural regions that process emotional significance (amygdala and striatal areas) and those that regulate emotional response (i.e., prefrontal cortical regions). Indeed, when depressed participants viewed sad facial expressions after a period of treatment, Chen *et al.* (2008) reported increased functional connectivity between left amygdala and several prefrontal cortical regions implicated in emotion regulation.

In sum, these findings suggest that although atypical brain activation seems to present in patients with depression, these abnormalities appear to be temporary and can be alleviated with treatment. Thus, they may only be present when patients are experiencing severe episodes of depression.

7.2.4. Summary of depression

■ Behavioural evidence indicates that individuals with depression tend to attribute emotional significance falsely to neutral facial expressions (Leppänen *et al.*, 2004), and that they have particular difficulties in interpreting mildly happy expressions (Surguladze *et al.*, 2004).

■ Further evidence suggests that individuals with depression might also have difficulties in regulating their responses to emotional stimuli, such that they respond to these stimuli in an inappropriate manner (Keedwell *et al.*, 2005a, 2005b).

■ Neuroimaging evidence suggests the negative cognitive bias often seen in depressed individuals might be attributed to under-activation of neural areas that process positive emotion and over-activation of those areas that process negative emotion (Fu *et al.*, 2004). Further, reports of reduced functional connectivity between cortical and limbic structures provide a potential biological basis for behavioural difficulties in regulating emotional reactions (Anand, Li and Wang, 2005).

■ These neurological abnormalities have been shown to alleviate in response to treatment, suggesting they are temporary effects that might only present during major depressive episodes (Costafreda *et al.*, 2009; Fu *et al.*, 2007, 2008).

7.3. SOCIAL ANXIETY DISORDER

Social anxiety disorder is characterized by a great fear and avoidance of being in social situations, and particularly the fear of being scrutinized by others. Individuals with the disorder report physical symptoms when they do find themselves in social situations, such as blushing, nausea, sweating, trembling or stammering. It has been estimated that social anxiety disorder might affect as many as 13 per cent of the population (Magee *et al.*, 1996), with even the most conservative estimates suggesting a prevalence of four per cent (e.g., Wittchen, Nelson and Lachner, 1998). It is thought that the disorder can have a genetic basis (Lieb *et al.*, 2000), and is particularly likely to develop in childhood (Beidel, Turner and Morris, 1999) or during or shortly after adolescence (Kessler, Stein and Berglund, 1998). The disorder also has a high degree of co-morbidity with other psychiatric disorders, particularly low self-esteem, depression and substance abuse (Kessler, Stein and Berglund, 1998). Given faces are important social stimuli, it is not surprising that individuals with social anxiety disorder might find this type of stimulus particularly threatening. Hence, several studies have investigated face processing in individuals with the disorder. These findings are discussed in the remaining section of this chapter.

7.3.1. Emotional expression impairments

In particular, it has been found that individuals with social anxiety disorder demonstrate biases in interpreting facial expressions of emotion. For example, Garner *et al.* (2009) examined the recognition of faces depicting ambiguous emotional expressions that were morphed between anger and happiness, fear and happiness, or anger and fear. Interestingly, participants with social anxiety disorder performed at a lower level than controls in the two conditions involving fear, but at a normal level in the anger and happiness condition. Hence, these findings suggest that individuals with the disorder might have a particular problem processing fearful facial expressions.

In another study, Joorman and Gotlib (2006) investigated sensitivity towards angry emotional expressions, by creating morph continua that began with neutral expressions and showed increasing levels of happiness, sadness or anger. The authors found that social anxiety participants required lower levels of anger in a face to identify correctly the expression compared with controls, indicating that they might be biased towards detecting this emotion in facial stimuli. Similar findings were found in a study that used an alternative paradigm. Specifically, Mohlman, Carmin and Price (2007) asked participants to sort a stack of cards according to their emotional expression. The researchers found that social anxiety participants sorted angry expressions more rapidly than control participants, and were more likely to misclassify neutral expressions as depicting anger.

These findings received additional support from an eye-tracking study that also suggests individuals with social anxiety disorder might be particularly impaired at processing angry expressions. Indeed, Horley *et al.* (2004) examined the visual scanpath in social anxiety participants while they viewed a series of emotional faces, and found differences in scanning strategy compared with control participants. Specifically, they found extended scanpaths, such that a greater distance of the face was covered between fixations, and an avoidance of the eye region. The authors interpreted these findings as evidence of hyper-scanning of facial stimuli, and a fear or avoidance of making eye contact with others. Interestingly, this pattern of findings was most prominent for faces displaying angry expressions. Hence, both behavioural and eye movement findings suggest that individuals with social anxiety disorder might be particularly impaired at processing facial expressions of anger.

7.3.2. Neurophysiological evidence

Further support for behavioural findings of impaired recognition of angry facial expressions has been provided by two studies that recorded event-related potentials while social anxiety participants viewed angry faces. Specifically, Kolassa and colleagues (Kolassa *et al.*, 2006; Kolassa and Miltner, 2007) reported that social anxiety participants had an increased N170 response in the right temporoparietal region when they viewed angry faces, compared both with healthy control participants and individuals with a clinical fear of spiders. Further, the magnitude of the P100 response was found to be correlated with higher scores on the Fear Survey Schedule, but only in the social anxiety participants. The authors suggested that these heightened early responses to angry faces might underpin the hypervigilance often observed in individuals with the disorder.

Several fMRI studies have examined neural activation while participants with social anxiety view emotional faces. In one study, Gentili *et al.* (2008) reported that, when viewing both emotional and neutral faces, participants with the disorder demonstrated increased activation in neural areas responsible for emotional processing, including the left amygdala, insula and bilateral superior temporal sulcus. Further, they also noted reduced activation in areas that process attention and non-emotional facial information, including the left FFA, dorsolateral prefrontal cortex and bilateral intraparietal sulcus. Gentili and colleagues suggest that this pattern of findings might underpin behavioural symptoms of the disorder, such as hyper-vigilance towards emotional faces, but also a wariness of them.

Finally, two further studies have noted abnormal patterns of neural activity when social anxiety participants view neutral faces. Specifically, Cooney *et al.* (2006) found increased activation in the left amygdala when social anxiety but not control participants viewed neutral faces, and Phan *et al.* (2006) found that the extent to which this activation increased was positively correlated with the severity of the social anxiety symptoms. These findings support the behavioural findings discussed above, which suggest that individuals with social anxiety disorder tend to attribute emotion falsely to neutral faces.

7.3.3. Summary of social anxiety disorder

■ Behavioural evidence suggests that individuals with social anxiety disorder are impaired at processing expressions of fear (Garner *et al.*, 2009) and anger (Joorman and Gotlib, 2006), and mistakenly attribute emotion to neutral faces (Mohlman, Carmin and Price, 2007).

- Both eye-movement (Horley *et al.*, 2004) and event-related potential (Kolassa *et al.*, 2006; Kolassa and Miltner, 2007) evidence suggests that individuals with the disorder might be hyper-vigilant in their attention to facial stimuli in social situations, particularly those expressing anger.
- Neuroimaging evidence demonstrates that neural areas responsible for processing facial emotion are over-activated in these individuals, and less attention is consequently paid to other aspects of facial information (Gentili *et al.*, 2008; Cooney *et al.*, 2006).

CHAPTER SUMMARY

Behavioural findings from facial expression recognition studies suggest that this process is impaired in a different manner in each of three major neuropsychiatric illnesses: schizophrenia, depression and social anxiety disorder. Indeed, schizophrenia is associated with general deficits in facial expression recognition (but particularly fear), and these deficits may predate illness onset, worsen as the disorder progresses and be associated with the magnitude of positive psychotic symptoms that present in an individual with the disorder. On the other hand, depression is associated with a bias away from labelling positive expressions as happy, whereas individuals with social anxiety disorder have particular problems in processing angry and fearful faces. Interestingly, all three disorders have been associated with the false attribution of emotional significance to neutral faces.

The abnormalities in facial expression labelling in each of these psychiatric illnesses is paralleled by functional abnormalities in neural regions supporting facial expression perception, suggesting potential biological abnormalities might underpin the deficits. It has been suggested that abnormal functional connectivity between the amygdala, hippocampus and parahippocampal gyrus may lead to the over-attribution of salience to ambiguous, potentially threatening faces in schizophrenia (Russell *et al.*, 2007). In depression, the negative attentional bias and inability to label positive expressions as happy may be explained by increased limbic activity in response to negative expressions but decreased activity for positive emotional expressions (Anand, Li and Wang, 2005). In social anxiety disorder, the neural areas responsible for processing facial emotion are over-activated such that less attention is directed to other aspects of facial information, and this may explain the hyper-vigilance towards emotional faces that is often observed in the disorder (Gentili *et al.*, 2008; Cooney *et al.*, 2006).

Given that abnormal processing of facial expression might directly give rise to some of the affective and social symptoms in these disorders, further research into these functional and neural abnormalities may improve our understanding of the pathophysiological mechanisms underpinning each illness. Moreover, continuous monitoring of the ability to process emotional expression in neuropsychiatric disorders might also help in the prediction or monitoring of response to treatment.

FURTHER READING

Fu, C. H., Williams, S. C., Cleare, A. J., Scott, J., Mitterschiffthaler, M. T., Walsh, N. D., *et al.* (2008) 'Neural Responses to Sad Facial Expressions in Major Depression Following Cognitive Behavioral Therapy', *Biological Psychiatry,* 64, 505–12.

Gentili, C., Gobbini, M. I., Ricciardi, E., Vanello, N., Pietrini, P., Haxby, J. V., *et al.* (2008) 'Differential Modulation of Neural Activity throughout the Distributed Neural System for Face Perception in Patients with Social Phobia and Healthy Subjects', *Brain Research Bulletin,* 77, 286–92.

Horley, K., Williams, L. M., Gonsalvez, C. and Gordon, E. (2004) 'Face to face: Visual Scanpath Evidence of Abnormal Processing of Facial Expressions in Social Phobia', *Psychiatry Research,* 127, 43–53.

Leppänen, J. M. (2006) 'Emotional Information Processing in Mood Disorders: A Review of Behavioral and Neuroimaging Findings', *Current Opinion in Psychiatry,* 19, 34–9.

Marwick, K. and Hall, J. (2008) 'Social Cognition in Schizophrenia: A Review of Face Processing', *British Medical Bulletin,* 88, 43–58.

Morris, R. W., Weickert, C. S. and Loughland, C. M. (2009) 'Emotional Face Processing in Schizophrenia', *Current Opinions in Psychiatry,* 22, 140–6.

GUIDANCE QUESTIONS

Use the following questions to guide your reading of this chapter and the recommended papers.

1. Is the processing of the same emotional expressions disrupted in schizophrenia, depression and social anxiety disorders?
2. Is the deficit in the recognition of emotional expressions a face-specific impairment in schizophrenia?
3. To what extent are the deficits related to symptomology and symptom extremity in each disorder?
4. Is it true to say that evidence suggests a common impairment in the amygdala might underpin the deficit in each of the three disorders?

8 Focus Chapter: What are the Theoretical Implications of Acquired and Neuropsychiatric Disorders of Face Processing?

In this section of the book, acquired and neuropsychiatric disorders of face processing have been discussed. However, in addition to these disorders being of clinical significance, they have also greatly informed our knowledge about the structure and functioning of the normal face-processing system. Indeed, it is particularly clear from Chapters 5 and 6 that both prosopagnosia and the Capgras delusion have informed the development of functional models of face processing.

In the current chapter, the theoretical implications of acquired and neuropsychiatric disorders of face processing are discussed in more detail. First, the implications for functional models are discussed, with particular reference to neuropsychological double dissociations. You may find it useful to refer to Chapter 1 while you read this section. Second, neurological patients have also contributed to the debate about the specificity of the face-processing system, and this is discussed in the remainder of the chapter. It might help you to read the Focus Chapter presented at the end of Section 1 (Chapter 4) before you read the second section of the current chapter.

8.1. IMPLICATIONS FOR FUNCTIONAL MODELS OF FACE PROCESSING

8.1.1. The cognitive neuropsychological approach

In Chapter 1, the influential functional model of face processing posited by Bruce and Young (1986) was discussed. To recap briefly, the face recognition pathway within the model is composed of four functional components that process faces in a sequential manner. First, in structural encoding, an incoming facial percept is transformed from a view-dependent to a view-independent representation. This latter representation is compared with all stored representations of familiar faces in the face recognition units. If a match is achieved, familiarity is signalled and semantic information is accessed via the person identity nodes, and finally the person's name is generated. Importantly, the model assumes that, after structural encoding, other aspects of facial perception that are not related to identity (e.g., emotional expression) are processed independently of the face recognition pathway.

Although the model was proposed to provide a cognitive architecture for the undamaged fully developed adult face-processing system, Bruce and Young used findings from neuropsychological patients to inform their theory. Further, the pattern of preserved and impaired abilities observed in case reports of individuals with face-processing impairments has also been used to test the predictions of the model. That is, if the assumptions made in the model are correct, the patterns of impairment that do and do not present in neurological patients should follow those predictions.

The study of patients with face-processing impairments after neurological damage is representative of the cognitive neuropsychological approach. This method of investigation uses 'double dissociations' between patients to test and modify a model of the normal cognitive system. In particular, one key double dissociation was used to inform Bruce and Young's model. Specifically, the authors posited that facial expression and facial identity are processed independently, and this hypothesis was largely based on the pattern of preserved and impaired processing abilities observed in neurological patients. This evidence is discussed in the next section.

8.1.2. The functional separation of the identity and expression pathways

As stated above, the primary evidence that supported the proposed independence of identity and expression processing came from a double dissociation between two neurological disorders. One half of this dissociation comes from individuals with prosopagnosia, who cannot recognize familiar people from their face yet can still recognize different emotional expressions (see, for example, Tranel, Damasio and Damasio, 1988). The other half of the dissociation comes from reports of patients who are impaired at recognizing particular emotional expressions, despite intact identification abilities (see, for example, Hornak, Rolls and Wade, 1996; Young *et al.*, 1993).

However, Calder and Young (2005) have questioned whether these two types of patient actually form a true double dissociation. Indeed, the authors argue that the double dissociation offered by neurological patients does not offer true evidence for independent processing streams, as the two processes are not functionally comparable. Specifically, Calder and Young suggest that, when tested appropriately, most cases of acquired prosopagnosia also show some level of disruption in expression processing, and therefore do not represent true cases of preserved expression recognition in the context of impaired identity recognition. Further, deficits in expression processing are often undetected in these individuals, because tasks of identification are more difficult than tasks of expression recognition. Indeed, face identification tasks require the provision of individuating information about familiar faces, whereas expression tasks generally ask participants to select the correct expression from a choice of up to six alternatives. According to Shallice (1988), the relative difficulty of the two tasks is important as neurological injury decreases cognitive resources, and performance can be impaired to a greater extent on more difficult tasks.

In addition to suggesting that there are actually few cases of prosopagnosia with intact expression processing abilities, Calder and Young also argue that many of the cases that have been thought to support the existence of independent processing streams actually do not feature true prosopagnosics, but patients with prosopamensia (impaired recognition of faces only encoded after illness onset; see, for example, Tranel *et al.*, 1988), general amnesia or semantic impairments (see, for example, Etcoff, 1984). However, more convincing evidence of a case of prosopagnosia with preserved facial expression recognition comes from Riddoch *et al.* (2008), who reported this pattern in patient FB. Yet, on the basis of a previous case report by Baudouin and Humphreys (2006), Riddoch *et al.* suggest that FB's apparently normal performance in recognizing expressions may reflect the use of compensatory strategies. Indeed, Baudouin and Humphreys (2006) reported that FB did not process expressions in the normal holistic manner, but instead used salient individual features to cue recognition (e.g., a smiling mouth indicates happiness, whereas a furrowed brow indicates anger).

Further, evidence that is more recent suggests the other half of the dissociation has been over-simplified, such that facial expression recognition cannot simply be the converse of facial identity recognition. Indeed, evidence suggests that a single processing stream cannot be responsible for the processing of all emotional expressions, as dissociable neural systems have been identified for particular expressions such as fear and disgust (e.g., Krolak-Salmon *et al.*, 2003). Instead, it is more likely that selective disruption of facial expression recognition reflects damage to a more general emotion system rather than one dedicated to the analysis of facial expression (Calder and Young, 2005).

In sum, Calder and Young concluded that at present there is no convincing evidence of a true double dissociation between facial identity and facial expression that is actually restricted to the facial domain and that has been tested appropriately. Hence, although this double dissociation has traditionally been used as evidence to support the proposed independence of the expression and identity pathways in Bruce and Young's model, recent discussions suggest that cases that convincingly form this double dissociation have not yet been reported. However, this is not to suggest that all evidence that informed Bruce and Young's model from individuals with prosopagnosia has been questioned. Indeed, the model's assumption that face processing occurs in a sequential manner has withstood the test of time, and the neuropsychological basis for this assumption is discussed in the next section.

8.1.3. The sequential nature of the face recognition system

Much of the evidence that supports the architecture of Bruce and Young's model comes from individuals who have acquired prosopagnosia and can no longer recognize faces. Further, it seems that face-processing impairments in prosopagnosia can manifest in different ways, and these can be mapped onto the Bruce and Young model. For example, Young, Hellawell and de Haan (1988) described three individuals with prosopagnosia (PG, RG and LH) who were all impaired at the level of structural encoding. Indeed, these patients had impairments in face perception, and could not complete tasks that involved matching of simultaneously presented facial images. Further, the patients could not complete any of the later stages of processing that follow structural encoding, supporting the sequential nature of Bruce and Young's model.

Further evidence supporting the sequential nature of processing comes from other patients who have impairments at later stages of the model. For instance, de Haan, Young and Newcombe (1987) reported the case of PH who could complete face-matching tasks (implying structural encoding was intact), but could not make familiarity decisions in response to familiar and novel faces, nor access semantic or name information. Hence, the impairment in this patient appears to be located at the level of the face recognition units, or the connection between this module and structural encoding. Further, De Haan, Young and Newcombe (1991) reported patient ME who appeared to have an impairment at the level of the person identity nodes. Indeed, ME could match facial images and process familiarity, but could not access semantic or name information in response to familiar faces. Finally, Flude, Ellis and Kay (1989) presented patient EST who could not retrieve the name of familiar people, indicating a problem at the level of name generation and providing further evidence of the functional independence of this stage of processing from general semantic processing. Importantly, this patient could successfully process faces at all the other stages of the model.

Although these case studies support the sequential nature of the Bruce and Young model, they have also been used to propose the existence of functional subtypes of prosopagnosia (see Chapter 5). Indeed, two broad types of prosopagnosic patient seem to exist: those who have problems at the level of structural encoding and experience problems in face perception as well as face recognition, and those who can perceive faces correctly but cannot make familiarity judgments, indicating a problem at the level of the face recognition units. De Renzi *et al.* (1991) termed the former type of patient 'apperceptive' prosopagnosics, and the latter type 'associative' prosopagnosics. Importantly, the pattern of performance noted in these two types of prosopagnosia have been used to inform theories of covert or unconscious recognition, particularly in relation to the Bruce and Young model. Indeed, it seems that covert recognition can only be noted in associative patients and not apperceptive patients, indicating that faces must be correctly perceived for subthreshold activation of the relevant face recognition unit and person identity node to signify recognition (see Chapter 5 for further explanation).

8.1.4. Covert recognition and the functional model

In Chapter 5, the various types of covert face recognition that have been observed in individuals with prosopagnosia were explained. Indeed, it can be seen that two broad types of covert recognition have been identified so far, and these have had important implications for the development of the Bruce and Young model. First, some authors have provided evidence of *behavioural* covert recognition, using techniques such as face-name priming or the face interference task. Such behavioural demonstrations of covert recognition can be accommodated by explanations that are based within the main cognitive pathway to recognition that is identified in the Bruce and Young model (see Chapter 5). Further, some authors have created single-route neural network models that, when lesioned, can display covert but not overt recognition (Young and Burton, 1999; Farah, O'Reilly and Vecera, 1993). Hence, the Bruce and Young model in its original form seems to be able to provide a theoretical basis for demonstrations of behavioural covert recognition in prosopagnosic patients.

However, further investigations have demonstrated evidence of covert recognition in prosopagnosia using the skin conductance response. This measure is a *physiological* rather than a behavioural measure of covert recognition, which measures changes in the skin's electrical conductivity in response to familiar and novel stimuli. Clearly, a physiological measure of covert recognition has a different basis to behavioural measures, and cannot be accommodated within the original model of Bruce and Young. Hence, evidence of the physiological measure of covert recognition was used as evidence to propose the existence of a second affective route to recognition, along with the proposed double dissociation with Capgras delusion (see Chapter 6). Indeed, although individuals with prosopagnosia are impaired at recognizing faces, indicating a problem in the cognitive route to recognition, they retain the ability to demonstrate an emotional response to familiar faces, as measured by the skin conductance response. On the other hand, individuals with the Capgras delusion can recognize people from their face indicating the cognitive face-processing pathway is intact, but they have incorrect emotional responses to familiar faces, indicated by the absence of the skin conductance response in response to familiar faces. Hence, patients with Capgras delusion show the reverse pattern of impairment to prosopagnosic patients.

Further, patients with Capgras delusion also provide evidence to suggest that physiological measures of covert recognition can be dissociated from behavioural measures of covert recognition, and must therefore be accounted for by independent pathways. Indeed, if it were the case that both behavioural and physiological covert recognition occur within the same route, patients with Capgras delusion should not demonstrate the phenomenon on either type of measure. However, Ellis *et al.* (2000) investigated this issue with patient BP, who suffered from Capgras delusion. In line with the earlier evidence suggesting two dissociable routes to recognition, BP did not show any evidence of a normal skin conductance response in response to familiar faces, but the authors did note evidence of behavioural covert recognition on two separate indicators.

The proposed double dissociation between prosopagnosia and Capgras delusion and their associated deficits and abilities has therefore provided strong evidence for two parallel routes to recognition. However, several authors have questioned whether such dual-route functional models really do provide an adequate account of the cognitive basis of Capgras delusion. This issue is discussed in the next section.

8.1.5. Capgras delusion and the cognitive neuropsychiatric approach

As stated above, the mere addition of a second affective route to recognition does not necessarily provide a complete explanation for the basis of the Capgras delusion, given some patients have been reported who lose emotional responsiveness after brain injury yet do not go on to experience Capgras delusion (see, for example, Tranel, Damasio and Damsio, 1995). Thus, although reduced autonomic responses may be a necessary condition that is required for Capgras delusion to occur, this factor alone does not seem to provide a sufficient explanation. In Chapter 6, the proposition that an 'integrative device' needs to be added to the model was discussed. Indeed, Ellis and Lewis (2001) suggest that this device might compare the outputs of the identification and affective routes, and Capgras delusion would result when there is conflict between the outputs of the two routes. That is, the disorder would arise when a patient does not receive the emotional response they expect in response to a particular face, bringing about a misattribution that results in the delusional belief.

Coltheart, Langdon and MacKay (2007) developed this concept further, by suggesting that two abnormalities must be present for any delusional misidentification disorder to occur. The first abnormality is specific to each disorder, and in the case of Capgras delusion is characterized by the absent autonomic response to a familiar face. The second abnormality, however, is more general, and prevents the patient from rejecting the delusion despite the evidence against it. Importantly, this perspective posits that Capgras delusion results from the interaction of several factors, and is therefore more typical of the cognitive neuropsychiatric than the cognitive neuropsychological framework. In recent years this latter approach has developed as an offshoot from cognitive neuropsychology, and, given that Capgras delusion can result from either neurological damage or psychiatric illness, the disorder has provided an ideal starting point to test cognitive neuropsychiatry's explanatory power.

Essentially, the additional psychiatric factors that are encompassed by cognitive neuropsychiatric explanations highlight key differences between the cognitive neuropsychological and cognitive neuropsychiatric approaches (Young, 2000). Indeed, the cognitive neuropsychological approach is only interested in cognitive processes, and does not see additional psychiatric factors as informative, given they do not represent dissociable functions. On the other hand, the cognitive neuropsychiatric approach pushes the logic used in cognitive neuropsychology to the limit, by giving psychiatric abilities the same status as cognitive abilities. The advantage of this approach is that it bridges normal psychiatry (which has traditionally posited psychodynamic explanations of the Capgras delusion) with the information processing approach of cognitive neuropsychology, allowing theories of delusions to have a firm and testable theoretical basis.

In sum, patients with a variety of neurological illnesses have not only allowed theories of the cognitive basis of face processing to develop, but have also contributed to the growth of more general approaches that are of use in a wide range of neurological and psychiatric settings. However, in addition to their contributions to the development of models of faces processing, neurological patients have also helped to inform a key theoretical debate in the face-processing literature. This issue is discussed in the next section.

8.2. ARE FACES SPECIAL?

As described in Chapter 4, an ongoing debate in the psychological literature is concerned with the notion that we have specialized cognitive and neural mechanisms for face processing, as opposed to the expertise hypothesis which states that we use these mechanisms to process any visual entity with which we have sufficient experience. A key part of this debate has used evidence from individuals with face-processing deficits. Indeed, the key double dissociation that supports the face-specificity viewpoint is the existence of prosopagnosic patients without problems in object recognition, and visual agnosic patients (who are impaired at recognizing certain categories of objects) without a concurrent impairment in face recognition. The latter half of this dissociation has been documented in the literature without contention (e.g., Bruyer *et al.*, 1983; Assal, Favre and Anderes, 1984). Indeed, many papers have examined the case of CK, who has severe problems in object but not face recognition (Moscovitch, Winocur and Behrmann, 1997; Moscovitch and Moscovitch, 2000).

However, the issue of whether prosopagnosic patients can present without any problems in object recognition has been the subject of further debate, although several authors have reported such individuals. Indeed, there have been reports of prosopagnosic patients who retain the ability to identify individual cars (Sergent and Signoret, 1992), places (Evans *et al.*, 1995), spectacles (Farah *et al.*, 1995), flowers (Evans *et al.*, 1995), and fruit and vegetables (Riddoch *et al.*, 2008). In addition, McNeil and Warrington (1993) reported the case of WJ, a farmer who became prosopagnosic after neurological injury, but could still recognize individual sheep from his flock. Interestingly, the double dissociation to this case was reported by Assal, Favre and Anderes (1984), who described a farmer who lost the ability to recognize his cows but could still recognize human faces.

However, supporters of the expertise hypothesis claim that these reports of apparently normal object recognition in prosopagnosic patients do not necessarily imply separable mechanisms. Indeed, Gauthier *et al.* (1999) suggest that face recognition tasks are simply more difficult than object recognition tasks, and this difference in difficulty has not been appropriately controlled in most studies, obscuring abnormal performance on object recognition tests. This point is illustrated by studies that have reported prosopagnosic patients who display normal recognition scores in object processing tasks, yet have longer response latencies than control participants (Gauthier *et al.*, 1999; Laeng and Caviness, 2001). However, Rossion, Caldara *et al.* (2003) did find normal response times in a prosopagnosic patient performing an object recognition task, countering the criticisms described above and supporting the face specificity viewpoint. Further evidence that counters the criticisms of expertise supporters comes from studies that have demonstrated that prosopagnosic patients can still learn to discriminate between individual Greebles (see Chapter 4) after several hours of training (e.g., Behrmann, Marotta *et al.*, 2005; Riddoch *et al.*, 2008). Indeed, the expertise hypothesis would predict that prosopagnosic patients should not be able to gain expertise in any category of object.

One of the further problems that has been encountered in investigations that examine object processing abilities in prosopagnosic patients is that often these individuals have extensive lesions that have not only damaged the fusiform face area, but also surrounding cortical regions that have been implemented in object processing. Thus, it is not surprising that most prosopagnosic patients do present with at least some difficulties in object processing, but this is not necessarily supportive of the expertise hypothesis. Some recent studies have addressed this issue by providing neuroimaging data that specify the extent of the damage in prosopagnosic patients, alongside their performance on object recognition tests. For instance, Barton *et al.* (2004) reported object recognition difficulties in eight of their nine prosopagnosic patients, but further neuroimaging data demonstrated that the one patient who did not show a strong impairment in object recognition had a more restricted lesion that appeared to affect only the fusiform face area (De Gelder *et al.*, 2003), whereas the other patients had more extensive lesions. Although this case clearly supports the face-specificity argument, more data are required from additional prosopagnosic patients to make a convincing argument.

Finally, further evidence that supports the specificity viewpoint comes from an impairment that occasionally presents alongside prosopagnosia, termed 'metamorphopsia'. In this condition, patients view faces in a deformed manner. Interestingly, one case of metamorphopsia has been found to also affect the perception of objects (Seron *et al.*, 1995), but other reports have found that the deficit is restricted to faces. For instance, Davidoff and Landis (1990) described a woman with normal object perception, who saw deformations on the left side of faces. Further, Landis, Cummings, Christen *et al.* (1986) described the experience of a woman with prosopagnosia and metamorphopsia while travelling on a bus. Specifically, the woman looked at the face of a poodle that belonged to another passenger, and then saw the poodle's face instead of human faces when she viewed the other passengers. Given that the poodle's face only replaced human faces and not any other category of object, this case provides further support for the face specificity argument.

CHAPTER SUMMARY

■ The cognitive neuropsychological approach uses double dissociations between neurological patients to infer the architecture of a normal adult processing system.

■ In face processing, a double dissociation between patients with converse patterns of identity and expression processing deficits (see, for example, Tranel, Damasio and Damasio, 1988; Young *et al.*, 1993) has been used to infer the functional separation of expression and identity pathways. However, this double dissociation has been criticized on the basis that the two processes are not of equal difficulty and there seem to be specific processing streams for different emotional expressions (Calder and Young, 2005).

■ Further evidence from prosopagnosic patients has supported the sequential nature of face processing (see, for example, Young, Hellawell and de Haan, 1988).

■ A double dissociation between prosopagnosia and the Capgras delusion has been used to propose a second affective route to recognition (Ellis and Young, 1990). Supporting evidence comes from investigations into covert processing in these two types of patient (see Bauer, 1984; Ellis *et al.*, 2000).

■ The cognitive neuropsychological approach has been extended by the cognitive neuropsychiatric approach, which gives added status to other abnormalities that the former approach would find irrelevant (e.g., Coltheart, Langdon and MacKay, 2007).

■ A further double dissociation has been reported between prosopagnosic patients (see Sergent and Signoret, 1992) and those with visual agnosia (see Moscovitch and Moscovitch, 2000), which has been interpreted as support for the face specificity rather than the expertise hypothesis. However, there are currently few convincing cases of prosopagnosic patients with intact object processing abilities.

FURTHER READING

De Haan, E. H., Young, A. W. and Newcombe, F. (1987) 'Face Recognition without Awareness', *Cognitive Neuropsychology*, 4, 385–415.

Dunn, J. C. and Kirsner, K. (2003) 'What can We Infer from Double Dissociations?', *Cortex*, 39, 1–7.

Ellis, H. D., Lewis, M. B., Moselhy, H. F. and Young, A. W. (2000) 'Automatic without Autonomic Responses to Familiar Faces: Differential Components of Covert Face Recognition in a Case of Capgras Delusion', *Cognitive Neuropsychiatry*, 5, 255–69.

McNeil, J. and Warrington, E. (1993) 'Prosopagnosia: A Face-Specific Disorder', *Quarterly Journal of Experimental Psychology A*, 46, 1–10.

Moscovitch, M., Winocur, G. and Behrmann, M. (1997) 'What is Special about Face Recognition? Nineteen Experiments on a Person with Visual Object Agnosia and Dyslexia but Normal Face Recognition', *Journal of Cognitive Neuroscience*, 9, 555–604.

Tranel, D., Damasio, A. R. and Damasio, H. (1988) 'Intact Recognition of Facial Expression, Gender, and Age in Patients with Impaired Recognition of Face Identity', *Neurology*, 38, 690–6.

Young, A. W., Hellawell, D. and de Haan, E. H. F. (1988) 'Cross-Domain Semantic Priming in Normal Subjects and a Prosopagnosic Patient', *Quarterly Journal of Experimental Psychology Section A: Human Experimental Psychology*, 40, 561–80.

DISCUSSION QUESTIONS

1. Read the case reports of the neurological patients specified in the 'Further Reading' section.
2. How have each of the patients informed theories related to face processing?
3. Do any of the patients match up to form double dissociations?
4. Are there any limitations in the methodologies that have been used to investigate different abilities in these patients? Might these limitations restrict the conclusions that can be drawn from these patients?

PART III

Developmental Disorders of Face Processing

9 The Development of Face Processing

Given that faces provide us with a multitude of information that is critical for successful social interaction, the development of the face-processing system has received much attention in the literature. Indeed, researchers have examined both the development of face-processing skills in typically developing children, and in children with developmental disorders that present with impairments in face recognition. In this section of the book, research that has investigated face processing both in unimpaired and impaired children is discussed.

Initially, the current chapter focuses on the development of the normal face-processing system. Indeed, much research has examined this issue, and two key themes have emerged in the literature. First, many authors have investigated the initial state of the face-processing system at birth, and questioned whether we are born with an intrinsic predisposition to attend to faces, or whether our expertise in face processing only develops in response to interaction with faces. Second, other researchers have investigated the age at which adult-like levels of expertise in face processing are reached. In this chapter, both of these issues are discussed.

9.1. ARE WE BORN WITH THE ABILITY TO RECOGNIZE FACES?

Much research indicates that newborn babies are drawn to facial stimuli, and it is thought that this early interest in faces is fundamental in providing the visual system with the experience it requires to develop expertise in face processing. However, what remains unclear is whether we are born with an innate attentional bias that specifically draws us to facial stimuli, or whether this bias is simply the by-product of a more general preference for visual stimuli that happens to include face-like configurations. In this section, two theories are discussed that have informed this debate. First, Johnson and Morton's (1991) CONSPEC/CONLERN theory posits that we are born with an innate attentional bias that draws us specifically to facial stimuli, whereas Nelson's (2001) 'perceptual narrowing' hypothesis does not make such an assumption. These two theories are reviewed in this section.

9.1.1. The CONSPEC/CONLERN theory

Johnson and Morton (1991) proposed the CONSPEC/CONLERN theory in response to a seemingly puzzling set of experimental findings (Johnson *et al.*, 1991). Specifically, these authors examined face-tracking abilities in a group of newborn babies within an hour of birth. The authors monitored the babies' head and eye movements while they tracked a moving schematic face, scrambled face and a blank face. Interestingly, the newborns preferred to look at the schematic face rather than the scrambled or blank faces, but additional investigation noted that this preference had disappeared by two months of age. Based on this evidence, Johnson and Morton suggested that two separate systems might contribute to the development of face-processing skills in infants. First, the authors suggested that an innate subcortical system draws babies' attention to moving face-like stimuli. They termed this system 'CONSPEC'. Second, they suggested that the cortical face-specific 'CONLERN' system takes over from CONSPEC at approximately one month of age. This second system develops in response to experience with faces, and is capable of retaining fine details about individual faces, allowing face recognition to occur.

Thus, the CONSPEC/CONLERN theory suggests that an initial biological predisposition to attend to faces brings about the visual experience that is necessary for an infant to develop face expertise and eventually adult-like levels of face recognition ability. The next two sections evaluate the CONSPEC and CONLERN components of the model in turn.

9.1.2. Evaluation of CONSPEC

Much attention has been directed towards evaluating the CONSPEC component of Johnson and Morton's model. In particular, it has been suggested that the attentional bias that draws newborns to facial stimuli might not be face-specific at all. Instead, this bias can be attributed to certain visual patterns that just happen to match the properties of faces. This 'sensory hypothesis' proposes that newborns only prefer to look at faces because they match the contrast sensitivity of the newborn visual system (Kleiner and Banks, 1987). That is, the eyes can clearly be seen against the background of the skin, which is contained within the circular outline of the face.

However, there is much evidence to suggest that the sensory hypothesis is incorrect, as newborns still favour face-like configurations when contrast-sensitivity is controlled. For instance, Valenza *et al.* (1996) examined visual preferences in newborn babies between 25 and 155 hours after birth. They found that the babies preferred to look at faces rather than scrambled faces when the contrast of the visual elements was held constant.

Other authors have suggested that the early attentional bias towards facial stimuli can be explained by a preference for 'top-heaviness' (Simion *et al.*, 2002). These authors demonstrated that newborn infants preferred to look at head-shaped stimuli that contained five black squares arranged in a T-shape, as opposed to an inverted T. Indeed, such a top-heavy arrangement of the component features resembles the configuration of facial features. Converging evidence was provide by Macchi Cassia, Turati and Simion (2004), who found that newborns preferred to look at a photograph of a scrambled face with more features in the top half of the image, as opposed to an unmanipulated version of the same face.

Hence, the early preference for faces might simply reflect a general visual preference for head-shaped stimuli with more elements in the top half. Interestingly, neuroimaging investigations using adult participants have found that, although not being perceived as face-like, such top-heavy visual stimuli activate the fusiform face area (FFA; Caldera *et al.*, 2006), and elicit a N170 response that is similar in amplitude to that observed in response to faces (Le Grand, Barrie and Tanaka, 2005).

Further problems for CONSPEC come from findings that suggest newborn infants prefer to look at their mother's face as opposed to that of a stranger, indicating some degree of recognition in the first day of life (Bushnell, 2001). Following such findings, Johnson and de Haan (2001) presented a modification of the CONSPEC theory, suggesting that a system based in the hippocampus can represent individual faces, but only as isolated stimuli. That is, this system is not able to merge representations of the same face in order to create a view-independent representation. However, Turati, Bulf and Simion (2008) demonstrated that babies between 12 and 72 hours of age could form fairly sophisticated representations of individual faces that are to some extent viewpoint-independent. Thus, this evidence provides problems even for the modified CONSPEC theory.

Nevertheless, Johnson (2005) continued to support the existence of the CONSPEC system, suggesting that newborns have at least one bias in visual processing that ensures they fixate on faces. Interestingly, recent neuroimaging evidence supports the existence of a rapid, low spatial frequency, subcortical face detection system involving the superior colliculus, pulvinar and amygdala (e.g., Bailey *et al.*, 2005; Winston, Vuilleumier and Dolan, 2003). Further, a correlation has been noted between the level of activation observed in this subcortical system and the activation of cortical face-processing areas (George, Driver and Dolan, 2001; Kleinhans *et al.*, 2008).

As an additional note, further evidence suggests that we actually might have more complex face-processing abilities from birth (Quinn and Slater, 2003). Indeed, newborn infants prefer to look at attractive faces (Slater *et al.*, 2000), are sensitive to the presence of eyes in a face (Batki *et al.*, 2000), and prefer faces with direct rather than averted gaze (Farroni *et al.*, 2002). Such findings suggest we might have an innate predisposition to attend to faces, but this may be more complex than originally thought. Yet, it is possible that these preferences can be explained by the current assumptions of CONSPEC. Indeed, when faces are observed through a spatial frequency filter that simulates the newborn visual system, evidence suggests that a mechanism that is sensitive to facial configurations might be preferentially activated by facial averageness (recall from Chapter 3 that this is linked to facial attractiveness), the presence of open eyes and direct eye gaze. Hence, it seems that CONSPEC might not only be responsible for face detection, but also for prioritizing faces that appear to seek social interaction with the infant. These findings suggest that further refinement of the theory might include a developmental basis for more general social cognition.

9.1.3. Evaluation of CONLERN

Although there has been much debate surrounding the concept of CONSPEC, the CONLERN component of the model has been more readily accepted. Indeed, regardless of whether or not we have an initial predisposition to attend to faces, it is clear that visual experience is needed to develop a preference for facial stimuli and an expert face-processing system. For instance, Mondloch *et al.* (1999) reported that 12-week-old babies preferred face-like stimuli compared with newborn and six-week-old babies.

However, the CONLERN system was underspecified in the original model, and the theory was updated by Johnson (2001). Specifically, Johnson suggested that functional brain development involves the sequential 'coming on-line' of several independent cortical regions. Indeed, more complex processes are thought to require the maturation and interaction of such independent regions. This is reflected in the development of the neural face-processing system, where particular cortical regions (e.g., the fusiform gyrus) become specialized for processing faces. Further, Johnson suggests that functional brain development involves a process of specialization where regions go from initially having very broadly tuned functions to having increasingly fine-tuned (more specialized) functions. Hence, Johnson suggests that some regions of cortex gradually become increasingly specialized for processing faces.

Findings from the neuroimaging literature appear to support this hypothesis. Indeed, recent studies show evidence that face-selective areas of cortex become increasingly specialized as children age (see, for example, Golarai *et al.*, 2007; Scherf *et al.*, 2007). In addition, Sugita (2009) reported that monkeys reared without exposure to faces had similar face-processing abilities to human newborns. Further, after interaction with faces, the monkeys appeared to undergo a similar process of specialization to that noted for human children.

9.1.4. The perceptual narrowing hypothesis

Interestingly, Johnson's (2001) CONLERN system has much in common with another theory of the development of the face-processing system, namely the 'perceptual narrowing hypothesis' (Nelson, 2001). This theory assumes that we are born with an undefined crude face-processing system that undergoes a process of perceptual narrowing in response to experience with faces. Indeed, it is thought that the system very quickly becomes fine-tuned to process the faces it encounters most frequently in an optimal manner.

Critically, the perceptual narrowing hypothesis is similar to CONLERN, but does not require the CONSPEC system. Instead, Nelson suggests that, as a result of evolutionary pressures, the human cortex is both flexible and open to learning at birth. Further, he posits that regions within inferotemporal cortex have the potential to become specialized for face recognition, and this occurs in response to increased exposure to faces. More specifically, Scott, Pascalis and Nelson (2007) suggest that this process occurs as neural circuits that respond to frequently perceived faces are strengthened, whereas those that respond to faces that are rarely seen are weakened. Interestingly, this theory is similar to a parallel hypothesis that accounts for the development of language. Indeed, young infants seem to be able to discriminate between different phonemes in almost any language, but this ability disappears at a later age when the child is only sensitive to the language that they are exposed to in their everyday environment (e.g.,, Kuhl, 1998).

Evidence supporting the perceptual narrowing hypothesis has come from investigations into the other-race effect (the finding that we are better at recognizing faces from our own race as opposed to other races), which has been found to be more pronounced in adults and older children than infants. For instance, Kelly *et al.* (2007) investigated the recognition of same- and other-race faces in three-, six- and nine-month-old infants. Specifically, the babies were shown images of African, Middle Eastern, Chinese and Caucasian faces until they habituated to each face. The infants were then shown pairs of faces containing one of the habituated faces and a novel face. The authors measured the time that the babies viewed each face in the pair, assuming that when the baby looked at the novel face for a longer period, this signified recognition of the habituated face. Interestingly, in support of the perceptual narrowing hypothesis, Kelly *et al.* found a progressive narrowing with increasing age in the ability to recognize other-race faces.

A similar effect has been noted in the recognition of human faces compared with those of other species. For instance, Pascalis, de Haan and Nelson (2002) investigated the recognition of human and monkey faces in six- and nine-month-old babies, in addition to adult participants. The authors reasoned that, if the perceptual narrowing hypothesis is correct, the younger participants should be able to discriminate between both monkey and human faces, whereas older participants should only be able to recognize the human faces. Indeed, Pascalis *et al.* found that although all participants could discriminate between the human faces, only the 6-month-olds could discriminate between the monkey faces. Presumably this effect occurred because the adults had undergone prolonged exposure to human faces, bringing about perceptual narrowing of the face-processing system to only be sensitive to human faces. On the other hand, young infants still have a broadly tuned perceptual window.

It is also of note that the processing of emotional expression also seems to be susceptible to perceptual narrowing. Indeed, Leppänen and Nelson (2009) suggest that this process begins at the age of 5–7 months, and lasts for several years. Evidence supporting the hypothesis that experience plays an important role in the development of expression recognition comes from studies that have examined this process in children who have experienced atypical early environments. For example, maltreated children find it more difficult to recognize facial expressions than non-maltreated children (see, for example, Camras, Grow and Ribordy, 1983). More specific findings were presented by Pollak and colleagues (2000, 2009), who found that children who are abused by their parents display abnormalities in the processing of angry facial expressions.

Finally, event-related potential (see Chapter 2) investigations also support the role of experience in the development of the ability to recognize emotional expressions. Indeed, Moulson et al. (2009) investigated this process in three groups of three-year-old Romanian children: those who had always lived in institutions, those who had been institutionalized but now lived in foster care and those who had never been institutionalized. The authors measured event-related potential responses while the children viewed facial expressions of emotion, and found smaller and later responses in the institutionalized children compared with the non-institutionalized children, with responses for the foster children falling between the other two groups. Interestingly, however, there were no differences between the groups for specific facial expressions. Hence, these findings suggest that atypical experience with facial expressions results in abnormalities in interpreting facial emotion, supporting the hypothesis that perceptual narrowing may also play a role in the development of this ability.

9.1.5. Interim summary

- Johnson and Morton suggest a pre-specified subcortical mechanism (CONSPEC) guides newborns' attention to faces. Later, a cortical system (CONLERN) takes over and infants learn about individual faces. However, demonstrations that newborns are capable of face recognition soon after birth (Bushnell, 2001) are problematic for the CONSPEC component of the model.
- Other theories suggest infants attend to faces merely because they are optimal stimuli for the newborn visual system (Kleiner and Banks, 1987; Simion et al., 2002).
- Much evidence supports the perceptual narrowing hypothesis (Nelson, 2001), and early experience with faces does seem to 'fine-tune' face-processing skills (Kelly et al., 2007; Pascalis, de Haan and Nelson, 2002).

9.2. WHEN DO ADULT-LIKE FACE-PROCESSING SKILLS DEVELOP?

9.2.1. The developmental time-course of face processing

It is clear from the above discussion that, even from birth, infants have surprisingly sophisticated face-processing abilities. Nevertheless, these abilities are clearly not at the level experienced by adults, and the face-processing system must undergo a period of development to reach these levels. Some studies have investigated the development of face recognition ability throughout childhood, and noted a rapid improvement up to 10 years of age, followed by a small dip in puberty, and a smaller increase up to the age of 16 years (e.g., Flin, 1980). Such findings receive support from recent event-related potential studies that indicate the face-specific N170 component continues to develop until well into adolescence. For example, Taylor, Batty and Itier (2004) reported that, although the latency of the N170 decreases consistently until approximately 14 years of age, a U-shaped function was noted for its amplitude, with smaller amplitudes at 11 to 12 years than older or younger ages.

Interestingly, although this small decline in puberty has not been noted in all investigations, a similar pattern has been reported in language processing, suggesting it might reflect a more general cognitive dip that occurs around this time. Indeed, McGivern *et al.* (2002) suggest that some degree of cortical reorganization occurs in prefrontal cortex during puberty, and as a result, general information processing abilities may become less efficient.

Regardless of this issue, experimental studies of face recognition ability indicate that adult-like levels of performance are not reached until mid-adolescence, and many studies have investigated the mechanisms underpinning this difference in performance. It has been of some debate whether improvements in face recognition ability throughout childhood actually reflect development of the face-processing system itself, or simply increases in more general visuocognitive abilities that support this process, such as improvements in memory or attention. This issue is discussed in the remainder of this chapter.

9.2.2. Improvements in face-specific processing mechanisms

In Chapter 1, experimental paradigms that have examined the processing strategies used by adults in face recognition were discussed. In particular, the techniques that are used to examine the use of the face-specific configural processing strategy were described, with evidence that suggests adults display an 'inner-face advantage' for the processing of familiar as opposed to unfamiliar faces. These effects have also been used as markers that indicate the onset of adult-like face-processing abilities. Hence, this section discusses evidence about the age at which children might develop these processing strategies, and considers whether the development of these abilities parallels the improvement in face recognition performance that is observed from childhood through to adulthood.

Much of this debate has focused on the 'encoding switch hypothesis' (Diamond and Carey, 1977), which attempts to account for experimental findings about the use of featural and configural information in children. Specifically, these authors suggested that young children process faces in a qualitatively different manner to older children and adults, such that they switch from a featural to a configural processing strategy at 10 years of age. Indeed, Diamond and Carey suggested that this change in processing strategy parallels the increase in face recognition performance that is noted in children around this age.

The encoding switch hypothesis was based on findings from studies that investigated the effects of paraphernalia (e.g., adding a hat or a scarf) on face recognition. For instance, Diamond and Carey (1977) showed children images of different faces wearing hats. In a later test phase, children were presented with pairs of faces containing one studied and one novel item. Further, the hat was either on the studied face or the novel face, and children were asked to select the face they thought they had seen before. The authors noted that children under 10 years simply picked the face with the hat, whereas older children were more likely to select the correct face. Diamond and Carey interpreted these findings as evidence that children switch from using featural to configural information at the age of 10 years.

However, more recent studies using paraphernalia have provided contradictory findings, drawing the encoding switch hypothesis into question. Indeed, Freire and Lee (2001) investigated face recognition ability in children aged between four and seven years. Initially, the children memorized a face that wore a hat, and then were asked to select the familiar face from an array displaying four faces, where the hat was added to either the studied face or one of the novel faces. In addition, the novel faces differed from the studied face either on the basis of configural or featural information. Interestingly, the authors noted that performance was better in the featural condition, although children were still misled by paraphernalia. Further, even though performance was lower in the configural condition, children still performed above chance levels. That is, although performance was easily disrupted by paraphernalia, the children could still recognize faces on the basis of configural information. Thus, the authors concluded that, although paraphernalia does impair recognition performance, the effect cannot be attributed to a lack of configural processing.

Further problems for the encoding switch hypothesis are encountered in studies using the classical configural processing paradigms described in Chapter 1. For instance, De Heering, Houthuys and Rossion (2007) used the composite face task to investigate configural processing ability in four-, five- and six-year-old children, as well as adults. Participants were required to decide whether the top halves of aligned or misaligned faces were the same or different. A similar interference effect was noted for incongruent faces in the aligned condition for all participants, indicating the automatic influence of configural processing in even very young children. Further studies have examined configural processing in young children using the face inversion effect. Indeed, Picozzi *et al.* (2009) adopted this paradigm in a study using three- to four-year-olds, and found that inversion disrupted the processing of faces to a greater extent than it did for shoes.

In addition, other authors have used the part–whole paradigm, in which participants are asked to encode whole faces, and then are presented with individual features for recognition either in the context of the whole face or in isolation. Adults tend to recognize the features more accurately in the whole condition, presumably because of the influence of configural processing, and the same effect has been noted in four-year-old children (see Pellicano, Rhodes and Peters, 2006). However, Hay and Cox (2000) provided evidence that the part–whole advantage is greater in nine-year-olds as opposed to six-year-olds, suggesting the effect does take some time to develop. Finally, other work has suggested that sensitivity to the spatial relations between features is present in infants as young as three months of age (Quinn and Tanaka, 2009).

Although the findings reviewed above indicate that the ability to discriminate facial configural information is present from early infancy, other work has indicated that both young and older children perform poorly when asked to use configural information for recognition purposes. For instance, Mondloch, Le Grand and Maurer (2002) found that 10-year-old children performed at a similar level to adults when they were asked to recognize unfamiliar faces that had undergone featural changes, whereas 14-year-olds did not demonstrate adults' levels of performance in a similar task where faces had undergone configural changes. Thus, although young infants might be able to perceive configural information in faces, it seems that the ability to use this information for actual recognition does not develop until adolescence.

In Chapter 1, evidence was also reviewed that suggests adults use the inner (i.e., eyes, nose and mouth) rather than outer features to recognize familiar faces, but use the outer features to recognize unfamiliar faces. Some studies have investigated the age at which this inner face advantage develops in children. For instance, Ge *et al.* (2008) examined this question in four-, eight- and 14-year-olds, who were asked to identify 10 of their classmates under four conditions: using the whole face, only the external features, only the internal features or isolated features. The authors noted that all three groups demonstrated the inner face advantage; and converging evidence has been reported in other studies using nine-year-olds (see Campbell, Walker and Baron-Cohen, 1995), seven-year-olds (see Bonner and Burton, 2004) and five-year-olds (see Wilson, Blades and Pascalis, 2007). Hence, it appears that the inner-face advantage is also present in young children, providing further evidence against the encoding-switch hypothesis. However, it is striking that evidence suggests that this effect is largely underpinned by more accurate recognition of the eye region as opposed to other features of the face. Indeed, several studies have reported that children are better at recognizing the eyes as opposed to the mouth or nose (Ge *et al.*, 2008; Hay and Cox, 2000).

Although much behavioural evidence has provided evidence against the encoding switch hypothesis, neuroimaging evidence suggests that important developments in the face-processing system do occur around 10 years of age. For instance, Taylor, Batty and Itier (2004) reported that face inversion did not influence the N170 until eight to 11 years of age. Similarly, Gathers *et al.* (2004) reported that activation in the fusiform gyrus is not greater for faces compared with objects until 10 years of age, although they did note such activation more posteriorly in the inferior occipital region. Interestingly, Passarotti *et al.* (2003) found more diverse activation in the fusiform region for children as opposed to adults. Hence, although behavioural evidence suggests that young children process faces in a qualitatively similar way to adults, neuroimaging evidence suggests that the cortical face-processing system continues to develop throughout childhood.

A recent study reported by Germine, Duchaine and Nakayama (2011) presents behavioural evidence that is even more striking. Specifically, these authors tested over 60 000 participants aged from pre-adolescence to middle age on their ability to learn new faces. In three experiments, Germine and colleagues found that face learning ability improves up until the age of 30, although the recognition of inverted faces and name recognition peaked at a much earlier age. This evidence suggests that the face-processing system may not reach maturation until a much later age than previously envisaged.

9.2.3. Improvements in more generalized processing mechanisms

The evidence discussed so far indicates that, although children's face recognition ability is *quantitatively* poorer than adults, children and adults seem to use *qualitatively* similar mechanisms to process faces. Hence, as faces are essentially being processed in the same manner by children as adults, the difference in recognition performance may be explained by more generalized mechanisms. Interestingly, evidence from the eye-witness literature might provide some insight into this issue. Indeed, Pozzulo and Lindsay (1998) reported a meta-analysis that summarized findings from eye-witness studies using children as participants. The authors noted that children as young as five years of age display adult-like performance in their ability to identify perpetrators from line-ups. However, when the perpetrator is not present in the line-up, children up to 14 years of age make more false identifications than adults.

This finding is clearly different from behavioural studies that indicate a large increase in face recognition ability up to the age of 10 years. This difference in findings between the two types of study can be attributed to several factors. First, most cognitive studies do not take demand characteristics into consideration. That is, findings from eye-witness studies with target-absent line-ups suggest that children assume the correct face is always present, and make an identification even when they might not necessarily recognize the face. Second, there is clearly an increased memory burden in cognitive studies of face recognition ability, where many face are normally presented for recognition. In contrast, eye-witness studies only require the recognition of one individual, and hence there are lower demands on more generalized processes such as memory, concentration and attention.

In sum, although it seems that young children have the processing mechanisms that are necessary to match adult levels of face recognition, they do not achieve these levels in experimental settings, perhaps because of poor attention and concentration, and an increased susceptibility to demand characteristics.

9.2.4. Interim summary

■ The ability to recognize faces markedly improves up to the age of 10 years, suffers a dip during puberty and continues to improve until mid-adolescence (Flin, 1980; Taylor, Batty and Itier, 2004).

■ The encoding switch hypothesis (Diamond and Carey, 1977) suggests that this pattern can be attributed to a shift from featural to configural processing around the age of 10 years. However, much evidence refutes the hypothesis, and suggests that young children and even infants are capable of using configural processing (e.g., Freire and Lee, 2001; Quinn and Tanaka, 2009) and the inner features to process faces (Ge *et al.* (2008). Thus, young children appear to process faces in a qualitatively similar manner to adults, indicating the strategies they use to process faces cannot explain their quantitatively poorer recognition performance.

■ Despite these behavioural similarities in processing strategy, neuroimaging evidence suggests that the cortical face-processing system continues to develop throughout childhood and well into adolescence (Gathers *et al.*, 2004; Passarotti *et al.*, 2003). Recent behavioural evidence also suggests that some components of face processing might reach maturity at the age of 30 years (Germine, Duchaine and Nakayama, 2011).

■ Further, in opposition to cognitive studies, eye-witness investigations suggest that adult-like face recognition performance is in fact reached by five years of age, but lower levels of attention, concentration and memory, and a greater susceptibility to demand characteristics, explain why children perform at a poorer level in cognitive face recognition experiments (Lindsay, 1998).

CHAPTER SUMMARY

A widespread network of cortical and subcortical structures are involved in face processing. Indeed, some evidence suggests that subcortical structures may be functioning from birth and orient attention towards faces, enhancing development of the cortical face-processing system. Neuroimaging evidence suggests that this system continues to develop into adolescence, where it eventually becomes more focal and less distributed. Nevertheless, face-specific behavioural processing strategies appear to be available to children from a young age, and their poorer performance relative to adults in laboratory-based face recognition experiments may be attributed to weaknesses in more generalized processes.

FURTHER READING

Freire, A., and Lee, K. (2001) 'Face Recognition in 4- to 7-Year-Olds: Processing of Configural, Featural, and Paraphernalia Information', *Journal of Experimental Child Psychology*, 80, 347–71.

Germine, L. T., Duchaine, B. and Nakayama, K. (2011). 'Where Cognitive Development and Aging Meet: Face Learning Ability Peaks after Age 30', *Cognition*, 118, 201–10.

Johnson, M. H. (2005) 'Sub-Cortical Face Processing', *Nature Reviews Neuroscience*, 6, 766–74.

Morton, J. and Johnson, M. H. (1991) 'CONSPEC and CONLERN: A Two-Process Theory of the Development of Infant Face Recognition', *Psychological Review*, 98, 164–81.

Nelson, C. A. (2001) 'The Development and Neural Bases of Face Recognition', *Infant and Child Development*, 10, 3–18.

Pozzulo, J. D. and Lindsay, R. C. L. (1998) 'Identification Accuracy of Children versus Adults: A Meta-Analysis', *Law and Human Behavior*, 22, 549–70.

Taylor, M. J., Batty, M. and Itier, R. J. (2004) 'The Faces of Development: A Review of Early Face Processing over Childhood', *Journal of Cognitive Neuroscience*, 16, 1426–42.

GUIDANCE QUESTIONS

Use the following questions to guide your reading of this chapter and the recommended papers.

1. Describe and evaluate the CONSPEC component of the CONSPEC/CONLERN theory.
2. What are the similarities between CONLERN and the perceptual narrowing hypothesis?
3. What is the encoding switch model, and to what extent does experimental evidence support this theory?
4. How have more applied studies of face processing in children informed our knowledge about the developmental trajectory of face recognition ability?

10 Developmental Prosopagnosia

Chapter 5 discussed acquired prosopagnosia (AP), a rare disorder characterized by a deficit in face recognition that occurs after neurological damage. However, other people simply fail to develop normal face-processing abilities. This form of the disorder had been termed 'developmental prosopagnosia' (DP). Like those with AP, these individuals have a selective impairment in face recognition despite intact lower-level visual and intellectual abilities, but have never suffered any neurological damage (Jones and Tranel, 2001).

Although perhaps most authors use the term 'developmental prosopagnosia' to adhere to the definition offered by Jones and Tranel (2001), the term has also been used interchangeably. Indeed, it has been used as an umbrella term to encompass face recognition impairments that occur alongside other developmental conditions (e.g., autistic spectrum disorder or Turner's syndrome (e.g., Kracke, 1994: see Chapter 11)), or that result from brain damage or visual abnormalities at an early age (e.g., Barton, Cherkasova and O'Connor, 2001). Further, some individuals report other family members who are also suspected to suffer from the disorder, suggesting in some cases DP might have a genetic origin. Some authors refer to these individuals as 'congenital' or 'hereditary' prosopagnosics, although other authors describe any case without known neurological damage or concurrent developmental disorder as 'congenital' or 'hereditary' in origin, regardless of evidence of a genetic link (e.g., Kennerknecht *et al.*, 2006).

From the above discussion, it can be seen that the terminology used to refer to lifelong cases of prosopagnosia is inconsistent. In this book, the more conservative term 'developmental prosopagnosia' is used to refer to all individuals who have suffered a face recognition impairment since birth, in the absence of any known socio-developmental disorder (SDD) or neurological trauma. Thus, the term is used to encompass cases with or without a suspected genetic link, but not those who have suffered neurological trauma at any point in life (including *in utero* or during birth), or who present with a concurrent SDD.

10.1. A BRIEF HISTORY OF DP

It was initially thought that DP was an extremely rare disorder (e.g., de Haan, 1999; Jones and Tranel, 2001). In 1963, Bornstein briefly described some prosopagnosic cases that appear to be developmental in origin, but McConachie (1976) was the first to publish a formal case study of a DP. Specifically, this author described the case of AB, an intelligent 12-year-old girl who reported severe difficulties in recognizing both unfamiliar faces and her peers when they wore school uniforms. Interestingly, AB's mother also reported problems in recognizing faces. De Haan and Campbell (1991) performed a follow-up study with AB, 15 years after the original report. They found that, as an adult, AB still presented with obvious difficulties in face recognition, but also suffered from impairments in recognizing emotional expressions and within-class objects.

A handful of other cases of DP were also reported in the 1990s (see, for example, Bentin, Deouell and Soroker, 1999; Kracke, 1994; Temple, 1992). However, at the beginning of the twenty-first century it became apparent that DP is not as rare as originally thought, and larger numbers of people who believe they had the disorder came forward for testing. Hence, the past decade has seen substantial leaps in our understanding of the condition, although much work remains to be done.

Given the large numbers of people with DP who have recently made themselves known to researchers, some authors have attempted to estimate the prevalence of the disorder. In an initial study, Kennerknecht *et al.* (2006) presented data that screened 689 German secondary school pupils and medical students for prosopagnosia, using self-report measures and semi-structured interview. They concluded that 17 members of their sample suffered from what they termed as 'hereditary prosopagnosia' (they assumed that all the prosopagnosics had a familial basis to their disorder), corresponding to a prevalence rate of 2.47%. In a later paper, this group of researchers performed a similar survey in 533 medical students at the University of Hong Kong, and diagnosed 10 students with 'hereditary prosopagnosia', translating to a prevalence rate of 1.9% (Kennerknecht, Yee-Ho and Wong, 2008). However, these estimates should be treated with some caution, as diagnosis of prosopagnosia in both studies relied on self-report measures, and were not confirmed using objective laboratory-based tests of face recognition ability.

However, in a recent paper, Bowles *et al.* (2009) screened the face recognition ability of 241 Australian adults using the Cambridge Face Memory Test (Duchaine and Nakayama, 2006b), a computerized test that has been thoroughly validated and standardized, and has been found to diagnose prosopagnosia reliably in many cases (see Chapter 14). Based on the number of cases of DP found in their sample, Bowles *et al.* calculated a prevalence rate of between 2.0 and 2.9 per cent, depending on how conservative they were in the calculation of cut-off scores that were used to indicate impairment. However, even taking the most conservative estimate of a prevalence of two per cent (i.e., one in 50 people), it is clear that many individuals suffer from DP.

10.2. THE AETIOLOGY OF DP

10.2.1. Is there a genetic basis for DP?

As described above, some authors refer to their cases of DP as 'congenital' or 'hereditary' because other family members also appear to suffer from the disorder. Such reports raise the possibility that DP might therefore be genetic in origin, and there is increasing evidence to support this claim. Indeed, many case reports in the literature describe at least one first-degree relative who is also suspected to suffer from prosopagnosia (see, for example, Bate *et al.*, 2009), and further reports considering entire families of prosopagnosics have recently been published (Duchaine, Germine and Nakayama, 2007; Grueter *et al.*, 2007; Kennerknecht *et al.*, 2006; Schmalzl, Palermo and Coltheart, 2008). In fact, Kennerknecht *et al.* (2006) concluded that the segregation patterns observed in their families of self-reported prosopagnosics are consistent with a dominant autosomal inheritance (i.e., the gene need only be abnormal in one parent), a finding that is rarely observed for higher visual functions. Yet, no gene has yet been associated with DP, and given the complexity of the human face-processing system, it is likely that many different genetic deficits might contribute to development of the disorder.

Familial reports of DP are given additional weight by a recent study that examined face recognition ability in monozygotic (identical) and dizygotic (non-identical) twins who did not have prosopagnosia (Wilmer *et al.*, 2010). These authors asked each twin to complete a series of face recognition tests, and correlated the scores achieved by each twin. Strikingly, it was found that the correlation of face-processing scores between monozygotic twins was more than double that observed for dizygotic twins, suggesting face recognition ability may indeed be highly heritable.

Despite this evidence and claims that DP almost always runs in families (Kennerknecht *et al.*, 2006), it is also clear that the disorder cannot be explained by genetics in a substantial number of cases reported in the literature. Indeed, many people with DP do not suspect that any of their first-degree relatives also suffer from the condition (e.g., Bate *et al.*, 2008; Duchaine and Nakayama, 2005). Based on this evidence, one might question how many people with DP actually have a genetic component to their disorder. In Kennerknecht *et al.*'s (2008) prevalence study described above, the authors concluded that all 10 of their prosopagnosics suffer from a hereditary form of prosopagnosia. However, this claim was questioned by Duchaine (2008), who suggested that closer inspection of the data revealed that only four of the 10 prosopagnosics reported family members who were also thought to have the condition. Hence, contrary to Kennerknecht and colleagues' (2006, 2008) hypothesis that DP almost always runs in families, Duchaine's amendment suggests that non-hereditary DP might actually be more common than hereditary DP, with a ratio of 3:2.

Additional data about the relative proportion of hereditary compared with non-hereditary DP was provided by Duchaine (2008) in the same paper. Specifically, Duchaine used an example of 19 objectively diagnosed cases of DP who had participated in a recent experiment in his laboratory. Of the 19 individuals, 11 reported close relatives with face recognition problems, four were unsure, and four were confident that none of their relatives had prosopagnosia. Duchaine used these figures to calculate a split of heritable to non-heritable cases of approximately 58:42, a figure that conversely suggests that heritable DP is more common than non-heritable DP.

In summary, although it is clear that more precise estimations of the ratio of heritable compared with non-heritable cases are still required using much larger numbers of individuals, it is evident that for some people with DP there is no genetic basis to the disorder. This brings about important theoretical questions concerning the cognitive and neural processes that might underpin DP in non-heritable cases. Several hypotheses about this issue are considered in the remainder of this section.

10.2.2. Is DP linked to other developmental disorders, such as autism?

Some authors have suggested that DP is simply a by-product of a SDD, given that face-processing deficits commonly present in these conditions (e.g., Schultz, 2005; see Chapter 11). Indeed, although the precise relationship between socio-emotional functioning and face recognition ability remains unclear (Bate *et al.*, 2010), it is certain that many individuals with SDDs also suffer from an impairment in face recognition (for reviews see Behrmann, Thomas and Humphreys, 2006; Dawson, Webb and McPartland, 2005; Schultz, 2005), and some individuals with DP have also been reported to show autistic spectrum symptoms (Duchaine, Nieminen-von Wendt *et al.*, 2003; Kracke, 1994). This has led to something of a 'chicken and egg' situation, in that it is not surprising that individuals with SDDs might experience difficulties in face processing given they are thought to avoid socially salient stimuli. Likewise, it is not surprising that DP can have devastating social consequences for some individuals, which might present as social withdrawal or a fear of social situations—symptoms that are commonly associated with SDDs. Hence, if it is true that there is a relationship between DP and SDDs, it is very difficult to speculate on the causal direction of that relationship. Schultz (2005) put forward a neurological theory that attributes face-processing impairments in autistic spectrum disorders to an early abnormality in the amygdala. You can read more about Schultz's theory in Chapter 11, but the pertinent point here is that Schultz hypothesizes that a failure in amygdala functioning in early childhood can bring about both impaired face-processing skills and difficulties in social interaction. Thus, Schultz raises the question that DP and some SDDs might be closely linked.

However, other authors have argued against this hypothesis, and believe that DP can (and mostly does) occur in the absence of any concurrent SDD. Indeed, many individuals with DP show no symptoms of SDD (Behrmann, Avidan *et al.*, 2005; Garrido, Duchaine and Nakayama, 2008), and it has been observed that some autistic individuals do not suffer from face recognition deficits (Barton *et al.*, 2004). Further research has demonstrated that the face recognition impairment that presents alongside autistic spectrum disorders is not as severe as that observed in prosopagnosia. Indeed, Barton *et al.* (2004) tested the face-processing abilities of 24 individuals with a variety of SDD diagnoses. Although eight of the SDD participants demonstrated no impairment in their face-processing abilities, the remaining 16 participants performed significantly poorer than controls on a range of face-processing tasks, but the performance of a prosopagnosic group was even worse than the SDD participants. Finally, in a recent paper, Duchaine *et al.* (2010) described two male patients with DP who were impaired at both face recognition and emotional expression processing. However, the authors found that neither met the diagnostic criteria for autism, as measured by performance on the Autism Diagnostic Observation Schedule and the Autistic-Spectrum Quotient Questionnaire. The authors also administered an animation task that was thought to tap theory of mind (the ability to attribute mental states to others), which is commonly impaired in individuals with autism. The two patients with DP performed within the normal range on this test, indicating that their social cognition was intact.

Thus, although investigation of individuals who suffer from face-processing impairments alongside SDDs is also of interest in informing our knowledge about other factors that may influence face recognition ability, the bulk of the available evidence supports the viewpoint that DP should be considered as an independent condition.

10.2.3. Is DP brought about by early visual deprivation?

It is currently unclear why DP might occur in the absence of either a genetic connection or a concurrent SDD. However, several case reports suggest that some people with DP experience uncorrected visual problems for substantial periods of time during childhood. This might simply have been uncorrected short- or long-sightedness, or might have involved amblyopia (lazy eye) or strabismus (crossed or wandering eyes). This is a pertinent issue in light of striking evidence that suggests early visual deprivation can bring about lasting difficulties in some aspects of face processing.

Specifically, Geldart *et al.* (2002) tested 17 individuals who had suffered from bilateral congenital cataracts that had deprived them of patterned visual input for at least the first seven weeks of life. When tested on their face-processing skills later in life (when they were aged between 10 and 38 years), the researchers found that the patients were impaired at tests requiring them to match faces according to facial identity, although they performed normally on other tasks assessing the perception of facial expression, gaze direction and lip speech. This pattern of findings supports models of the development of face processing that postulate the importance of early visual experience with faces for normal adult levels of face recognition ability to be achieved (e.g., de Schonen and Mathivet, 1989; Johnson and Morton, 1991).

The study of Geldart *et al.* suggests that visual experience with faces in infancy is vital for normal face-processing skills to develop, and it is possible that DP may sometimes originate from a failure to attend to faces in early childhood. Indeed, in Chapter 9 we learnt that faces are particularly salient to both infants and toddlers, and as such they direct considerable attention to these stimuli (Goren, Sarty and Wu, 1975; Johnson and Morton, 1991). Hence, some theories predict that diminished attention to faces may affect the tuning of face-processing mechanisms (Nelson, 2001). Some support for this hypothesis can be found in the DP literature. Indeed, Schmalzl, Palermo, Green *et al.* (2008) described a 4-year-old girl with DP (K), who displayed severe perceptual deficits with faces. The researchers used eye-tracking technology to demonstrate that K tended to avoid the inner features of the face compared with age-matched controls, particularly the eye region. Interestingly, reduced attention to the eyes has also been demonstrated in both AP (Rossion *et al.*, 2009) and SDDs (Dalton *et al.*, 2005). However, although it remains possible that such visual deficits might underpin DP in some cases, it is equally possible that higher-level deficits might bring about the failure to attend to faces.

Further, other people with DP have been described who experienced no visual abnormalities during childhood nor report any relatives with the disorder. Thus, having considered the neuropsychological history and accompanying deficits that might explain DP in some individuals, we now turn to look at the cognitive and neural profile that commonly presents in the disorder and might explain the basis of the face recognition impairment in some cases.

10.2.4. Is DP underpinned by a deficit in configural processing?

As described in Chapter 1, face processing is thought to rely on configural processing, and a common hypothesis is that any failures in face recognition may be attributed to a breakdown in this processing strategy. Hence, a possible cause of the symptoms of DP may lie in specific deficits in the processing of configural information. Several authors have investigated this possibility, testing either general configural processing strategies (i.e., using non-facial configural processing tests) or face-specific configural processing strategies (i.e., tests that use faces as stimuli).

First, two groups of researchers have demonstrated that general configural processing (i.e., that noted on non-facial tests) is impaired in their cases of DP. These papers used Navon stimuli (Navon, 1977) to assess information processing at both global (i.e., configural) and local (i.e., featural) levels. Navon stimuli consist of large letters (global level) that are constructed from smaller component letters (local level). The large letter either matches the small letters (i.e., the stimuli consists of a large letter H constructed from many small letter Hs), or the letters used at the two levels differ (i.e., a large letter S constructed from many small letter Hs). Participants complete many trials that are either congruent or incongruent across the two levels. In different blocks of the task, participants are asked to respond either to the large (global) or the small (local) letter. Control participants tend to respond more quickly to the global letter than they do to the local letter, particularly on congruent trials.

Behrmann, Avidan *et al.* (2005) used this task to investigate general configural processing in their group of five people with DP. In contrast to control participants, the researchers found that the DP group were slower at responding to global letters, but showed normal performance for local letters. Further, the participants with DP also experienced greater interference from inconsistent local information, and less interference from inconsistent global information. A similar pattern was noted in another study that investigated general configural processing abilities in a single case of DP (Bentin *et al.*, 2007). These studies indicate that configural processing might be impaired at a general level in DP. However, other reports suggest configural processing on the Navon task can be unimpaired in some cases of DP. Indeed, Duchaine, Yovel and Nakayama (2007) tested a large group of 14 people with DP on this task, and found no signs of impairment at the global level. Further, other studies have used alternative tasks to assess general configural processing strategy in DP and found no deficits. For example, Duchaine (2000) described case BC, who displayed normal configural processing in three non-facial tasks (word completion, snowy pictures and gestalt completion); and Le Grand and colleagues (2006) found no problems in configural processing in eight people with DP using a global-form task.

However, although generalized configural processing mechanisms might be intact in some people with DP, other evidence suggests that face-specific configural processing can be independently disrupted. This form of configural processing is commonly assessed using the face inversion effect (Yin, 1969). Recall from Chapter 1 that this effect refers to the finding that faces are disproportionately more difficult to recognize when viewed upside down compared with other classes of objects; and this decrease in performance has been attributed to the hypothesis that we cannot use configural processing for inverted faces (e.g., Leder and Bruce, 2000). Some authors have examined the effects of face inversion in their participants with DP, and found a smaller inversion effect compared with control participants, indicating configural face-processing mechanisms might be impaired (Behrmann, Avidan *et al.*, 2005; Duchaine *et al.*, 2004). De Gelder and Rouw (2000a) additionally found evidence of an 'inverted inversion effect' in their participants with DP. That is, the people with DP were more successful at recognizing inverted faces than control participants, presumably because they are more accustomed to using the suboptimal featural processing strategy for recognition. Finally, eye movement studies have indicated that individuals with DP display a more dispersed pattern of fixations when viewing facial stimuli, which has been interpreted as an impairment of configural processing (e.g., Schwarzer *et al.*, 2007).

In sum, although there is mixed evidence to suggest that generalized configural processing strategies might be impaired in DP, findings are more consistent when face-specific configural processing mechanisms have been investigated. However, many more studies with larger numbers of participants are required before any firm conclusions can be reached.

10.2.5. Are there any neurological abnormalities in DP?

It is important to note that it is not surprising that almost all studies fail to find any obvious lesions in their participants with DP using conventional magnetic resonance imaging; and indeed if such damage was observed, the individual is likely to have an acquired rather than developmental form of prosopagnosia. However, some structural abnormalities have been noted in cases of DP. Specifically, two studies have found volumetric differences in the temporal lobe of people with DP (Hasson *et al.*, 2003; Behrmann *et al.*, 2007). In one case, the entire temporal lobe was smaller compared with control participants, whereas six other people with DP had a smaller right anterior fusiform region. Strikingly, the authors reported that the size of this area negatively correlated with the severity of the face recognition impairment in each individual. That is, the smaller the area the more severe the prosopagnosia.

Further, Garrido *et al.* (2009) used voxel-based morphometry in 17 participants with DP, and reported reduced volume of grey matter in several neural regions that are thought to respond selectively to faces, including the right anterior inferior temporal lobe and the superior temporal sulcus/middle temporal gyrus bilaterally. Finally, Thomas *et al.* (2009) used diffusion tensor imaging to re-examine the six people with DP reported in the study of Behrmann *et al.* (2007), and found deficiencies in white matter fibres that connect ventral occipito-temporal regions with more anterior regions. In sum, these recent studies indicate that some structural and volumetric abnormalities can be associated with at least some cases of DP.

Other studies have investigated the activation of neural areas associated with face processing, and surprisingly some have found no abnormalities in DP compared with control participants. For example, Hasson *et al.* (2003) reported case YT, who showed a normal response to faces in both the left and right fusiform face area and the right occipital face area. However, YT did display a reduced selectivity for faces in the left occipital face area. In another study, Avidan *et al.* (2005) assessed face-selective activation in four people with DP, and reported stronger activation for faces than objects in the fusiform gyrus. Further, this response was reduced in the normal manner in both the fusiform gyrus and lateral occipital cortex after repetition of the faces (repetition suppression).

However, other studies have reported functional differences in face-specific areas between people with DP and controls. Duchaine *et al.* (2006) reported a single case of DP, Edward, who failed to show any face-selective voxels in two separate face localizer scans. Further, Bentin *et al.* (2007) described case KW, who also showed no face-selective voxels in ventral temporal cortex; and von Kriegstein, Kleinschmidt and Giraud (2006) reported case SO, who showed a weaker response to faces than objects in left fusiform face area and the temporal poles bilaterally.

Recall from Chapter 2 that healthy participants demonstrate a negative component approximately 170 ms after stimulus onset, that has been termed the 'N170 component' (Eimer, 2000). This response tends to be much stronger for faces than other categories of objects, and is thought to reflect the structural encoding stage of face processing in Bruce and Young's (1986) model. Hence, examination of event-related potentials and particularly the N170 has been performed to assess whether people with DP have problems in the early processing of faces. As noted in functional magnetic resonance imaging investigations, some people with DP demonstrate a normal pattern of face-selectivity as measured by the N170. For instance, Harris, Duchaine and Nakayama (2005) reported five people with DP who were presented with faces and houses while their response was measured using both event-related potentials and magnetoencephalography, a technique that has higher temporal resolution than event-related potentials but measures many of the same neural sources. The researchers found a mixed pattern of findings in their DP group: although three of the participants with DP had non-selective M170 responses, two had normal face-selective M170s and N170s. Hence, it is possible that the prosopagnosia observed in these latter individuals originates from deficits to later stages of processing.

Other people with DP have also demonstrated non-specific responses to faces according to measurement of the N170. For instance, the prosopagnosic YT reported by Hasson *et al.* (2003) was found to have a non-face-selective N170 that responded in a similar manner to faces as it did to objects, although this effect was thought to be driven by an increased response to objects rather than a decreased response to faces. Hence, the authors hypothesized that YT's face-processing system was being used to process both faces and objects, and that this could perhaps be attributed to an early processing deficit that failed to filter faces from other categories of visual stimuli. A similar pattern of findings was noted in the two people with DP reported by Kress and Daum (2003), and case MZ described by DeGutis *et al.* (2007).

In summary, although several different neural abnormalities have been identified in different participants with DP, an integrated understanding of the neural basis of DP remains to be achieved. These neurophysiological studies have also demonstrated a heterogeneous presentation of DP, indicating that the disorder can result from impairments to different mechanisms in different cases. In the final section of this chapter, we consider the varied behavioural presentation of DP that supports this hypothesis.

10.2.6. Are people with DP simply the tail-end of the normal face-processing continuum?

Finally, there is some evidence to suggest that DP might not be a disorder that is characterized by a qualitatively different type of processing, but that these individuals may simply be the people who reside at the poorer end of the normal face-processing continuum. Indeed, there is increasing evidence to suggest that there is much variation in face-processing ability across the population. Much of this evidence comes from the eye-witness literature, where it has been shown that some people are better at identifying perpetrators in line-ups than others (Olsson and Juslin, 1999; Bindemann *et al.*, 2012); although norming data that accompany neuropsychological tests also indicate that control participants can vary from near-chance to perfect performance (e.g., Burton, White and McNeil, 2010). Further, recent reports have identified certain characteristics that correlate with face recognition ability, including empathy (Bate *et al.*, 2010), extraversion (Li *et al.*, 2010), and a global processing bias (Darling *et al.*, 2009).

More convincing evidence that suggests the normal face-processing continuum might reflect a wider range of abilities than previously thought comes from a study reported by Russell, Duchaine and Nakayama (2009). These authors assessed the face-processing abilities of four individuals who believed they were exceptionally good at recognizing faces. These 'super-recognizers' performed beyond the range of control participants, and showed a larger face inversion effect. Interestingly, the authors commented that the super-recognizers were about as good at face recognition as people with DP are bad, and suggested that many cases of DP might simply reside on the tail end of normal face-processing ability, rather than experiencing a qualitatively different kind of processing. What is currently unclear is whether people with DP, 'normal' perceivers and super-recognizers all lie on the same continuum, where DP is simply the poorer end of that continuum, or whether DP is represented by a qualitatively different type of processing that puts them on a different trajectory to that of normal perceivers and super-recognizers.

10.3. CO-MORBID DEFICITS IN DP

From the above discussion, it is clear that there may be multiple causes of DP. It is perhaps, then, unsurprising that many authors have suggested that DP is a heterogeneous disorder, and different individuals present with a varying pattern of facial and non-facial co-morbid impairments. Interestingly, these associated deficits are similar to those that often co-occur with AP, suggesting the two types of prosopagnosia might involve deficits to similar mechanisms. However, it has not yet been determined whether DP can be partitioned into subtypes according to aetiology, and additionally whether this subdivision can predict the co-morbid impairments that present in each individual.

As noted for AP, DP can be accompanied by other deficits in face processing. For instance, in some individuals the face-processing impairment extends to face detection (Garrido, Duchaine and Nakayama, 2008), gender discrimination (Duchaine *et al.*, 2006), expression recognition (Duchaine, 2000; Duchaine *et al.*, 2006; Garrido *et al.*, 2009) or trustworthiness judgements (Todorov and Duchaine, 2008).

Chapter 5 illustrated how the pattern of face-processing deficits that are commonly observed in AP have been mapped onto functional models of face processing (e.g., Bruce and Young, 1986), and this has been used to propose the existence of two broad subtypes of the disorder. Specifically, *apperceptive* prosopagnosics are thought to be unable to create a correct percept of a face, whereas it is though that face perception is largely intact in *associative* prosopagnosia, but these individuals are unable to give any meaning to a correctly elaborated visual representation of a face (de Renzi *et al.*, 1991). In terms of the Bruce and Young (1986) model, it is thought that apperceptive prosopagnosia represents an impairment at the level of structural encoding, whereas the lesion in associative prosopagnosia is believed to be located either within the face recognition units, or in the link between the face recognition units and the person identity nodes.

It is currently unclear whether the apperceptive/associative distinction maps onto developmental cases of prosopagnosia, although there are reports of individuals who present with and without a deficit in face perception, suggesting the distinction can broadly be applied. However, it is important to note that the functional models that underpin the distinction in patients with AP are based on normal adult performance and disruption of a fully and normally developed adult face-processing system. As people with DP are unlikely to have ever developed an intact adult face-processing system, some caution must be applied when attempting to interpret the cognitive presentation of these individuals within such models (see Chapter 12).

Nevertheless, the apperceptive/associative subclassification is thought to be of particular theoretical importance in AP given evidence of a relationship between covert recognition and perceptual impairment. Specifically, in the acquired form of the disorder, covert recognition has been demonstrated in virtually all patients with an associative impairment, but only in some patients with an apperceptive impairment. This finding suggests that some residual capacity to encode face representations is required to demonstrate covert recognition. Hence, some authors have argued against the existence of covert processing in

DP, because they believe that the process relies on subthreshold activation of previously intact face representations (e.g., those created in a normal manner before onset of the disorder (Barton, Cherkasova and O'Connor, 2001)).

However, some authors have looked for evidence of covert recognition in their cases of DP, and, rather than finding no evidence of the process, have reported a pattern of findings that is similar to that observed in AP. Specifically, de Haan and Campbell (1991) and Bentin, Deouell and Soroker (1999) failed to find evidence of covert recognition in their cases of DP (AB and YT), but both individuals had impairments in face perception that would classify them as having the apperceptive form of prosopagnosia. On the other hand, two studies have demonstrated covert face recognition in cases of DP using eye movement measures of recognition (AA (Bate *et al.*, 2008)) and the skin conductance response (TA (Jones and Tranel, 2001)). Importantly, both of these two cases appear to be more representative of the associative form of prosopagnosia. Thus, although it is not clear whether the apperceptive/associative distinction maps onto DP in precisely the same manner as it does in AP, there is nevertheless some evidence to support this claim.

Finally, some people with DP also show deficits in particular aspects of non-facial processing, such as object recognition. Most people with DP reported in the literature do not show difficulties in basic-level object recognition (e.g., discriminating a car from a lorry (Duchaine *et al.*, 2006)), but many do seem to have problems recognizing particular items that are from the same category (e.g., recognizing a specific car among other cars (Behrmann, Avidan *et al.*, 2005; Duchaine and Nakayama, 2005; Duchaine, Nieminen-von Wendt *et al.*, 2003)). For example, eight out of the 14 people with DP described by Garrido, Duchaine and Nakayama (2008) showed impairments on at least one of seven tests that required participants to memorize and then recall particular objects from within the same category. The authors noted that five of the 14 people with DP appeared to have severe deficits in object recognition, and were impaired on at least four of the seven tests. However, six people with DP displayed normal performance on all seven tests, and preserved object recognition abilities has also been demonstrated in other cases of DP (Duchaine and Nakayama, 2005; Nunn, Postma and Pearson, 2001; Yovel and Duchaine, 2006). Lastly, although it has yet to be formally documented, many people with DP report difficulties with large-scale navigation and left–right confusion (see, for example, Duchaine, Parker and Nakayama, 2003).

CHAPTER SUMMARY

- ▪ DP is similar to AP in that it is characterized by a severe deficit in face recognition, but individuals with this form of the disorder have had the impairment since birth and have never experienced any neurological damage (Jones and Tranel, 2001).

■ It was initially thought that DP was a rare disorder, but recent estimates suggest two per cent of the population may experience DP (Bowles *et al.*, 2009).

■ There are several hypotheses about the aetiology of DP, and it seems in some individuals there is a familial basis to the disorder (see, for example, Duchaine, Germine and Nakayama, 2007; Schmalzl, Palermo and Coltheart, 2008), although a specific gene has not yet been associated with DP. Other researchers have suggested that some cases of the disorder might be connected to SDDs (Schultz, 2005), or a period of visual deprivation in childhood (Geldart *et al.*, 2002; Schmalzl, Palermo, Green *et al.*, 2008), or that it might result from deficits in configural processing (Behrmann, Avidan, *et al.*, 2005; de Gelder and Rouw, 2000a) or neurological abnormalities (Garrido *et al.*, 2009; Thomas *et al.*, 2009).

■ A recent report of 'super-recognizers' suggests there might be a much wider continuum of face-processing ability across the general population, in which DP simply represents those people who are quantitatively poorer at face recognition (Russell, Duchaine and Nakayama, 2009).

■ Behavioural investigations of DP have also revealed several co-morbid impairments that differentially present between individuals with the disorder. Hence, it is clear that DP is not a homogeneous disorder, and it is likely that it can result from a variety of developmental disruptions. However, current evidence does not yet allow us to discriminate between potential subtypes of the disorder.

FURTHER READING

Barton, J. J. S., Cherkasova, M. V., Hefter, R., Cox, T. A., O'Connor, M. and Manoach, D. S. (2004) 'Are Patients with Social Developmental Disorders Prosopagnosic? Perceptual Heterogeneity in the Asperger and Socio-Emotional Processing Disorders', *Brain,* 127, 1706–16.

Behrmann, M., Avidan, G., Marotta, J. J. and Kimchi, R. (2005) 'Detailed Exploration of Face-Related Processing in Congenital Prosopagnosia: 1. Behavioral Findings', *Journal of Cognitive Neuroscience,* 8, 551–65.

Duchaine, B., Murray, H., Turner, M., White, S. and Garrido, L. (2010) 'Normal Social Cognition in Developmental Prosopagnosia', *Cognitive Neuropsychology,* 25, 1–15.

Duchaine, B., Yovel, G., Butterworth, E. and Nakayama, K. (2006) 'Prosopagnosia as an Impairment to Face-Specific Mechanisms: Elimination of the Alternative Hypothesis in a Developmental Case', *Cognitive Neuropsychology,* 23, 714–47.

Russell, R., Duchaine, B. and Nakayama, K. (2009) 'Super-Recognizers: People with Extraordinary Face Recognition Ability', *Psychonomic Bulletin and Review,* 16, 252–7.

Wilmer, J. B., Germine, L., Chabris C. F., Chatterjee, G., Williams, M., Loken, E., Nakayama, K. and Duchaine, B. (2010) 'Human Face Recognition is Highly Heritable', *Proceedings of the National Academy of Sciences of the USA*, 107, 5238–41.

GUIDANCE QUESTIONS

Use the following questions to guide your reading of this chapter and the recommended papers.

1. To what extent does DP support the hypothesis that face recognition ability is highly heritable?
2. Is it likely there is one unitary cause of DP? Explain your answer with reference to the various factors that might underpin the condition.
3. How similar is DP to AP? Discuss with reference to the co-morbid impairments that commonly present with DP.

11 Face-Processing Deficits in Socio-Developmental Disorders

In this chapter, the types of face-processing impairment that present in three socio-developmental disorders are discussed: autistic spectrum disorder (ASD), Williams syndrome and Turner's syndrome. As you read the chapter, take note of the general neurocognitive presentation of each disorder, and how underlying behavioural and neural abnormalities might contribute to the face-processing deficits that occur in the three conditions.

11.1. ASD

ASD includes a range of neurodevelopmental conditions, the most common of which are autism and Asperger's syndrome. ASD has widespread effects on cognitive, perceptual and motor functioning; it is characterized by behavioural impairments in social functioning and communication, repetitive and restricted behaviours and interests, and a lack of theory of mind (the ability to understand that other people have thoughts, beliefs and emotions). It is clear that impairments in general social functioning and the ability to interpret the mental state of others are necessarily linked to various aspects of face processing. Hence, it is of no surprise that much research has found that face-processing mechanisms are commonly disrupted in individuals with ASD. This section describes the types of face-processing impairments that are often observed in ASD, and the theories that have attempted to account for these difficulties.

11.1.1. Which aspects of face processing are impaired in ASD?

A mixed pattern of findings has been reported for face recognition abilities in individuals with ASD. Indeed, although some studies have found their participants with ASD to be poor at face recognition, others have reported normal performance.

For example, Deruelle *et al.* (2004) compared a group of 11 children with autism to two groups of normally developing children, matched according to either verbal–mental age or chronological age. The children were required to complete a set of face-matching tasks, where they had to compare faces on the basis of identity, emotion, gaze direction, gender or lip-speech. The authors found that all aspects of face processing were impaired in the individuals with ASD, with the exception of identity-matching.

Other studies have reported mild face recognition impairments in their participants with ASD. For example, Boucher, Lewis and Collis (1998) performed a face recognition task that compared the performance of children with autism to both verbal and chronological age-matched controls. Specifically, the children were shown a series of faces of individuals who worked at their school intermixed with unfamiliar faces who 'worked at another school', and were asked to identify the familiar individuals. In group-level analyses, the researchers found that the autistic children correctly identified fewer faces than both groups of control children. However, when each individual child's score was taken into consideration, only four of the 19 children with ASD achieved a lower score than that achieved by the poorest control child. These latter analyses suggest considerable overlap in face recognition ability between children with ASD and unimpaired children.

A similar pattern of findings was noted in another study that examined face recognition ability in a group of 24 adults with ASD (Barton, Cherkasova, Hefter *et al.*, 2004). Interestingly, this study not only compared the performance of the participants with ASD to control participants, but also to a group of individuals with prosopagnosia. The authors found that, although eight of the participants with ASD had normal face recognition abilities compared with control participants, 16 participants with ASD did show significant face recognition impairments. However, the difficulties noted in the latter group of participants were not as severe as those observed in the prosopagnosic group.

Hence, the study of Barton *et al.* also suggests that not all individuals with ASD suffer from face recognition impairments, and those that do tend to suffer from milder impairments than those that are experienced in other disorders of face processing. However, it is also possible that the extent of the face recognition impairment in ASD might be related to the severity of the more general ASD symptoms in each individual. Support for this hypothesis comes from a study performed by Klin *et al.* (1999). These authors studied a large number of children with ASD, and found that those with autism displayed impaired performance on a face memory task compared with both verbal and non-verbal age-matched control groups. However, children who had less severe ASD symptoms (i.e., those with a diagnosis of pervasive developmental disorder – not otherwise specified) did not show impaired performance compared with the control children. Thus, although it may be the case that face recognition and identification impairments do not tend to be severe in any individual with

ASD, some evidence suggests there might be a continuum of impairment that is related to more general social functioning.

It is perhaps unsurprising that many more studies have examined other non-identity aspects of face processing, particularly those that are essential for social and emotional functioning. Indeed, in the study by Dereulle *et al.* (2004) described above, the processing of emotional expression, eye-gaze direction, gender and lip-speech were all found to be impaired. In particular, many researchers have examined the processing of emotional expression in ASD, given that individuals with the condition have difficulties interpreting the mental states of others. A more consistent pattern of findings has emerged in studies examining emotional expression processing in ASD, with most studies reporting some degree of impairment. Indeed, although many different experimental designs have been used by researchers, a general impairment in the recognition of emotional expressions has consistently been reported (e.g., Baron-Cohen, Spitz and Cross, 1993; Pelphrey *et al.*, 2002), and it has also been noted that individuals with ASD have difficulty integrating emotional information from different modalities (see, for example, Hobson, Ouston and Lee, 1988; Loveland *et al.*, 1997).

Some evidence suggests that the impairment does not extend to the recognition of all emotional expressions. For example, Humphreys *et al.* (2007) asked adults with autism and a typically developing control group to categorize morphs of all possible combinations of the six basic expressions (happiness, sadness, fear, anger, disgust, surprise) identified by Ekman and Friesen (1971). The researchers found that the ASD group showed a specific impairment in recognizing fearful faces, and a milder impairment in recognizing disgust and happiness. Interestingly, further analyses indicated that the extent of each participant's impairment in recognizing fear correlated with the severity of their ASD symptoms. A second experiment confirmed that the participants with ASD were capable of simply matching faces displaying the same facial expression, indicating that the underlying deficit was one of interpretation and not lower-level perceptual difficulties. This study is supported by an event-related potential investigation performed by Dawson *et al.* (2004). These authors reported that the electrophysiological responses recorded in three and four-year-olds with ASD did not differentiate a fearful face from a neutral face at either the early or later stages of processing. Further, as observed by Humphreys *et al.* (2007), the researchers additionally found that the speed of the response to fearful faces correlated with the severity of ASD symptoms in each child.

Finally, it should be noted that, despite the multitude of studies that have found impairments in emotional expression recognition in ASD, a few studies have failed to find impaired performance (Adolphs, Sears and Piven, 2001; Grossman *et al.*, 2000; Ogai *et al.*, 2003). Further, in a study of event-related potentials, Wong *et al.* (2008) found a normal pattern of responses to emotional faces in older children with ASD.

11.1.2. Why is face processing atypical in ASD?

From the above discussion, it is clear that, to some extent, the processing of facial stimuli is atypical in at least some individuals with ASD. Several different hypotheses for the basis of face-processing impairments in ASD have been suggested. These hypotheses are discussed in turn below.

11.1.2.1. Avoidance of facial stimuli

It is clear that making eye contact with others has an important role in social interaction and communication, and thus it is unsurprising that individuals with ASD tend to avoid looking at the faces of others, and particularly the eye region of the face (Baranek, 1999; Osterling, Dawson and Munson, 2002). This is a strong argument, given that attention to faces has been found to modulate the activation of the fusiform gyrus among typically developing adults (Wojciulik, Kanwisher and Driver, 1998). Hence, it is possible that this abnormality might contribute to the pattern of socio-cognitive deficits often observed in ASD, including difficulties in processing faces.

A study that investigated this possibility in a group of adults with ASD was reported by Klin *et al.* (2002). Specifically, the researchers monitored visual attention to faces during complex scene viewing, by recording eye movements while participants watched the movie 'Who's afraid of Virginia Woolf?'. Group-based analyses revealed that the ASD group paid less attention to the internal features (i.e., the eyes, nose and mouth) of faces seen in the movie compared with control participants. Further analysis revealed an interesting correlation between the time spent viewing the mouth region of the face and general social abilities, suggesting that viewing of the mouth might compensate for a lack of attention to the eye region. Specifically, those individuals who spent a longer period viewing the mouth had better social abilities than those who did not attend to the face at all.

Other studies of eye movements have supported the findings of Klin *et al.* (2002). For example, Pelphrey and colleagues (2002) noted that participants with ASD were more likely to look at the areas of faces without features compared with control participants, and spent more time looking at the mouth than the eyes. This tendency to avoid looking at the inner facial features has been shown in children as young as three years of age (De Wit, Falck-Ytter and von Hofsten, 2008); and Jones, Carr and Klin (2008) reported that two-year-olds with ASD also showed decreased attention to the eye region of the face and increased attention to the mouth. Further, it is of note that in the latter study, the extent of the reduced attention to the eye region was found to be correlated with an increase in social deficits. In contrast, however, two studies have found that participants with ASD spend longer on the eye region of the face than the mouth, but importantly the effect was less exaggerated than that noted in control participants (see Hernandez *et al.*, 2009; Sterling *et al.*, 2008).

As stated above, attention to facial stimuli has been found to modulate the activation of the key face-processing area of the brain, the fusiform gyrus. Many studies have used functional magnetic resonance imaging to examine fusiform activity in participants with ASD, and have consistently reported decreased activation compared with control participants (for a review see Schultz, 2005). Some evidence suggests this decrease in activation can be attributed to an avoidance of the eye region of faces. For example, Dalton *et al.* (2005) found that fusiform activity in participants with ASD was correlated with the amount of time each individual spent looking at the eye region of facial stimuli. Further evidence that supports this hypothesis was provided by Hadjikhani *et al.* (2004). These authors found that the reduction in fusiform activity in participants with ASD disappeared when attention was explicitly directed to the eye region of the face, and when larger facial images were used.

11.1.2.2. A deficit in configural processing

Much evidence has suggested that early abnormalities in the visual system could selectively impair face processing while leaving the processing of other categories of objects relatively intact. Such *weak central coherence* hypotheses are based on evidence that suggests face perception in ASD is biased towards the use of high spatial frequency (HSF) information, as opposed to the bias towards low spatial frequency (LSF) information that is seen in control participants (see, for example, Fiorentini, Maffei and Sandini, 1983; Schyns and Oliva, 1999). Support for this hypothesis comes from a study performed by Deruelle *et al.* (2004), who found that five to 13-year-old participants with ASD matched pairs of faces more successfully when provided with HSF rather than LSF information. In another study, Katsyri *et al.* (2008) found that adults with Asperger's syndrome were impaired at recognizing emotional expressions that only contained LSF information.

Such work is theoretically important, as it is thought that configural processing relies on LSF information, and featural processing on HSF information. Recall from Chapter 1 that face processing is believed to rely critically on configural processing, and it therefore follows that a deficit in this process might underpin the face-processing difficulties observed in ASD. This issue has been investigated using the face inversion effect. Remember that face inversion is thought to disrupt configural processing, forcing the perceiver to adopt a featural processing strategy, and bringing about disproportionately poorer recognition performance for faces than other categories of objects in unimpaired participants.

Several studies have examined face inversion in ASD and failed to find evidence of the effect, suggesting a reliance on featural rather than configural facial information (e.g., Rose *et al.*, 2007; Wallace, Coleman and Bailey, 2008). An electrophysiological study also failed to find evidence of the typical face inversion effect in participants with ASD. Specifically, McPartland *et al.* (2004) did not observe a faster N170 in response to upright compared with inverted faces, as noted for control participants. However, other studies have failed to find differences between ASD and control participants on face inversion tasks, indicating preserved configural processing. Indeed, Teunisse and de Gelder (2003) noted that the face inversion effect is not always absent in participants with ASD, and reported a correlation between recognition accuracy for upright faces and social intelligence. Further, Rouse *et al.* (2004) used the Thatcher illusion (see Chapter 1) to investigate second-order configural processing in their participants with ASD, and found no differences compared with control children.

A study performed by Lahaie *et al.* (2006) reveals some further insight into this issue. In an initial experiment, these authors found a similar face inversion effect in their ASD and control participants, suggesting configural processing was intact in the ASD group. In a second experiment, the authors used individual facial features to prime whole faces, and found that the level of priming achieved from single face features was significantly greater in ASD than control participants. This pattern of performance was interpreted as evidence that configural processing is not impaired in participants with ASD, but that these individuals simply prefer to use a featural processing strategy. Joseph and Tanaka (2003) provided evidence that supports these findings. Specifically, these researchers asked participants to recognize individual facial features that were presented either within a whole face or in isolation. Although control children were better at recognizing features when they were presented within the whole face, children with ASD only displayed the whole face advantage for mouths, and were particularly poor at processing the eyes. Hence, this study suggests that, although a configural processing deficit might be present in ASD, that deficit is not absolute as different strategies can be used to process different parts of the face.

Such evidence has been used as the basis of the *enhanced perceptual functioning* theory, another hypothesis that might explain face-processing difficulties in ASD (e.g., Mottron *et al.*, 2006). According to this model, individuals with ASD are more proficient at processing fine-detailed (local) information than unimpaired participants. Hence, this superior ability is used by default in perceptual processing, and interferes with the configural processing strategy that is thought to be essential for face processing. As a result, fine-detailed visual information is extracted and processed more easily by people with ASD, and dominates their perception at the expense of global information. Thus the enhanced perceptual functioning model, like the weak central coherence theory, provides an account of the relative advantage of local over global information processing observed in individuals with ASD.

11.1.2.3. Neural dysfunction

As described above, some authors have suggested that an avoidance of facial stimuli leads to decreased fusiform face area (FFA) activation. Indeed, many neuroimaging studies have reported decreased activation in the FFA while participants with ASD view facial stimuli (see, for example, Critchley, Daly, Bullmore *et al.*, 2000), although it is unclear whether this effect can always be attributed to an attentional avoidance of facial stimuli. For example, Pierce *et al.* (2001) found that when participants with ASD viewed faces, activation was either reduced or totally absent in the four key neural areas associated with face processing: the fusiform gyrus, the amygdala, the inferior occipital gyrus and the superior temporal sulcus. Reduced activation in the FFA and extrastriate areas has also been reported when participants with ASD view faces displaying different emotional expressions (see Deeley *et al.*, 2007).

Other evidence suggests that neural abnormalities in face processing might extend beyond simple under-activation of the FFA. Indeed, some evidence suggests that individuals with ASD might use a completely different neural system to process faces than that employed by unimpaired participants. For example, Schultz and colleagues (2000) noted increased activation in response to faces in the inferotemporal gyrus for ASD compared with control participants, an area commonly associated with object as well as face processing. Similarly, Hubl *et al.* (2003) found less activation in the FFA in participants with ASD, but more activation in the medial occipital gyrus, an area that is more typically associated with object processing. Importantly, these findings might account for the preference for processing fine-grained local information in ASD, as this processing strategy is thought to be used in object recognition.

Other authors have suggested that the face-processing deficits observed in ASD can be attributed to a specific dysfunction in the amygdala. Indeed, several studies have reported abnormal amygdala activation in participants with ASD during the processing of both emotional (Ashwin *et al.*, 2007; Pelphrey *et al.*, 2007; Wang *et al.*, 2004) and neutral (Bookheimer *et al.*, 2008; Kleinhans *et al.*, 2008) faces. Such evidence led Baron-Cohen *et al.* (2000) to propose the 'amygdala theory of autism', which posits that deficits in social intelligence (including face processing) in individuals with ASD might be attributed to a specific impairment in this neural structure. This theory was largely based on an functional magnetic resonance imaging experiment that failed to note amygdala activation while participants with ASD made mentalistic inferences from the eye region of facial stimuli.

An alternative account that is also based on abnormal amygdala activation was proposed by Schultz (2005) (see Figure 11.1). Specifically, the *amygdala/ fusiform modulation model* proposes that the preference for face-like stimuli seen in newborn infants is underpinned by functions in the amygdala that draw attention to social stimuli. This increased social attention is thought to consequently provide the scaffolding that supports social learning, and modulate activity in the fusiform gyrus. Schultz suggests the theory can account for both impaired face processing and more general social deficits in individuals with ASD. This is based on the observation that individuals with ASD do not attend to faces in the same manner as unimpaired individuals, because faces

Figure 11.1   *Schultz's (2005) amygdala/fusiform modulation model.*

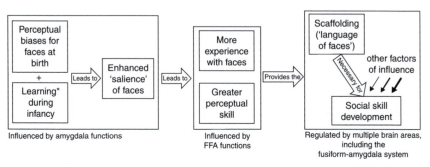

* A combination of associative and instrumental learning

have less emotional salience for people with ASD. As a result, individuals with ASD acquire less experience in processing facial stimuli, which leads to specific difficulties in face processing. Further, as faces are critical social stimuli, more general deficits in social interaction additionally develop.

However, there are some problems with the amygdala/fusiform modulation model. Indeed, the model assumes that the same abnormalities underpin both deficits in face processing and more general social difficulties in ASD, suggesting the two types of impairment necessarily must co-occur. Yet, we know that not all individuals with ASD have problems with face identification, suggesting the two types of impairment can be dissociated in individuals with ASD. Further, we have also discussed the reverse pattern of impairment. That is, there are many reports of individuals with developmental prosopagnosia who have suffered from a lifelong impairment in face processing, yet do not demonstrate any other symptoms of ASD.

In sum, several different hypotheses have been put forward to account for the range of face-processing difficulties often observed in individuals with ASD. Although each theory provides a plausible account that might explain the difficulties observed in at least some individuals, it is unclear how these different hypotheses might fit together to provide a unified account of face-processing deficits in ASD.

11.1.3. Summary of ASD

- A range of face-processing deficits can present in ASD. Sometimes, individuals have problems recognizing facial identity, gaze direction, gender, expression and lip-reading (Deruelle *et al.*, 2004; Boucher, Lewis and Collis, 1998). Most importantly, nearly all individuals with ASD have problems interpreting emotional expression.

- For some individuals with ASD, the impairment in recognizing emotional expressions seems to only affect certain expressions, most notably fear (Humphreys *et al.*, 2007).

■ There are several hypotheses about the behavioural and neural abnormalities that might underpin face-processing impairments in ASD. Although some authors suggest that individuals with ASD simply pay less attention to faces (Klin *et al.*, 2002; Pelphrey *et al.*, 2002), others postulate that the impairment can be attributed to a preference in using a featural or local processing strategy that is suboptimal for face processing (Dereulle *et al.*, 2004; Lahaie *et al.*, 2006).

■ Much neuroimaging evidence suggests that individuals with ASD display abnormalities in both the fusiform gyrus and the amygdala in response to facial stimuli, and some authors have theorized that individuals with ASD might process faces using object- rather than face-specific areas of the brain (Hubl *et al.*, 2003).

■ Schultz (2005) proposed the amygdala/fusiform modulation theory that may simultaneously account for both face processing and social interaction impairments in individuals with ASD. However, this account is challenged by findings that not all individuals with ASD are impaired at face processing (Deruelle *et al.*, 2004), and developmental prosopagnosics do not show ASD symptoms (Duchaine *et al.*, 2010).

11.2. WILLIAMS SYNDROME

Williams syndrome (WS) is a very rare genetic condition, and is thought to affect one in 20 000 live births (Morris and Mervis, 1999), although more recent estimates suggest its prevalence might be considerably higher (1:7,500; Stromme, Bjornstad and Ramstad, 2002). WS occurs as the result of a chromosomal abnormality, with a deletion of approximately 28 genes at chromosome site 7q11.23 (Tassabehji, 2003). Children with WS tend to have distinctive facial features, such as an elfin-like face, a broad brow, a flat nasal bridge, a short upturned nose, a wide mouth with full lips, and irregular dentition. They also have a low IQ, estimated typically to reside between 40 and 90 (Searcy *et al.*, 2004). However, their language skills are relatively unaffected and are sometimes above average, and they often have extraordinary musical ability. Children with WS additionally suffer from auditory abnormalities, such as fear of specific sounds (auditory allodynia) and a lowered pain threshold for loud noises (odynacusis). Finally, and most relevant to the current chapter, visuo-spatial skills also tend to be impaired in this condition.

Individuals with WS and those with ASD both display abnormalities in social interaction, but critically these are of a different nature. In ASD, the abnormality commonly manifests as social withdrawal and an inability to socialize appropriately with others, whereas individuals with WS are often described as 'hyper-sociable' and are unusually social, friendly and empathic (Jones *et al.*, 2000). Indeed, some researchers have proposed that a *social stimulus attraction* underpins social interaction in WS (Frigerio *et al.*, 2006), given that several studies have demonstrated that these individuals tend to look at faces for prolonged periods of time (Doherty-Sneddon *et al.*, 2009). Although this pattern of social interaction is clearly different to that seen in ASD, it should be noted that it is still abnormal, given it also differs from the levels of sociability observed in unimpaired individuals, albeit in a different direction.

11.2.1. Face-processing deficits in WS

In the previous section, it was noted that face-processing deficits often present in individuals with ASD. One hypothesis that has attempted to account for such impairments refers to findings that these individuals have poor social skills and avoid looking at faces. If this hypothesis is correct, we might predict that individuals with WS should be highly proficient at face processing, given they are hyper-sociable and spend unusually long periods examining faces in social situations. Hence, it came as no surprise when several studies found face recognition skills to be intact in individuals with WS, and these findings were initially interpreted as evidence that WS presents with a preserved face-processing module (e.g., Bellugi, Sabo and Vaid, 1988; Bellugi, Wann and Jernigan, 1994; Wang *et al.*, 1995).

However, other studies have examined the behavioural processes that underpin face recognition in WS and found some abnormalities. This has led to suggestions that, although face recognition performance may appear normal on the surface in WS, the mechanisms underpinning the process are nevertheless impaired. In particular, several investigations have found that individuals with WS have specific impairments in configural processing, and instead rely on a featural processing strategy when recognizing faces. Theoretically this is an important issue, given it has traditionally been thought that successful face recognition depends on configural processing, and a deficit in using this processing strategy has been hypothesized to underpin face-processing impairments in disorders such as prosopagnosia and ASD.

Karmiloff-Smith (1997) described findings from a face-matching task where 10 adult participants with WS did not differ from chronologically age-matched controls with respect to featural analysis, but were significantly worse when the task required configural analysis. In a later study, Deruelle *et al.* (1999) used the face inversion effect to investigate configural processing in 12 individuals with WS aged between seven and 23 years. Specifically, participants were asked to decide whether two pictures of faces were of the same or a different person when presented in upright and inverted conditions. The authors noted that the participants with WS were less subject to an inversion effect than control participants. In a further experiment, the authors investigated the processing of schematic faces and geometric shapes that had been altered on either a configural or a featural level. Once again, the participants with WS displayed impaired performance for configural but not featural trials, suggesting that individuals with the disorder might have a generalized rather than a face-specific impairment in configural processing.

However, two studies have challenged this conclusion, and suggested that configural processing is actually intact in WS. Indeed, Deruelle *et al.* (2003) compared 12 children with WS (aged 6–17 years) with chronologically and age-matched control groups in their ability to match facial stimuli to target faces that had been filtered for either LSF (broad patterns of light and dark preserved) or HSF (fine details preserved) information. The authors found that all three groups performed better in the LSF condition (requiring configural rather than featural processing), and performance in the WS group did not significantly differ from either control group. In another study that used a larger sample of adolescent and adult participants with WS ($n° = °47$), Tager-Flusberg *et al.* (2003) also provided evidence that suggests normal configural processing in WS. In this study, configural processing was tested using the part–whole paradigm, where participants were required to match individual facial features that were presented either in isolation or within the context of a whole face. Overall accuracy across conditions was higher in the control group, but the benefits of presenting the features within the whole face (corresponding to the use of configural processing) were similar both for those with WS and control participants. Tager-Flusberg and colleagues concluded that the impairments in configural processing noted in previous studies might simply be an artefact that resulted from small sample size.

There are, however, weaknesses with both of these studies that limit the strength of their conclusions. In the case of Tager-Flusberg's study, the part–whole paradigm does not necessarily tap the same aspects of configural processing as the tasks that have been used in other studies that reported impaired performance. Specifically, the part–whole task is thought to assess holistic (i.e., processing of the face gestalt) rather than second-order configural processing. Further, in Deruelle *et al.*'s (2003) study, the sensitivity of responses to the spatial frequency manipulation did not change with age in any of the participant groups. This suggests that any developmental changes in configural processing that could be tapped by the task had already plateaued, and thus it is difficult to draw any firm conclusions on the developmental trajectory of configural processing in WS from this data.

A study that addressed the latter issue was reported by Karmiloff-Smith *et al.* (2004), who built full developmental trajectories from childhood to adulthood for each task they used. In an initial experiment that used real faces, participants with WS were found to be poorer at configural processing when faces were upright, and less sensitive than controls to face inversion. A second experiment used a storybook context to assess face processing, and the face inversion effect emerged clearly in controls but only weakly in the WS developmental trajectory. Interestingly, although the configural processing abilities of controls correlated with their general face recognition abilities as measured by the Benton Facial

Recognition Test (BFRT (Benton and Van Allen, 1968)), no relationship between the two processes was noted in the participants with WS. In a final experiment, both schematic faces and non-facial stimuli were used to demonstrate a general configural processing deficit in the participants with WS, which again failed to correlate with their performance on the BFRT. Hence, the findings of Karmiloff-Smith and colleagues suggest that configural processing can be impaired in WS, and it is important to examine the full developmental trajectory of processing to observe these deficits.

Finally, other work has examined the recognition of facial expressions of emotion in WS. Again, if it is true that the level of attention directed to faces in social situations predicts expression recognition ability, we might expect individuals with WS to perform well in such tasks. However, several studies have revealed deficits in emotional expression recognition in participants with WS. For example, Gagliardi *et al.* (2003) found that recognition of all six of Ekman and Friesen's (1971) basic facial emotions was poorer on more difficult items in individuals with WS compared with chronological age-matched controls, although it did not differ from that of mental age-matched controls. The authors attributed the poor performance of participants with WS in recognizing more difficult expressions to a failure of configural processing. Indeed, they suggested that the act of forming particular expressions changes the overall configuration of the face, and individuals with WS have weak sensitivity to such differences. Porter, Shaw and Marsh (2010) reported more specific impairments in expression recognition in their participants with WS. Indeed, the individuals with WS were particularly impaired at recognizing angry expressions, although no abnormalities in their eye movement patterns were detected for the processing of these stimuli. However, the authors did note that the eye region of all the faces (regardless of expression) did not capture the attention of WS patients more quickly than controls, although they did spend more time looking at the eyes once they had focused on this region.

Another group of authors also reported deficits in expression recognition in their participants with WS, but did not attribute the impairment to poor configural processing mechanisms or difficulties processing the eye region of the face. Specifically, Tsirempolou *et al.* (2006) found that adolescents and adults with WS were particularly impaired at recognizing expressions of sadness and anger, even when compared with four-year-old control participants. Further, the participants with WS were also found to be severely impaired at judging eye gaze direction. The authors interpreted this latter finding as evidence that expression recognition deficits in WS do not reside in difficulties with configural processing, but in problems with interpreting the social meaning of the eyes, implicating dysfunction of the amygdala circuit. In the next section, this hypothesis is examined in more detail.

11.2.2. Neurophysiological evidence of impaired face processing in WS

11.2.2.1. FFA

Some key structural differences have been noted in significant neural areas in WS. Indeed, reductions in total brain-volume (Reiss *et al.*, 2004) and abnormalities in cortical thickness along parts of the fusiform gyrus (Thompson *et al.*, 2005) have been reported. However, perhaps the most striking finding comes from recent evidence that the FFA is approximately two times larger in individuals with WS than in typically developing participants (Golarai *et al.*, 2010). Interestingly, several reports have indicated that larger FFA volumes are associated with greater face recognition ability in unimpaired participants (see, for example, Golarai *et al.*, 2007), suggesting that a large FFA might underpin proficient face recognition skills in WS despite impaired configural processing ability.

Gupta (2011) suggests that the increased size of the FFA might be attributed to increased visual input received by primary visual cortex. Evidence supporting this hypothesis comes from a study performed by Galaburda and Bellugi (2000), who suggested that the average size of cortical neurons is greater in primary visual cortex in WS compared with control participants, despite normal cell packing density. Alternatively, Gupta raises the possibility that the larger FFA volume in WS might reflect functional reorganization of the fusiform gyrus in response to greater cumulative visual experience with faces during development. Indeed, consistent increased exposure to facial stimuli over critical points in development might lead to regional increases in the number and/or selectivity of face-responsive neurons (Grill-Spector, Gollarai and Gabrieli, 2008), as well as synaptic changes in the fusiform gyrus. Such an experience-dependent account of expansions of cortical representations have been reported in more generalized models of neural plasticity (Merzenich *et al.*, 1996; Weisberg, van Turennout and Martin, 2007), making this a logical hypothesis.

This suggestion receives further support from a study of event-related potentials that found an abnormally large N200 response in participants with WS, which correlated with performance on the BFRT (Mills *et al.*, 2000). The authors of this study suggested that the larger N200 response reflected increased attention to faces in the participants with WS, and hypothesized that this might bring about enhanced instantaneous responses to faces in the fusiform gyrus. Such a suggestion makes sense, given there is some evidence that the neural systems underpinning visual attention and face processing to some extent overlap. For example, Pessoa (2009) suggested that the attentional network recruits fronto-parietal regions such as the middle frontal gyrus, anterior cingulate cortex, inferior frontal gyrus and anterior insula; which are all areas involved in the processing of faces and emotional information. Interestingly, the participants with WS investigated by Golarai *et al.* (2010)

showed an increase in both volume and grey matter in two of these regions (the anterior cingulate cortex and anterior insula), in addition to other regions that are known to participate in face processing (including the amygdala, orbital prefrontal cortices and superior temporal gyrus). Hence, the larger volume and grey matter density of the attentional network might encourage individuals with WS to attend to faces, and bring about normal behavioural scores on tests of face recognition ability.

11.2.2.2. Amygdala

Other neuroimaging work has provided insight into the difficulties that individuals with WS have in recognizing emotional expression. Indeed, Haas *et al.* (2010) observed increased activation in the amygdala for happy but not fearful faces. A similar finding was reported by Meyer-Lindenberg *et al.* (2005), who observed reduced amygdala activation in participants with WS viewing fearful and threatening faces, but not when they viewed fearful and threatening scenes. These findings suggest that individuals with WS might not be able to inhibit an approach response to negative faces, although they can process the emotional significance of other categories of visual stimuli appropriately.

Interestingly, Meyer-Lindenberg *et al.* (2005) also found that individuals with WS showed no activation in orbitofrontal cortex when they viewed fearful and threatening faces. Further, they found no functional connection between orbitofrontal cortex and the amygdala or the dorsolateral prefrontal cortex, areas that are thought to regulate social cognition. The authors suggest these abnormalities might account for the social disinhibition and socially inappropriate behaviour that is often observed in WS. Finally, the medial prefrontal cortex was found to be persistently activated while the participants with WS viewed the negative faces, which might account for the hyper-sociability and increased levels of empathy that are commonly observed in the disorder.

11.2.3. Summary of WS

■ WS is a neurodevelopmental condition that is characterized by hyper-sociability and increased attention to facial stimuli. Hence, it is perhaps unsurprising that face recognition ability has been found to be preserved in individuals with this condition (see, for example, Bellugi, Sabo and Vaid, 1988; Bellugi, Wann and Jernigan, 1994; Wang *et al.*, 1995).

■ However, several studies have suggested that although face recognition does seem to be proficient in the disorder, the process is not underpinned by typical face-processing strategies and mechanisms. In particular, individuals with WS seem to be impaired in configural processing (see Karmiloff-Smith, 1997; Deruelle *et al.*, 1999).

■ Neuroimaging work has suggested that preserved face recognition ability in WS is supported by an abnormally large FFA (Golarai *et al.*, 2010). This might be brought about by the increased attention to faces that is often observed in individuals with the condition (Gupta, 2011).

■ Other studies suggest that the processing of emotional expression is also impaired in individuals with WS (see Gagliardi *et al.*, 2003; Tsirempolou *et al.*, 2006). Neuroimaging evidence has suggested that abnormalities in the amygdala and related structures might underpin this deficit and explain more general symptoms of hyper-sociability in the disorder (Haas *et al.*, 2010; Meyer-Lindenberg *et al.*, 2005).

11.3. TURNER'S SYNDROME

Finally, Turner's syndrome (TS) is another developmental disorder that commonly presents with face-processing deficits. This condition is one of the most common chromosomal disorders that occurs in women, and affects around one in 2500 live births. It occurs when one X chromosome is missing, resulting in ovarian failure and oestrogen deficiency. Women with TS have certain physical characteristics, such as short stature, webbing of the neck, micrognathia (undersized jaw), and low-set ears and hairline. They tend to have a strong verbal IQ, deficits in visuo-spatial perception, memory problems, poor motor abilities and poor attentional processes. They also have an increased risk of psychosocial difficulties, below average social competency and a tendency to be socially withdrawn (Skuse *et al.*, 1997).

Much less work has investigated face processing in TS. However, a handful of studies have investigated face recognition in this disorder using the BFRT and consistently reported impaired performance (Reiss *et al.*, 1993; Ross *et al.*, 1995; Ross, Kushnerand and Zinn, 1997; Romans *et al.*, 1998). Two further studies also found that women with TS were impaired in delayed face-matching tasks compared with control participants (Buchanan, Pavlovic and Rovet, 1998; Murphy *et al.*, 1994).

A more recent study performed an extensive assessment of face-processing ability in TS. Specifically, Lawrence *et al.* (2003) reported a series of experiments that examined face recognition, expression recognition and configural processing ability in a group of 23 women with TS. The researchers initially assessed face recognition ability using performance on four different tasks: the BFRT, Warrington's Memory Test for Faces (WRMF (Warrington, 1984)), a famous faces test, and an incidental face recognition test that assessed memory for faces that had been presented in previous components of the testing session. Analyses revealed that the participants with TS achieved lower scores on all four tests compared with control participants, although performance on the BFRT did not fall into the 'impaired' range according to the test's norming data (but see Chapter 14 for a discussion of the validity of the BFRT). The authors also reported findings from three tests of configural processing: the

Mooney faces test (which tests the ability to detect face-like configurations in high contrast stimuli), a face-matching test using upright and inverted stimuli, and a part–whole matching task. Interestingly, Lawrence *et al.* reported that the TS group performed in a similar manner to control participants on both the face inversion and part–whole tests, and in detecting faces on the Mooney faces test. Surprisingly, these findings indicate the participants with TS were sensitive to configural aspects of face processing.

Finally, Lawrence *et al.* also investigated emotional expression recognition in their participants with TS, and noted significant deficits in the recognition of fearful and angry expressions. The authors hypothesized that although the face-processing deficits observed in the women with TS could not be attributed to a failure in configural processing, they might be explained by abnormal amygdala functioning. Although very little neuroimaging research has been performed with participants with TS, a structural imaging study reported by Good *et al.* (2003) suggests the development of the amygdala might be compromised in the disorder.

In sum, although much work remains to be done to further our understanding of face-processing deficits in TS, early findings suggest that both facial identity and expression recognition tend to be impaired in these individuals, despite normal configural processing ability.

CHAPTER SUMMARY

In this chapter, impairments in processing both facial identity and facial expression have been discussed in three socio-developmental disorders. Interestingly, a different pattern of behavioural characteristics appear to underpin the face-processing impairments in each disorder. Specifically, those with ASD have very good visuo-spatial skills but impaired configural processing and social cognition; those with WS are hyper-sociable but are impaired at both visuo-spatial and configural processing tasks; whereas individuals with TS seem to have preserved configural processing skills yet impaired social cognition and visuo-spatial skills. This pattern of findings suggests multiple behavioural causes of impaired face-processing skills in socio-developmental disorders, although neurological abnormalities in the FFA and/or amygdala have also been observed in all three disorders. A more thorough discussion of this issue can be read in Chapter 12.

FURTHER READING

Behrmann, M., Thomas, C. and Humphreys, K. (2006) 'Seeing it Differently: Visual Processing in Autism', *Trends in Cognitive Sciences,* 10, 258–64.

Golarai, G., Hong, S., Haas, B. W., Galaburda, A. M., Mills, D. L., *et al.* (2010) 'The Fusiform Face Area is Enlarged in Williams Syndrome', *The Journal of Neuroscience*, 30, 6700–12.

Karmiloff-Smith, A., Thomas, M., Annaz, D., Humphreys, K., Ewing, S., *et al.* (2004) 'Exploring the Williams Syndrome Face Processing Debate: The Importance of Building Developmental Trajectories', *Journal of Child Psychology and Psychiatry*, 45, 1258–74.

Lawrence, K., Kuntsi, J., Coleman, M., Campbell, R. and Skuse, D. (2003) 'Face and Emotion Recognition Deficits in Turner Syndrome: A Possible Role for X-Linked Genes in Amygdala Development', *Neurophysiology*, 17, 39–49.

Pelphrey, K. A., Sasson, N. J., Reznich, J. S., Paul, G., Goldman, B. D., *et al.* (2002) 'Visual Scanning of Faces in Autism', *Journal of Autism and Developmental Disorders*, 32, 249–61.

Schultz, R. T. (2005) 'Developmental Deficits in Social Perception in Autism: The Role of the Amygdala and Fusiform Face Area', *International Journal of Developmental Neuroscience*, 23, 125–41.

GUIDANCE QUESTIONS

Use the following questions to guide your reading of this chapter and the recommended papers.

1. What types of face-processing impairment are observed in individuals with ASD, and do all individuals with ASD experience these impairments?
2. Describe and evaluate Schultz's (2005) model that accounts for face-processing impairments in individuals with ASD.
3. Is it true to say that face recognition is unimpaired in individuals with WS?
4. How does the neurocognitive presentation of TS differ to that observed in ASD and WS, and how might this account for the face-processing deficits often seen in the disorder?

12 Focus Chapter: What are the Theoretical Implications of Developmental Disorders of Face Processing?

12.1. CAN DEVELOPMENTAL DISORDERS INFORM ADULT MODELS OF NORMAL FACE PROCESSING?

The models of face processing that were discussed in Part I of this book describe the functional and neural architecture of the healthy adult face-processing system. Importantly, the development of these models has been informed by case studies of neurological patients who present with various patterns of deficits in face processing. The most convincing evidence that has informed these models comes from instances of 'double dissociations', or pairs of patients that present with converse patterns of impairment, indicating independent streams for certain processes. Indeed, in Chapter 8, instances of double dissociations between patients with either identity or expression processing impairments were discussed, in addition to the proposed double dissociation between acquired prosopagnosia and the Capgras delusion. Such double dissociations illustrate the 'lesion' approach of cognitive neuropsychology, and how the logic of this framework has been used to identify different stages in processing that can be selectively disrupted.

Importantly, however, the patients that were discussed in Chapter 8 acquired their injuries in adulthood, and presumably had a fully developed and normally functioning face-processing system before their injury. Further, the injuries sustained by these patients brought about a permanent and relatively stable impairment in face processing. Hence, it is logical to make theoretical inferences about each patient's pattern of preserved and impaired abilities using adult models of face processing.

However, it is debateable whether the same logic applies to case studies of individuals who present with developmental disorders of face processing. Indeed, it is possible that such individuals have had some form of atypical brain organization from birth, and consequently follow an abnormal trajectory that prevents normal processing skills from ever being developed. Thus, it is difficult to interpret developmental cases within the functional models of the face-processing system discussed above, given that the basic architecture of this system might not have developed in these individuals, and therefore it is unknown if the system can be selectively disrupted in the manner inferred for patients with acquired deficits.

For instance, some authors have described individuals with developmental prosopagnosia (DP), who retain the ability to recognize facial expressions of emotion (e.g., Duchaine, Parker and Nakayama, 2003; Humphreys *et al.*, 2007). If we apply the traditional cognitive neuropsychological approach to such patients, we would infer that this evidence suggests that the healthy human brain has independent streams for identity and expression processing. However, although we can certainly infer from these cases that we do not need to recognize a person's identity to interpret their affective state, they do not tell us whether the same mechanisms are used by these patients as normal perceivers. Indeed, Bishop (1997) has warned that cognitive neuropsychology and developmental disorders make 'uncomfortable bedfellows' that require different approaches.

Karmiloff-Smith, Scerif and Ansari (2003) take a similar viewpoint to Bishop, and highlight the possibility that developmental rather than representational abnormalities can provide a convincing explanation of the basis of face-processing impairments in these cases. For instance, some authors have investigated face-processing impairments in individuals who were born with congenital infantile cataracts that obscured their vision for the first few months of life. These cataracts were surgically removed when the participants were between three and six months of age, but critically prevented normal visual experience with faces before surgery. Interestingly, when these individuals were tested later in life (at the age of 10–39 years), they were found to have impairments in configural processing (Le Grand *et al.*, 2001) and in recognizing facial identity, although their perception of emotional expression and lip speech was normal (Geldart *et al.*, 2002). Based on these findings, it might be inferred that delayed development of visual perception in the critical first few months of life accounts for cases of DP where identity processing is impaired yet expression recognition is intact. Indeed, it might be that the processes that underpin the perception of emotional expression were unaffected by the delay in gaining visual experience with faces.

Although it is therefore clear that some caution must be applied when attempting to interpret developmental disorders within theoretical frameworks concerned with the normal adult system, it is equally clear that there are still critical benefits that can be gained from the study of developmental patients. For instance, in Chapter 5, the aetiology of acquired prosopagnosia was discussed, and it is evident that most cases of acquired prosopagnosia present with large lesions that are not restricted to the face-processing areas of the brain, and unsurprisingly these individuals often suffer from a range of co-morbid impairments. Further, cases of pure acquired prosopagnosia are exceptionally rare, meaning that there are limited opportunities to investigate this form of the disorder. On the other hand, the lack of brain damage in DP implies a cleaner presentation of the condition, and there is ample opportunity to investigate such cases given the much greater prevalence rate. Finally, although developmental cases might not provide reliable opportunities to test and refine theories of the nature of the healthy adult processing system, they have greatly informed our knowledge about the developmental trajectory of face processing. In the next section, this issue is discussed.

12.2. WHAT CAN DEVELOPMENTAL DISORDERS TELL US ABOUT DEVELOPMENTAL THEORIES OF FACE PROCESSING?

Importantly, the study of developmental disorders can inform theories concerned with (1) the state of the face-processing system at birth, and (2) the factors that are essential for the development of normal face-processing abilities during childhood.

In Chapter 9, the CONSPEC/CONLERN theory of the development of face processing was discussed. Importantly, the CONSPEC component hypothesizes that we are born with an innate pre-specified mechanism that draws our attention to facial stimuli. If it is the case that face-processing ability is to some extent innate, we would expect that there might be genetic influences in its development. Indeed, evidence supporting this hypothesis comes from a recent study that reported a higher correlation of face recognition skills in identical compared with non-identical twins (see Wilmer *et al.*, 2010). Further support for a genetic component in face recognition ability comes from cases of DP where there is a clear familial component to the disorder (see, for example, Duchaine, Germine and Nakayama, 2007; Schmalzl, Palermo and Coltheart, 2008). Interestingly, Kennerknecht *et al.* (2006) concluded that the segregation patterns observed in families of self-reported prosopagnosics are consistent with a dominant autosomal inheritance (i.e., the gene need only be abnormal in one parent), although a specific gene for DP has not yet been reported.

Despite these reports of large numbers of individuals with DP who might have a genetic component to their disorder, it is equally clear that many other cases have no apparent familial link, and other causal factors might underpin the deficit in these individuals. Some of the evidence discussed in earlier chapters points towards several factors that might be important in the development of normal face-processing abilities. These include early visual experience with faces, configural processing skills, visuo-spatial skills, level of socio-emotional functioning (including attention to faces) and neurological abnormalities.

First, several studies have highlighted the importance of early visual experience in the development of face-processing abilities. Indeed, in Chapter 9, studies that examined face-processing skills in young children who had been institutionalized were described (e.g., Moulson *et al.*, 2009). Specifically, these studies demonstrated that institutionalized children had poorer face-processing skills than non-institutionalized children and those that had been placed in foster care. Presumably these effects were noted because institutionalized children had much less interaction with faces than control children. However, the most striking evidence that demonstrates the importance of early visual experience in the development of face-processing skills comes from the individuals discussed above who were born with congenital infantile cataracts. Indeed, findings from these studies suggest that early experience with faces is critical for the development of both normal face recognition (Geldart *et al.*, 2002) and configural processing abilities (Le Grand *et al.*, 2001).

Clearly then, early visual experience has some influence on the development of certain aspects of face processing, yet there are still instances of individuals with DP who did not suffer early visual deprivation nor appear to have a genetic link to their disorder. Importantly, study of individuals with socio-developmental disorders (SDDs) who present with face-processing deficits further informs this issue. Indeed, in Chapter 11, the pattern of impairments that present in three SDDs were discussed: autistic spectrum disorder (ASD), Williams syndrome (WS) and Turner's syndrome (TS).

Interestingly, configural processing has been found to be impaired in some cases of DP, as well as in ASD and WS, suggesting this factor might contribute to the development of face-processing impairments. However, it is important to note that not all individuals with DP seem to be impaired in non-facial configural processing (see, for example, Duchaine, 2000; Le Grand *et al.*, 2006), although more consistent evidence of impairment has been observed in facial tests of the ability (Behrmann, Avidan *et al.*, 2005; Duchaine *et al.*, 2004). In addition, configural processing has also been found to be intact in TS, despite poor face recognition skills (Lawrence *et al.*, 2003). The pattern of performance noted in participants with WS is also intriguing, given that these individuals display good face recognition skills but are poor at configural processing. Hence, it appears that face-processing deficits are not necessarily linked to configural processing abilities in all developmental cases.

A similarly intriguing pattern of findings has been noted for visuo-spatial skills and socio-emotional functioning, both of which provide sensible hypotheses about the abnormalities that might impinge the development of face-processing abilities. Indeed, it seems logical that impaired socio-emotional functioning might bring about a face-processing impairment, perhaps because of an avoidance of faces or their critical features; and that poor visuo-spatial skills are essential for accurate perception of a face and therefore its recognition. Yet, a varying relationship between these two functions and face recognition ability has been noted in the three SDDs. Specifically, visuo-spatial skills have been found to be poor in both WS and TS, yet normal in ASD; and although socio-emotional functioning is impaired in ASD and TS, individuals with WS tend to show hyper-vigilance towards faces. Hence, this pattern of findings suggests that although several factors are critical for the development of normal face-processing skills, there is likely to be a complex interaction between these factors and their influence on normal development, and the mere absence of just one of them might not be enough to bring about face-processing impairments.

However, some caution must be applied in drawing conclusions from the pattern of performance noted in SDDs. Indeed, we cannot firmly infer a causal link between any of the factors discussed above and the impairment in face processing. Further, some hesitation must be applied in concluding that socio-emotional functioning in WS is normal, given evidence suggests that these individuals demonstrate hyper-vigilance towards faces, which is abnormal in its own right. Thus, the pattern of impairments displayed in WS cannot simply be perceived as being the converse to those observed in ASD and TS. Finally, there is evidence to suggest that the magnitude of the face-processing impairment that presents in SDDs is not as large as that observed in prosopagnosia (Barton *et al.*, 2004), suggesting a different aetiological underpinning of each disorder. Therefore, although both appropriate socio-emotional functioning and normal configural processing and visuo-spatial skills are likely to have some role in the development of normal face-processing abilities, we cannot firmly conclude that they are of essential importance based on the evidence from SDDs alone.

Finally, it is of note that neurological impairments have been noted in all four disorders. Critically, abnormalities in either the structure or function of the core face-processing areas (i.e., the fusiform and occipital face areas) have been noted in each condition, suggesting a biological basis for the disruption in face recognition ability. Further, abnormalities in activation of the amygdala have been noted in the three SDDs, and it is likely that the specific pattern of findings observed for each of the conditions might explain the socio-emotional symptoms and other co-morbid cognitive impairments specifically associated with that disorder. Importantly, it is likely that deficits in the critical face and emotion processing areas of the brain do not occur in isolation, yet the precise relationship between the functioning of each structure has yet to be unravelled.

In sum, several factors appear to contribute to the development of normal face-processing skills. Indeed, there is strong evidence to suggest that genetic influences and early visual experience with faces play important roles in this process. However, other developmental cases are unlikely to have been affected by either of these influences, yet they still suffer from face-processing impairments. Further evidence suggests that a varying pattern of cognitive, perceptual and socio-emotional difficulties might underpin the difficulties experienced by these individuals, but the precise relationship between each variable and face recognition ability remains unclear. It is likely that the specific pattern of symptomology noted in each disorder is linked to the specific neural abnormalities that tend to present in the condition, and further that there is some biological basis to the development of face-processing impairments. Hence, investigation of a range of developmental disorders with increasingly sophisticated biological and neurological methodologies will no doubt further inform our knowledge about the precise nature of the developmental trajectory of face processing.

12.3. WHAT CAN DEVELOPMENTAL DISORDERS TELL US ABOUT THE FACE-SPECIFICITY DEBATE?

In Chapter 4, the key debate concerned with the specificity of the face-processing system was introduced. Specifically, although supporters of the 'domain-specificity' hypothesis suggest that we have dedicated cognitive and neural systems that are specialized only for the processing of faces, supporters of the 'domain-general' or 'expertise hypothesis' suggest that these systems are also used to process objects with which we have sufficient expertise.

In Chapter 9, Diamond and Carey's 'encoding switch hypothesis' was introduced. This theory supports the expertise hypothesis, given that it suggests children switch from a featural to a configural processing strategy at approximately 10 years of age, presumably when they have gained ample visual expertise with faces. However, other evidence from typically developing children has drawn the encoding switch hypothesis into question (McKone, Kanwisher and Duchaine, 2007). Indeed, using a variety of classic paradigms, it has been shown that very young children and even babies are capable of configural processing (Bushnell, 2001; Turati, Bulf and Simion, 2008). Further, evidence suggests that infants lose the ability to discriminate monkey faces by nine months of age (Kelly *et al.*, 2007), implying that we may be born with the ability to discriminate any type of face from birth, but that this ability is later refined to those faces that we encounter most often. Hence, this evidence supports the domain-specificity viewpoint.

In Chapter 8, evidence from neuropsychological patients with acquired disorders of face processing was discussed in reference to the face-specificity debate. Indeed, some authors have suggested that domain-specificity is supported by evidence of a double dissociation between prosopagnosic patients with intact object recognition skills, and visual agnosic patients who retain the ability to recognize faces. Interestingly, similar findings have been reported in the developmental form of prosopagnosia, suggesting that DP and acquired prosopagnosia may truly be parallel disorders, and supporting the face-specificity argument.

Indeed, some Individuals with DP present with abnormalities in the occipital and temporal regions that show face-selectivity in controls, although such impairments have not been observed in all cases. Further, Duchaine and colleagues (2004, 2006) have described in detail the pattern of preserved and impaired abilities in 'Edward', an individual with severe DP. Specifically, the authors found that although Edward suffered from a profound impairment in face recognition, he retained the ability to match inverted faces, discriminate between objects from the same category, and to recognize non-facial entities with which he had natural (i.e., bodies) and learnt (i.e., Greebles) expertise. Hence, Duchaine and colleagues argued that Edward's prosopagnosia could only by accounted for by a face-selective explanation.

Other evidence supporting this conclusion comes from the seemingly genetic contribution to some cases of DP, indicating that face recognition ability may be to some extent heritable and thus supported by specialized mechanisms. On the other hand, however, many individuals with DP do present with co-morbid impairments in object recognition, suggesting that even in genetic cases the disorder is not always restricted to impairments in face processing. Further, McKone, Kanwisher and Duchaine (2007) point out that this genetic influence might not necessarily be face-specific and instead represent some other 'unknown factor', such as a lack of attention to the mother's voice which consequently brings about reduced early visual experience with faces.

Case reports of individuals with ASD also describe a mixed pattern of visual recognition impairments, with some cases only presenting with deficits in the recognition of faces, whereas others also have problems recognizing exemplars from other categories of objects. For instance, some studies have found poor memory for non-social stimuli in their participants with ASD (see, for example, Boucher and Warrington, 1976; Boucher and Lewis, 1992), whereas Blair *et al.* (2002) found normal recognition of buildings and leaves in individuals with ASD. However, as these studies have not considered objects that are of specific expertise to the participants, there is some limitation to the strength of the conclusions that can be drawn from these reports.

Nevertheless, some authors have posited theories of the biological basis of ASD that are grounded in the expertise hypothesis. Indeed, in Chapter 11, Schultz's (2005) amygdala/fusiform modulation model was discussed. This model posits that, in newborn infants, the amygdala draws attention to faces, modulating activity in the fusiform gyrus. Because faces have less emotional salience for people with ASD, these individuals acquire less experience in processing facial stimuli, leading to specific difficulties in face processing and in more general social cognition. Hence, Schultz argues that the expertise hypothesis fits well with his model, and provides evidence against the idea of face-specific processing in the fusiform gyrus. However, the model does encounter some problems in its hypothesis that the development of face-processing ability and social cognition go hand-in-hand. Indeed, if this hypothesis is correct, we would expect all individuals with DP also to have ASD, and vice versa. Yet, there are many case reports to suggest that the two disorders often do present in isolation (e.g., Duchaine *et al.*, 2010; Barton *et al.*, 2004).

Finally, the pattern of performance noted in the patients infantile cataracts discussed above provides more convincing support for the expertise hypothesis. Indeed, research has indicated that individuals who were deprived of visual experience for the first few months of life not only fail to develop the ability to recognize faces (Geldart *et al.*, 2002), but also do not develop normal configural processing mechanisms (Le Grand *et al.*, 2001). This evidence suggests that expert face-processing skills are only acquired in response to appropriate experience with faces.

CHAPTER SUMMARY

- Several authors have warned against the interpretation of developmental disorders within adult models of face processing, given that these individuals might have followed an unusual developmental trajectory (see Bishop, 1997; Karmiloff-Smith, Scerif and Ansari, 2003).
- However, there are advantages of using developmental cases for theoretical investigations, given that they often offer a cleaner presentation than acquired cases, and are more readily available for testing. Further, investigation of these individuals has begun to inform our knowledge about the factors that influence the development of normal face-processing ability.
- There is increasing evidence for a genetic contribution to face recognition ability in at least some individuals (see, for example, Duchaine, Germine and Nakayama, 2007; Schmalzl, Palermo and Coltheart, 2008), and striking evidence from people who experienced congenital infantile cataracts suggests early visual experience with faces is essential (Geldart *et al.*, 2002; Le Grand *et al.*, 2001).
- Investigation into individuals with SDDs also suggests that configural processing ability, visuo-spatial skills and socio-emotional functioning might contribute to the development of face-processing skills, but the precise influences of these factors are currently unclear.
- Neurological abnormalities are likely to underpin these deficits, and further research might shed further light on the precise mechanisms that are required for normal face recognition to develop.
- Mixed evidence about the face-specificty debate has been provided from developmental disorders, and further insight into the basis of these conditions is required to truly understand their theoretical implications. Despite this, evidence from cataract patients provides more convincing support for the expertise hypothesis (see Geldart *et al.*, 2002; Le Grand *et al.*, 2001).

FURTHER READING

Bishop, D. V. M. (1997) 'Cognitive Neuropsychology and Developmental Disorders: Uncomfortable Bedfellows', *The Quarterly Journal of Experimental Psychology A: Human Experimental Psychology,* 50, 899–923.

Duchaine, B., Yovel, G., Butterworth, E. and Nakayama, K. (2006) 'Prosopagnosia as an Impairment to Face-Specific Mechanisms: Elimination of the Alternative Hypothesis in a Developmental Case', *Cognitive Neuropsychology,* 23, 714–47.

Geldart, S., Mondloch, C. J., Maurer, D., De Schonen, S. and Brent, H. P. (2002) 'The Effect of Early Visual Deprivation on the Development of Face Processing', *Developmental Science,* 5, 490–501.

Karmiloff-Smith, A., Scerif, G. and Ansari, D. (2003) 'Double Dissociation in Developmental Disorders? Theoretically Misconceived, Empirically Dubious', *Cortex,* 39, 161–3.

Le Grand, R., Mondloch, C. J., Maurer, D. and Brent, H. P. (2001). 'Neuroperception: Early Visual Experience and Face Processing', *Nature,* 410, 890.

McKone, E., Kanwisher, N. and Duchaine, B. C. (2007) 'Can Generic Expertise Explain Special Processing for Faces', *Trends in Cognitive Sciences,* 11, 8–15.

DISCUSSION QUESTIONS

1. Bishop (1997) stated that cognitive neuropsychology and developmental disorders make 'uncomfortable bedfellows'. To what extent is this true, and are there any further limitations to the theoretical implications that can be drawn from developmental disorders?
2. To what extent does evidence from developmental disorders support the CONSPEC and CONLERN components of Johnson and Morton's (1991) model (see Chapter 9)?
3. If a gene were found that brings about deficits in face processing, do you think that all people who have this gene will be affected?
4. In the next section of the book, research that has attempted to treat disorders of face processing is discussed. Before reading this section, can you design any intervention studies that might help such individuals, based on your knowledge about the factors that might underpin the disorders? Would the same intervention be suitable for all patients? Are there any patients who might not benefit from any type of intervention?

PART IV

The Impact, Assessment and Treatment of Face-Processing Deficits

13 Living in a World without Faces

In this book, a range of acquired, neuropsychiatric and developmental disorders of face processing have been considered. Although the aetiology, prevalence and co-morbidity of face-processing deficits greatly vary between these conditions, it is clear that difficulties in processing faces can have a large impact on everyday social and occupational functioning. In some disorders (e.g., acquired or developmental prosopagnosia), these difficulties largely revolve around the inability to recognize familiar people from their faces. In other conditions (e.g., schizophrenia or depression), it is mainly the ability to accurately interpret different emotional expressions that is affected.

Most of us take these skills for granted, and perhaps find it hard to imagine a world in which we cannot accurately process facial stimuli. Indeed, we rely on faces not only to recognize our family, friends, work colleagues and acquaintances, but also to interpret the feelings, intentions and wishes of others. We also live in a society where it is considered rude or inappropriate to stare at people's faces for a long period. Hence, even the most basic of social interactions fundamentally depend upon the ability to process faces quickly and accurately.

In this chapter, the psychosocial impact of face-processing deficits is considered. However, despite the obvious social consequences of these difficulties, very little work has directly explored the impact of face-processing deficits on everyday life. Most attention has been directed towards the psychosocial impact of developmental prosopagnosia (DP), and this is perhaps unsurprising given its high prevalence rate and the amount of media attention this disorder has received in recent years. Thus, this chapter will mainly focus on the experiences of individuals with DP in considering the psychosocial impact of face-processing deficits. Many of the quotes that you will read in this chapter are taken from an online discussion forum where individuals with DP post their comments about coping with the disorder in everyday life.

13.1. EVERYDAY CONSEQUENCES OF DP

Many individuals with DP describe embarrassing social and occupational situations where they have failed to recognize a person, missed romantic opportunities or deliberately avoided situations that they believe they cannot cope with (Barton, 2003; Duchaine, 2000; Duchaine and Nakayama, 2005, 2006a). The following quotes provided by individuals with DP demonstrate how the disorder can affect the development and maintenance of interpersonal relationships with others:

> I find social situations difficult – I avoided a street party recently because I knew that after it all the neighbours we didn't previously know would recognize me and expect me to recognize them – and I knew I wouldn't.

> I frequently don't know who people are, and I run into a lot of issues around that. Seeing the disappointment in people's faces. Finding that people think I don't like them or have a problem with them.

Other individuals with DP describe the embarrassing consequences of DP in the workplace:

> I have only recently figured out that this disorder is likely the root of what has been a confusing, decade- long problem with not remembering people – and hurting a lot of feelings in the process. A few instances have been truly mortifying, such as looking blankly at a client I had lunched with the previous day.

> I once worked in the same building as someone for a year and spoke to him several times, then to my horror saw him twice, talking to himself, and realized they were two different people. Both tall, slim, short dark hair – I was doomed.

> I try to use hair and context to help me, but if someone changes their hairstyle or colour it is very unlikely I'll recognize them, and I have introduced myself to a colleague whom I saw in a different office than normal, thinking she must be a new person, when she was someone I had frequent contact with.

13.2. COMPENSATORY STRATEGIES USED IN DP

Many adults with DP report the use of compensatory strategies that help them either to identify people, or to disguise their failure of recognition. These strategies have often been developed after years of suffering from the disorder, and can be quite elaborate in nature.

Often, individuals with DP can identify familiar people in many situations, simply by putting together cues from the person's non-facial appearance with contextual information. For instance, a gentleman with DP who goes to visit his sister at her home might be able to infer that the tall man who answers the door and has a grey beard is his brother-in-law, Bob. This is achieved by putting together distinctive characteristics about the man's appearance with the knowledge that he expects to meet this person in that particular location. However, it is important to realize that when someone with DP does successfully recognize a person using this strategy, he or she is not using their face-processing system to achieve recognition, they are simply circumventing their problem using alternative cues and logic. The following quotes from two individuals with DP illustrate this point:

> I make a huge effort to remember people's clothes, hair, tattoos, make-up, or anything just to be able to say hello on the street, whereas I wouldn't even recognize my own mother in an unexpected place.

> I rely very heavily on hairstyles, but obviously this falls down with any changes. I failed to recognize my husband in the swimming pool as his hair had washed back...he had to wave and shout to me!

As these quotes describe, compensatory strategies based on appearance and contextual cues do not always work. Indeed, they often break down when meeting a familiar person in an unexpected location, or when a person changes something about their appearance (e.g., a change in hairstyle or colour, or the removal of a distinctive mole on their chin). This can often lead to an embarrassing situation for both the individual with DP and their acquaintance, and can be put down to rudeness or a lack of effort on the part of the prosopagnosic.

13.3. MORE ELABORATE COMPENSATORY STRATEGIES

Some compensatory strategies that are used by individuals with DP are even more elaborate, and can help them to function in everyday social and occupational situations. Some of these strategies are summarized in the quotes below:

- 'I have figured out the amount of people I can handle at the same time, and only engage in private activities that meet these criteria.'
- 'I always make very specific meeting arrangements and tend to be the earliest person there so the others have to find me, and not vice versa.'
- 'I never use anyone's name, because it could be the wrong one.'
- 'I find that I recognize motion very easily. I can often recognize someone at a distance just by looking at the way they walk.'
- 'In a meeting or classroom, I draw a plan of where everyone sits with a name.'

- ◼ 'I meet just one or two new people at once, look for their most distinguishing features or something permanent about their person, and make a mnemonic about it.'
- ◼ 'Just for safety, I smile at practically everyone I meet.'

These strategies might help some individuals with DP to navigate the social world, and to cope with what can be to others a very distressing disorder. However, such strategies might also obscure the severity of an individual's difficulty in processing faces. This issue is further discussed in the next chapter, in reference to the need for sophisticated tests of face-processing ability that prevent impaired individuals achieving a 'normal' score, by blocking the use of compensatory strategies.

13.4. THE PSYCHOSOCIAL IMPACT OF DP

As described above, some individuals use compensatory mechanisms to help with everyday functioning, and although they still experience some embarrassing failures of recognition, their psychosocial well-being is not affected in a major way. However, there have been reports of more devastating consequences for some individuals with DP, particularly as the condition can interfere with social interaction. For example, some authors have suggested that DP might predispose some individuals to develop social anxiety disorder, a condition characterized by fear and avoidance of social situations that have the potential to bring about embarrassment or humiliation (American Psychiatric Association, 2000).

Recently, the first systematic in-depth description of the consequences of DP for psychosocial functioning and occupational disability was published, in an attempt to determine whether professional intervention might be needed (Yardley *et al.*, 2008). The authors found that all of the 25 individuals with DP they interviewed reported persistent and sometimes traumatic difficulties in social situations. Often, these difficulties bring about a state of chronic anxiety, where the individual worries about offending others. Most of the individuals with DP also described feelings of embarrassment, guilt and failure; and explained that they deliberately try to avoid social situations in which face recognition is important. The authors determined that the longer-term consequences of DP could include an over-dependence on others, a restricted social circle, more limited employment opportunities, and a loss of self-confidence. Perhaps the most striking conclusion of the report is the statement that 'the potential for negative psychosocial consequences and occupational difficulty posed by DP is as great at that posed by conditions which are currently afforded professional recognition and support, such as stuttering and dyslexia' (Yardley *et al.*, 2008, p. 445).

Yardley and colleagues recommend that an increase in public awareness about DP could reduce the social anxiety suffered by individuals with the condition, and make it easier for individuals with DP to explain their difficulties to friends and employers. As we will see in the next section, this is a pertinent issue, yet we still have some way to go before the necessary recognition of the condition is achieved.

13.5. PUBLIC AWARENESS OF DP

In the past decade, DP has received much media attention, which can largely be attributed to estimates that the condition affects a relatively large portion of the population (see, for example, Kennerknecht *et al.*, 2006). Despite this interest, there is still a lack of awareness that the condition exists, both among sufferers themselves, and among the population at large. Indeed, individuals who have suffered from face-processing impairments since birth or early childhood might simply not be aware that face recognition is typically effortless and reliable for others. Further, their problem may not seem severe owing to their development of compensatory strategies for everyday recognition. Even if they do become aware that they are poorer at face processing than other people, they are unlikely to suspect that this may be attributed to a neurological problem, let alone be a recognized condition. Indeed, despite recent media coverage of DP, most people are not aware of its existence, and are very surprised to learn about the condition. Some individuals with DP are quite open about their difficulties, and find that telling others about their problem is a positive step in dealing with everyday failures in recognition:

'Tell everybody about it, especially at places that count like work. That divides the responsibilities of recognizing somewhat.'

'I've been trying the strategy of launching into a long-winded explanation of my condition to everyone I meet...It's been really helpful in my new job, where people that encounter me tell me who they are if I seem to be having trouble placing them. The fact that this happens with people that work right next to me, or that I talk to on a regular basis is what makes this odd to them, and several have thanked me for letting them know about my condition so that it doesn't bother them as much. My boss is considering helping me draft an email to the entire company about the issue, just to let people know.'

However, many other people are reluctant to share information about their condition with others, and are often worried about how public knowledge of their difficulties might affect their career progression. This is obviously an issue that needs to be addressed by increasing awareness of prosopagnosia both among the general public, and in occupational settings. Indeed, as Yardley and colleagues (2008) pointed out, professional recognition and support networks are already in place for other developmental and cognitive disorders such as dyslexia, and the psychosocial consequences of prosopagnosia appear to sometimes be comparable to those observed in other conditions.

13.6. PROSOPAGNOSIA IN CHILDREN

Finally, very little attention to date has been directed towards the existence of prosopagnosia in children. It is generally well known that face-processing deficits are often observed in autistic spectrum disorders, and many professionals will draw parents' attention to this knowledge as a matter of course. However, there is little awareness of DP among teachers, educational psychologists and other caregivers. This is a pertinent issue given estimates that two per cent of the population might suffer from DP (Kennerknecht *et al.*, 2006), translating to 300 000 children in the UK alone. As public awareness of the condition is currently low, DP is likely to go undetected in most of these children, unless they are members of a family containing other individuals with DP.

It is not difficult to imagine that DP could have a devastating effect on children, particularly in the UK where most schools have strict rules about physical appearance and the wearing of school uniforms, preventing the provision of distinctive cues that can be used to aid recognition. It is currently unknown whether children with DP are likely to be labelled as being socially withdrawn or experiencing behavioural problems, but it is important that such issues are addressed in future research.

CHAPTER SUMMARY

- Most individuals with DP experience embarrassing everyday failures of recognition both in social and occupational settings.
- Some individuals deal with these failures well, and have even developed compensatory strategies that help them navigate the social world fairly successfully.
- However, some individuals with DP experience more devastating effects, and might suffer from social anxiety disorder or depression in response to their difficulties (Yardley *et al.*, 2008).
- It is important that awareness of the disorder is raised among the general public, in occupational settings and in schools.

FURTHER READING

Yardley, L., McDermott, L., Pisarski, S., Duchaine, B. and Nakayama, K. (2008) 'Psychosocial Consequences of Developmental Prosopagnosia: A Problem of Recognition', *Journal of Psychosomatic Research*, 65, 445–51.

GUIDANCE QUESTIONS

Use the following questions to guide your reading of this chapter and the recommended papers.

1. Does every individual with DP suffer severe psychosocial consequences that result from the disorder? Explain your answer with reference to the development of compensatory strategies that can aid recognition.
2. Much media attention has recently been directed to DP. Has this helped public awareness of the condition, or is there still more work to be done? You can search for recent media reports on the Internet to help inform your answer.

14 The Assessment of Face-Processing Deficits

This book has illustrated how face-processing impairments can present in many acquired, neuropsychiatric and developmental disorders. From both a practical and theoretical viewpoint, it is important to consider how these different types of face-processing difficulty might be assessed. Sometimes, a person who is experiencing face-processing impairments might be referred to a clinical or cognitive neuropsychologist for formal assessment. Other individuals might not seek formal intervention for their difficulties, but nevertheless volunteer to participate in a particular research project. In either case, an initial assessment of that individual's face processing and other cognitive abilities should be performed. This chapter discusses the neuropsychological and cognitive tests that might be administered in such an assessment, alongside other considerations that the person administering the tests might need to take into account.

14.1. INITIAL CONSIDERATIONS

Given the many different types of face-processing disorder that exist, it is initially important to establish an individual's neuropsychological background. This will guide the selection of tests that are used in the assessment session. Indeed, it would make sense to perform a wider variety of tests that assess identity perception with a patient who is suspected to have prosopagnosia than with one who is thought to experience difficulties interpreting particular emotional expressions as a result of schizophrenia. Some of this information may already be provided, but further details might be sought through informal interview. For example, the following questions could be asked.

■ Has the person ever suffered a brain injury or neurological illness? If so, did they suffer from the current (or any other) impairment before the trauma?
■ Do they have/suspect they might have a concurrent socio-emotional disorder? Does anyone else in their family suffer from such a disorder?

172

- Have they ever suffered from uncorrected vision for any length of time?
- Does anyone else in their family suffer from face-processing impairments?
- Do they have a history of or current neuropsychiatric disorder?
- Do they suffer from any other cognitive, perceptual or memory impairments?

Depending on their specific case history, the nature of the problem should also alert the assessor to other potential difficulties that they might wish to assess in the course of the session. For example, the discussion in Chapter 5 suggested that individuals who acquire prosopagnosia after neurological trauma often have more widespread cognitive difficulties, given the lesion is often not limited to only the face-processing areas of the brain. Hence, other difficulties might require assessment either in the current session or via referral to a specialist in that area, and the assessor should additionally be aware that any co-morbid impairments might influence performance on the battery of tests planned for the current session.

14.2. NEUROPSYCHOLOGICAL TESTS AND DEFINING IMPAIRMENT

Having performed an initial informal interview, the assessor might then proceed to run a series of neuropsychological or cognitive tests. These tests can be used to assess a variety of cognitive and perceptual processes, and can be selected to evaluate the particular processes that are of interest. After each test is administered, the participant's score is calculated and then compared with the performance of unimpaired control participants. Fortunately, these comparison data are provided with most tests, and the assessor does not need to collect his or her own control data. These data are often referred to as 'norming data', and usually provides us with the average score for a large group of unimpaired participants, together with a 'cut-off' score that signifies the lower boundary of the normal range. An individual's score on a particular test that is lower (or occasionally higher, if measuring the number of errors) than the relevant cut-off score is classified as impaired. Often, the cut-off is calculated by taking the control mean minus two standard deviations of the control group's performance.

Sometimes, neuropsychological tests are accompanied by more precise norming data that provide separate cut-offs according to several variables. Commonly, these variables include the age, gender and IQ of the control group. The assessor would therefore need to know these details to compare a person's performance to the appropriate norms. Although it is of course easy to access information about age and gender, it can be more difficult to assess IQ, particularly when a person has suffered a brain injury. Fortunately, there are some tests that can be used to provide a reliable assessment of pre-morbid IQ. For example, the

Wechsler Test of Adult Reading (Wechsler, 2001) is a reading test composed of 50 irregular words. The participant is presented with a card displaying the list of words, and is asked to read each word aloud while the assessor counts how many are pronounced correctly. Because the test only uses irregular words, it assumes the reader actually has to be familiar with each word and its meaning to pronounce it correctly. That is, they cannot pronounce the word by building its component phonemes. The total number of words pronounced correctly is thought to correlate with that person's IQ because, unlike many intellectual and memory abilities, reading recognition has been found to be relatively stable in the presence of cognitive decline associated with normal aging or brain injury. Reading tests such as the Wechsler Test of Adult Reading are also commonly used with non-brain damaged cases, because they allow for a rapid yet reliable estimation of IQ when longer in-depth assessments are not required.

14.2.1. Why do we need neuropsychological tests?

It might be argued that we do not need neuropsychological tests to ascertain whether a person is impaired at particular aspects of processing. Indeed, some researchers have argued that self-report alone is a satisfactory indicator of performance, and computerized or laboratory-based tests lack the ecological validity needed to provide a reliable assessment of everyday cognitive and perceptual abilities. For example, in Chapter 10 a study that used self-report data to estimate the prevalence of developmental prosopagnosia (DP) was discussed (Kennerknecht et al., 2006). Following later criticisms of this method, the authors defended their use of self-report to diagnose prosopagnosia by claiming that performance on experimental tests of face recognition might not accurately reflect the complexity of the face-processing system. Further, Stollhoff et al. (2011) reported a significant correlation between the self-reported difficulties of a group of congenital prosopagnosics and their performance on a range of experimental tests. The authors therefore claimed that diagnoses of prosopagnosia based on self-report data are just as reliable as those based on laboratory-based tests.

Despite these claims, most authors agree that gaining objective measures of face processing is a necessary procedure, and that more recent tests of face processing provide a more ecologically valid method of assessment than previous tests (see below). Another argument in favour of using objective rather than subjective measures of face-processing ability is that some individuals are not aware of the severity of their problem in comparison to unimpaired perceivers. This is perhaps less of an issue in acquired prosopagnosia, where a person can usually report the differences between his or her experiences of everyday face processing before and after their accident. For these individuals, the difference is usually quite striking in the context of sudden onset of the disorder (i.e., waking from a coma to find they can no longer recognize faces), and therefore they are aware of the change in their face-processing skills. Further, a family member will usually confirm that this problem is a result of the trauma, rather than a pre-existing condition.

Awareness of face-processing difficulties can be more difficult in developmental cases, where a 'normal' period of recognition has never been experienced that can be used as a point of comparison. Indeed, many individuals with DP are unaware that their face-processing abilities are different to those of others, particularly when entire families of individuals are affected. In other cases, individuals with DP are aware that they often fail to recognize familiar people, but attribute their difficulties to some personal characteristic, such as rudeness, laziness or inattentiveness. These individuals often report feelings of relief when they learn about prosopagnosia for the first time, and realize that face-blindness is actually a recognized neurological condition and their difficulties may not be the result of a 'flawed personality'.

Finally, it is perhaps more difficult for people to self-assess whether they are poor at other aspects of face processing, such as judging gender, age or attractiveness. Indeed, errors in identity recognition in social situations become immediately obvious following a person's reaction to the failure of recognition, but such feedback is not so readily available for other aspects of face processing. Further, some social judgements about faces (e.g., judging facial attractiveness), are commonly thought to be subjective, and any difficulties in this domain may therefore go unnoticed. Whether or not a person has object recognition difficulties is also hard to self-evaluate. Indeed, it is not often that our memory for different exemplars of particular objects is tested in everyday life (e.g., many laboratory-based tests evaluate memory for specific guns or houses). Hence, because we cannot always rely on people's self-assessment of their difficulties, it is critical that we do have objective and standardized measures of processing abilities that can easily be administered in laboratory-based settings.

14.3. THE COGNITIVE NEUROPSYCHOLOGICAL APPROACH: TESTING FUNCTIONAL STAGES OF FACE PROCESSING

Neuropsychological tests are useful because they not only provide assessment of different components of a particular processing system, but performance on these tests can also be used to evaluate the location of a patient's lesion with respect to functional models. Hence, many neuropsychological tests have been created with a theoretical basis: they are believed to test a particular component in a given model.

Throughout this book, the dominant functional model of face processing that was proposed by Bruce and Young (1986; see Chapter 1) has consistently been referred to. Further, these functional stages of face processing have been applied to neurological models, in which face processing consists of several hierarchical stages and parallel processes in a distributed cortical network (Gobbini and Haxby, 2007; Haxby *et al.*, 2000). In later chapters of this book, the interpretation of particular disorders of face processing have been discussed with reference to the Bruce and Young model. Indeed, the model has been used to partition prosopagnosia into its two broad subtypes (associative and apperceptive), and has been adapted to explain covert recognition in prosopagnosia and the misidentification that is observed in the Capgras delusion. Finally, Chapter 12 discussed whether the Bruce and Young model can be used to accommodate developmental disorders of face processing.

These issues aside, it is clear that the model can be used to generate hypotheses about the functional site of a lesion in individuals with impaired face-processing skills. As discussed in Chapter 1, functional models reduce individual cognitive and perceptual processes to 'boxes' and 'arrows', and these processes are believed to be hierarchical in nature. Hence, if a particular module or a connection between modules is lesioned, all subsequent stages of processing must also be impaired. This means that a patient might report a problem in face recognition, but the actual impairment itself is in their ability to perceive a face (e.g., at the level of structural encoding). According to the model of Bruce and Young, all processes below structural encoding must also be affected, even though the lesion itself is located within an earlier component.

An assessor might therefore set out to evaluate all functional stages of the model of Bruce and Young when testing a new client. However, one can imagine that there might be some disruption in early- and mid-visual processes that are causing the face-processing problem, and these processes might be located outside of the face-processing system. Such processes are therefore not encompassed in the Bruce and Young model. For example, face-processing problems might result from a problem in very early visual analysis, rather than a deficit residing within the face-processing system itself. These early processes are generally very quick and easy to assess.

The remainder of this chapter discusses the various stages of processing where a deficit might occur, and recommends particular tests that can be used to evaluate performance at each functional stage. Figure 14.1 provides a summary of these stages, merging the Bruce and Young (1986) and Gobbini and Haxby (2007) models with earlier stages of visual processing. As a final note, it is commonly recommended that at least two different tests are used to assess processing at each stage, to provide a more thorough evaluation of an individual's abilities.

14.3.1. Low-level vision (processing of local details)

It is thought that local elements of a visual stimulus are detected by simple and complex cells in the primary visual cortex (area V1). It is useful to test this basic visual perception, given any general impairment in low-level perceptual abilities

Figure 14.1 *A schematic diagram of face-processing stages in the brain.*

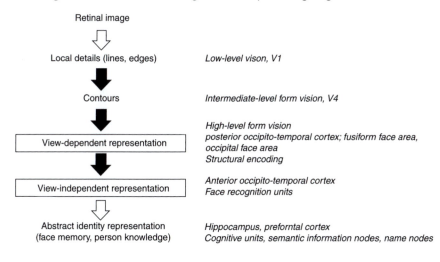

might bring about a general perceptual problem that would affect, among other things, face processing.

Basic visual acuity is usually tested using a chart of letters commonly known as a 'Snellen chart' (named after a Dutch ophthalmologist who developed the chart in 1862). You may be familiar with the Snellen chart from your own visits to an optician. The chart is traditionally printed with 11 rows of letters that get progressively smaller in size. Perceivers are required to cover each eye in turn and read aloud the letters on the chart, working from the top to the bottom, until they can no longer distinguish the letters. The smallest row that can accurately be read aloud indicates the visual acuity in that particular eye.

Contrast sensitivity is commonly measured using the Pelli–Robson contrast sensitivity test (Pelli, Robson, and Wilkins, 1998). In this test, participants view rows of letters on a chart that are the same size, but progressively decrease in contrast as participants proceed through the test. This test provides a quick means to assess a client's contrast sensitivity thresholds.

Other aspects of basic visual perception can be tested using batteries such as the Birmingham Object Recognition Battery (Humphreys and Riddoch, 1993). This consists of many subtests that are designed to assess functioning at various stages of the visual system. Several these tests assess lower-level visual abilities. Commonly reported tests in case-reports of prosopagnosia include the Length Match, Size Match, Orientation Match, and Position of the Gap Match tests. In the Length Match test, participants are required to judge whether two lines are of the same length; in the Size Match test they judge whether two circles are of the same size; in the Orientation Match test they decide whether two lines are parallel or not; and in the Position of the Gap Match test they decide whether the position of the gap in two circles is in the same position or not.

14.3.2. Intermediate-level form vision (contours)

Once information about local elements is processed, it is thought that more sensitive response cells in higher cortical areas integrate this information. In particular, the extrastriate area V4 in the ventral visual pathway has been implicated in this process, as single-cell recordings in monkeys have identified a type of cell that is primarily responsive to global concentric structure (Gallant *et al.*, 1996; Kobatake and Tanaka, 1994). Specifically, it is believed that the global concentric units in V4 may provide a critical link between the processing of local detail by cells in V1 and the later extraction of information about facial identity (Wilkinson *et al.*, 2000).

Assessment of intermediate-level form vision has been performed in a variety of ways. For example, Glass patterns (Glass, 1969) are stimuli that are used to assess sensitivity to structure in global form. In these stimuli, a pattern of random dots is superimposed over an identical pattern and rotated, creating a percept of concentric swirl. The ratio of paired signal dots to unpaired noise dots in the signal patterns is then reduced until the participant can no longer discriminate accurately between the signal pattern and a pattern comprised only of noise dots (see Figure 14.2). Previous work has indicated that adults detect the signal pattern accurately when it is carried by only 12 per cent of the dot pairs (Lewis *et al.*, 2004).

In a recent study, Lee *et al.* (2010) examined perception of closed curvature using radial frequency patterns. Radial frequency patterns are circular contours that are defined by sinusoidal modulation of a circle's mean radius in polar coordinates. That is, as the radial amplitude of the circle increases, deformation

Figure 14.2 *Example stimuli used to test sensitivity to global form.*

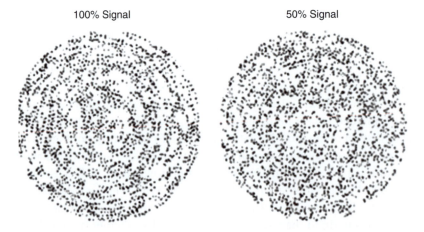

The pattern on the left has 100 per cent of the dots paired to form a global swirl, whereas the pattern on the right has 50 per cent paired signal dots and 50 per cent randomly placed noise dots.

from circularity increases. In this test, participants are asked to decide which of two briefly presented circles has a deformed contour. It has been suggested that, because curvatures and circles are key attributes of faces, this test most effectively probes the intermediate form vision that is specific to face and object recognition (Wilkinson, Wilson and Habak, 1998; Wilkinson *et al.*, 2000).

14.3.3. Face detection

Face detection is the process of finding a face in a visual scene. Despite being a crucial component of face processing, it is not reflected in most models. Nevertheless, face detection is an important stage of processing that warrants assessment. Many studies up to now have used categorization tasks to assess face detection, where participants decide if a stimulus is a real face or a scrambled face, or a face or an object (e.g., Le Grand *et al.*, 2006). In a recent study that was designed to provide a more ecologically valid measure of face detection, Garrido, Duchaine and Nakayama (2008) asked participants to detect whether or not a face was present in (1) an array of small images, or (2) in an array of two-tone face parts (see Figure 14.3). The authors found that impaired participants took longer to complete these tasks than unimpaired participants.

14.3.4. Face matching

Face-matching ability specifically tests the structural encoding component of the model of Bruce and Young. A prosopagnosic with an impairment at the

Figure 14.3 *Examples of the face detection stimuli used by Garrido, Duchaine and Nakayama (2008).*

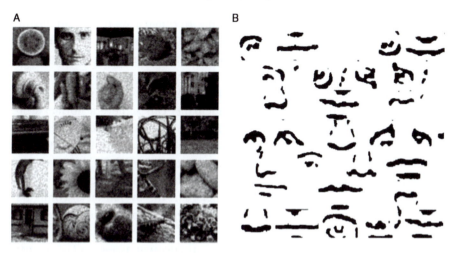

Participants were asked to detect facial configurations in (A) an array of small images, and (B) an array of two-tone face parts.

stage of structural encoding is thought to have an impairment in face perception, and, as such, all subsequent aspects of face processing will also be impaired. Hence, a patient with an impairment at the level of structural encoding would be expected to be impaired at face matching, expression recognition, other perceptual judgements (e.g., age, gender) and face recognition itself. Such a patient would fall into the apperceptive subtype of prosopagnosia, as specified by De Renzi *et al.* (1991). As structural encoding is thought to be where a perceiver turns an incoming percept of a face into a view-independent percept, a specific test of this function is the ability to complete a face-matching task (note that judgements of expression, age and gender are performed a subsequent stage, and even though we would expect these processes to also be impaired in an apperceptive patient, they are not direct tests of the structural encoding module).

It is theoretically important to test face-matching ability both for faces that are displayed from the same viewpoint, and for those that are displayed from different viewpoints. This is because it is thought that incoming facial percepts are transformed from viewpoint-dependent to viewpoint-independent representations during structural encoding (see Figure 14.1). Indeed, there is neuroimaging evidence that suggests different neural regions are involved in these two tasks (Pourtois *et al.*, 2005), and some prosopagnosic individuals have been found to be able to match faces from the same viewpoint but not those presented from different viewpoints (see, for example, Laeng and Caviness, 2001; Marotta, McKeeff and Behrmann, 2002).

There are few standardized tests of face-matching ability, particularly those that take viewpoint manipulations into account. The process has traditionally been assessed using the Benton Facial Recognition Test (BFRT (Benton and Van Allen, 1968)). The BFRT can be administered in either a short-form containing 27 items, or a long form containing 54 items. In the first six trials, participants view a target face and six test images. They are asked to select which of the test images depicts the same person as the target image. From trial seven onwards, there are three correct answers in each trial. Some trials are more difficult than others, as pose or lighting has been manipulated. In recent years, the BFRT has been criticized on the grounds that participants can achieve a normal score when the internal features of the facial stimuli are obscured and only external information can be used to cue recognition (Duchaine and Weidenfeld, 2003; Duchaine and Nakayama, 2004). Further, as the test presents the target face and the test faces simultaneously, successful performance can be achieved using a feature-by-feature matching strategy, rather than the overall facial configuration. This may mask impairments in face perception, particularly if response time is not monitored.

A recent test that is thought to provide a more adequate assessment of face perception skills is the Cambridge Face Perception Test (CFPT (Duchaine, Germine and Nakayama, 2007)). In the CFPT, participants are presented with 16 trials,

Figure 14.4 *An example trial from the CFPT.*

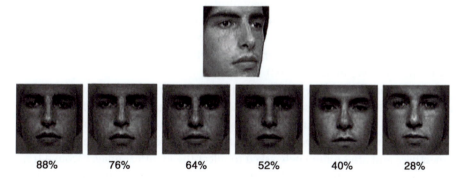

| 88% | 76% | 64% | 52% | 40% | 28% |

The numbers presented underneath each image indicate the proportion of the original image that is present. In the actual test, these test images are presented for sorting in the same format but in a random order.

eight upright and eight inverted. In each trial, participants view a target face at the top of the screen, and six test faces below that are presented in an array (see Figure 14.4). The test faces are displayed from a different viewpoint than the target face, and have been morphed to contain different proportions of the target face: 28%, 40%, 52%, 64%, 76% and 88%. The participant has one minute to sort the faces according to their similarity to the target face. The deviation of the participant's order from the correct order is calculated for each trial, and summed for upright and inverted trials.

Finally, a further face-matching test was recently developed by Burton, White and McNeil (2010), termed the 'Glasgow Face Matching Test'. In this test, participants view pairs of faces that have been photographed from the same frontal viewpoint, but using different cameras. Participants are required to state whether the same person is displayed in the two images. The authors produced two different versions of the test: a full version containing 168 pairs, and a shortened version containing the 40 most difficult pairs. Although the authors primarily developed the test for use in security settings where employees are often required to match two frontal views of faces (i.e., in passport control), they also note that the test can be of use in neuropsychological assessments of individuals with face-processing disorders.

14.3.5. Face memory

Face memory has traditionally been tested using the Warrington Recognition Memory for Faces test (Warrington, 1984). In this test, participants view a set of 30 faces in a study phase, then are required to select the familiar face from pairs of faces containing one studied and one novel item. However, this test has received similar criticisms to the BFRT. Indeed, the images of the familiar faces presented during the study and test phases are identical, and hence the test can be completed using 'picture-matching' rather than face recognition skills. Further, the images used in the test are not cropped to only display the internal facial features, and information from clothing, hairstyle and background can be used to cue recognition. Evidence supporting this weakness was provided by Duchaine and Weidenfeld (2003).

The Cambridge Face Memory Test (CFMT (Duchaine and Nakayama, 2006b)) is now the dominantly used test to assess face recognition ability. In this test, participants are asked to memorize six faces in an initial introduction phase. They view each of the target faces from left-profile, frontal and right-profile perspectives, and are immediately asked to select the identical images from a triad of faces containing the target face and two distractor items. After reviewing the six faces for a 20-second interval, participants complete a further 30 trials, again consisting of triads of faces. In this section of the test, faces are displayed from novel perspectives or under novel lighting conditions. After a final 20-second review of the six target faces, participants complete the remaining 24 trials, where noise has been added to the images (i.e., the faces look blurred). This test has been thoroughly standardized (e.g., Bowles *et al.*, 2009) and is particularly successful in removing any image-specific cues that might aid performance (see Figure 14.5). Further, the test is thought to be more ecologically valid by asking participants to only learn six faces.

Many laboratories also ask participants to take part in face recognition tests that use famous faces as stimuli. Such tests are particularly useful as they can be used to assess various aspects of the face-processing system simultaneously. For example, participants can be shown a set of famous faces intermixed with novel faces. For each face, the participant might only be required to make a familiarity decision, i.e., decide if the face is familiar or novel. Such a test would assess processing in the face recognition units. The assessor could then ask the participant to provide semantic information about each celebrity, or to name them. This would test the person identity nodes, semantic information units and name generation stages. Assessors should be aware that often participants are unable to name familiar people when put on the spot, and this is not necessarily indicative of an impairment. The assessor should ask the client to provide semantic information about the celebrity when they cannot access the name. If this is successful, the assessor should be aware that the client might not suffer from prosopagnosia, but possibly from proper name anomia (a failure to recall names, but face recognition itself is intact). Finally, some caution should be exercised in the use of famous face tests, as some participants might simply be unfamiliar with the target celebrities, as they may take little interest in the media or entertainment industry. For this reason, it is recommended that the individual is asked to rate their familiarity with each celebrity from name cues, and any celebrity they would not expect to recognize, regardless of their face-processing impairment, should be removed from the overall test and the proportion correct adjusted accordingly. For this reason (and in circumstances

Figure 14.5 *Example images from the CFMT.*

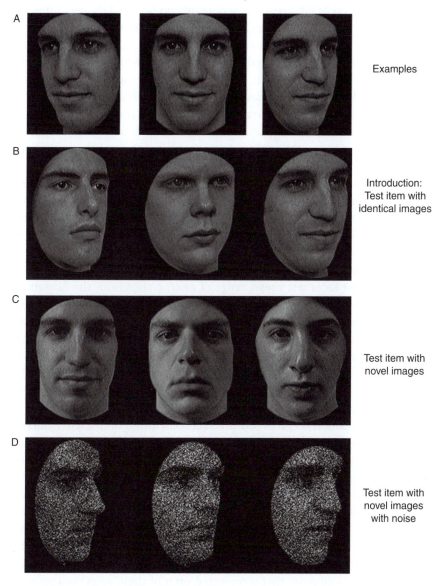

Participants are required to memorize six faces from three viewpoints (A), then immediately select the identical image (B) from triads of faces. After reviewing the target faces, participants recall the studied images when presented in a novel format (C) and in novel images with noise (D).

where young children are being tested), it might be more fruitful to use faces that are personally familiar to the individual, rather than famous faces.

In sum, the CFMT and CFPT are the dominant tests that are currently used to diagnose prosopagnosia, although not all prosopagnosics display poor performance on the CFPT. However, the tests are thought to be particularly reliable given that people who perform very poorly on famous face tests often also perform poorly on the CFMT and CFPT. The tasks are also subject to a large face-inversion effect in normal individuals, indicating they are successfully measuring face-specific processes (Duchaine and Nakayama, 2006b; Duchaine, Yovel, and Nakayama, 2007). As a result, both tests have become widely used by face recognition and prosopagnosia researchers since their publication (e.g., Bate *et al.*, 2008; DeGutis *et al.*, 2007; Herzmann *et al.*, 2008; Iaria *et al.*, 2009).

14.3.6. Non-identity face perception

Perhaps because of the multitude of disorders that present with impairments in processing emotional expressions, several standardized tests that assess this ability have been developed. However, there are three tests that tend to be used more frequently than others: the Ekman 60 Faces Test (Young *et al.*, 2002), the Emotional Hexagon Test (Young, *et al.*, 2002) and the Reading the Mind in the Eyes Test (Baron-Cohen *et al.*, 1997, 2001).

The Ekman 60 Faces test uses a range of photographs from the Ekman and Friesen (1976) series of Pictures of Facial Affect, to test recognition of basic facial expressions (i.e., those depicting anger, disgust, fear, happiness, sadness and surprise). Participants are asked to complete six practice trials followed by 60 test trials. Stimuli are presented in a random order for five seconds per face, followed by a blank screen. Participants are required to use the mouse to click on-screen buttons representing each of the six basic emotions. The test is not timed: participants can take as long as they wish to make their response.

Whereas the Ekman 60 Faces test involves recognition of discrete emotional expressions, the Emotion Hexagon test uses computer image manipulation techniques to test facial expression recognition with stimuli of graded difficulty (see Figure 14.6). The rationale underlying the Emotion Hexagon test is that, whereas the Ekman and Friesen (1976) faces were developed to provide relatively unambiguous examples of each emotion, in some circumstances it is useful to be able to test recognition of less clear-cut expressions. The left-hand panel of Figure 14.6 demonstrates the pairs of expressions that participants find it most difficult to discriminate between. Young *et al.* (2002) took images from the Ekman and Friesen (1976) stimulus set that represented each of these pairs, and morphed them to create 120 trials. Because the images have been morphed to greater or lesser degrees between two emotional expressions, interpretation of the expression is more difficult. Participants are required to interpret the expressions in the same manner as described for the Ekman 60 Faces test. Specific details of the image manipulation procedures used to create these images can be found elsewhere (e.g., Calder *et al.*, 1996).

Baron-Cohen and colleagues (1997, 2001) developed the Reading the Mind in the Eyes Test to assess the attribution of more subtle emotions in adults.

Figure 14.6   *Example stimuli from the Emotional Hexagon test.*

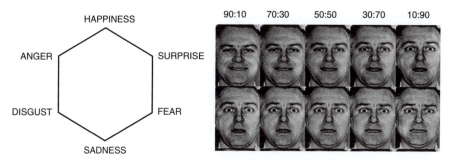

The image on the left displays a hexagonal representation of the manner in which emotional expressions are most often confused. Emotions that are most likely to be mistaken for other emotions are located at adjacent points around the hexagon. The image on the right displays two example continua of 90 per cent, 70 per cent, 50 per cent, 30 per cent and 10 per cent morphs used in the Emotion Hexagon test. The top row displays a blend of happiness and surprise, and the bottom row displays a blend of surprise and fear.

Participants view 36 trials, each displaying the eye region of a face. They are required to select the emotion that is depicted by the image from four response options (see Figure 14.7). Unlike the previous two tests, response options consist of many different and often subtly differing emotional states. A children's version of this test is also available.

Finally, no standardized tests currently exist that test the ability to make gender, age or attractiveness judgements. However, some researchers have created their own tests to assess these abilities (e.g., Le Grand *et al.*, 2006).

14.3.7. Object processing

As seen throughout this book, evaluation of whether a patient's difficulties are limited to face processing or extend to other categories of visual stimuli is important from both a theoretical and practical viewpoint. Indeed, assessment of both processes is important to inform the key theoretical debate about the specificity of face processing. Further, we know that face and object processing deficits often co-occur, and therefore it is important to assess both processes.

Basic object recognition and naming can be assessed using simple tasks, such as the Object Decision Task that is presented in the Birmingham Object Recognition Battery. In this test, the participant is presented with a series of line drawings that depict animals or tools. However, in some trials, the drawings represent 'unreal' objects that do not exist (i.e., the picture shows half of one object combined with half of another object). The participant is asked to decide whether each of 64 (short-form) or 128 (long-form) drawings represents a real

Figure 14.7 *A test item from the Reading the Mind in the Eyes test.*

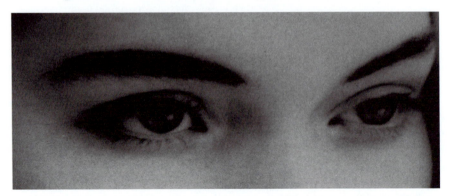

The participant is asked to select the word that they think most accurately describes the emotion expressed in the face. In this trial, the options are reflective (the correct answer), aghast, irritated or impatient.

or unreal object. An alternative image set that can be used is that developed by Snodgrass and Vanderwort (1980). The Visual Object and Space Perception Battery (Warrington and James, 1991) is also commonly used to evaluate both object and space perception, and is based on the assumption that these processes are functionally separable. The subtests in the Visual Object and Space Perception Battery require very simple responses, each of which focuses on one component of visual perception while minimizing the involvement of other cognitive skills.

It is also necessary to perform tests that assess memory for particular exemplars of given object categories. Until very recently, no standardized object memory test has been available, although researchers often developed their own object memory tests, commonly using guns, cars or houses as stimuli (e.g., Duchaine and Nakayama, 2005). However, Dennett *et al.* (2012) recently published the Cambridge Car Memory Test, which has an identical format to the successful CFMT, but uses cars rather than faces as stimuli.

CHAPTER SUMMARY

■ When assessing a person with face-processing difficulties, it is important to perform an initial interview to get an overview of the problem. Broadly speaking, this interview allows the neuropsychologist to suspect either an acquired, neuropsychiatric, developmental or congenital disorder.

■ The testing session can then be structured according to the predictions of the initial diagnosis, with attention also directed towards assessment of co-morbid impairments that are known to present alongside that type of disorder.

■ It is very important to use neuropsychological tests to confirm impairments. We cannot rely on self-report alone, given some patients over- or under-report their difficulties.
■ There are existing neuropsychological tests that assess each stage of visual perception and the face-processing system. These tests generally come with norming data that allow us to decide if performance at each level is intact or impaired compared with control participants.
■ Traditional tests that have been used to diagnose face-processing impairments have been criticized on the grounds that the face-processing system is not required to achieve a normal score. More recent tests have overcome these problems.

FURTHER READING

Burton, A. M., White, D. and McNeil, A. (2010) 'The Glasgow Face Matching Test', *Behavior Research Methods,* 42, 286–91.
Duchaine, B. and Weidenfeld, A. (2003) 'An Evaluation of Two Commonly Used Tests of Unfamiliar Face Recognition', *Neuropsychologia,* 41, 713–20.
Duchaine, B. and Nakayama, K. (2003) 'Developmental Prosopagnosia and the Benton Facial Recognition Test', *Neurology,* 62, 1219–20.
Duchaine, B. and Nakayama, K. (2006) 'The Cambridge Face Memory Test: Results for Neurologically Intact Individuals and a Test of its Validity Using Inverted Face Stimuli and Prosopagnosic Subjects', *Neuropsychologia,* 44, 576–85.

GUIDANCE QUESTIONS

Use the following questions to guide your reading of this chapter and the recommended papers.

1. Why is it important to gain background information about a person before neuropsychological testing starts?
2. What are the benefits and disadvantages of relying on self-report measures alone?
3. Why are more recent tests of face processing more successful than previous tests (e.g., the BFRT and Warrington Recognition Memory for Faces test)?

15 Treatment of Face-Processing Deficits

Despite increasing awareness that many people suffer from face-processing deficits, there have been few attempts to improve face-processing skills in these individuals. Indeed, there is no formal programme of treatment currently offered by clinical services, although some investigators have attempted to improve face processing in small numbers of research participants. This chapter describes the attempts that have been made so far, and highlights recent developments in the literature and potential directions for future research.

15.1. TREATMENT OF FACE RECOGNITION IMPAIRMENTS

15.1.1. Attempts to remedy face recognition deficits in acquired prosopagnosia

A few early studies attempted to remedy the face recognition impairment in cases of acquired prosopagnosia, but met with little success. This is perhaps not surprising given the complexity of many cases of acquired prosopagnosia, and the many other cognitive impairments that commonly co-occur with the disorder.

First, Ellis and Young (1988) studied an eight-year-old prosopagnosic child, KD, for a period of 18 months. KD had acquired severe prosopagnosia after anaesthetic complications at three years of age. She also had object agnosia, and the underlying deficit seemed to be an inability to construct adequate representations of visual stimuli. The researchers asked KD to complete four training programmes that required (1) simultaneous matching of photographs of familiar and unfamiliar faces, (2) paired discriminations of computer-generated schematic faces, (3) paired discriminations of digitized images of real faces and (4) the learning of face-name associations. Unfortunately, none of the programmes brought about an improvement in KD's face-processing skills.

In another study, De Haan, Young and Newcombe (1991) attempted to rehabilitate an adult with severe acquired prosopagnosia, PH. This individual had profound face recognition impairments, but was found to display covert recognition on several behavioural tasks. Based on this knowledge, the authors used a category-presentation method to try to improve the patient's face-processing skills. Specifically, PH was presented with the faces of famous people who were all involved in the same occupation. The researchers informed PH about the occupation performed by that set of people, and then asked him to identify the faces. Unfortunately, PH was only successful in recognizing faces from one of the six occupational categories that were used in the study, and the improvement was not maintained in a follow-up test two months later.

More recently, Powell *et al.* (2008) examined the rehabilitation of face recognition impairments in 20 patients with general impairments of face processing alongside a broader pattern of cognitive deficits (note that these patients did not suffer from a 'pure' prosopagnosia). The patients took part in three different training procedures derived from contemporary face-processing theories, and the procedures were specifically designed to enhance the learning of new faces:

- **Semantic association training.** In this procedure, participants were provided with additional verbal information about the learnt faces. The theoretical basis for this technique came from findings that suggest faces are often only known to be generally familiar to a perceiver, without being uniquely identified (Young, Hay and Ellis, 1985). According to the interactive activation and competition model of face processing (Burton, Bruce and Johnston, 1990; see Chapter 1), such a 'familiar only' state is represented by partial activation of a person identity node. This incomplete activation is enough to signal familiarity, but not to enable retrieval of identity-specific semantic information. Powell *et al.* (2008) therefore reasoned that because semantic memories of people are often reasonably intact after brain injury (albeit inaccessible from facial cues), the participants might benefit from activation of identity-specific semantic knowledge to help facilitate the processing of faces that would not otherwise be recognized.
- **Caricature training.** In this training programme, participants were presented with caricatured versions of the faces they were required to learn. This technique was based on Valentine's (1991) multidimensional face space model, which predicts that, by exaggerating distinctive features of a face, caricaturing moves the facial representation away from the centre of face space and hence the representation of most other faces (see Chapter 1). Thus, this procedure should make caricatured faces more distinctive and easier to remember.
- **Part-recognition training.** In the final procedure, participants' attention was directed towards particular facial features during training. Indeed, face processing is thought to rely on configural processing (see Chapter 1), and it has been hypothesized that a disruption in this process might underpin face-processing deficits in a variety of disorders. If this is true, Powell *et al.*

(2008) reasoned that training should attempt to maximize the use of residual processing abilities (i.e., the use of a featural processing strategy).

Participants were required to attend four days of training. On three of the days they took part in one of the training procedures described above. Each procedure was applied to a different set of ten unknown faces, viewed six times, and participants were required to memorize each face using the relevant technique. On the remaining day, participants took part in a control version of the task, where they simply viewed each of the ten faces six times, and did not apply a training strategy while attempting to memorize the faces. The order of the four sessions was counterbalanced between participants. After each set of faces had been memorized, participants took part in a face recognition test where they viewed the 10 studied faces intermixed with 10 novel faces. Participants were required to decide whether they have seen each face in the study (training) phase. Powell *et al.* also tested a control group of 12 patients who had similar face recognition impairments to the experimental group. This group of participants were required to learn all four sets of faces under control conditions. That is, no training strategy was applied to the learning of any of the face sets.

The researchers found that all three of the training procedures resulted in more accurate discrimination of the studied faces compared with the control condition where no training strategy was applied. Further, the authors demonstrated that the finding could not be attributed to the face recognition tests in the three experimental conditions being easier than that used in the control condition, as the control group of participants performed at a similar level across all four versions of the test (see Figure 15.1). Powell *et al.* also noted that the pattern of associated cognitive deficits in each participant did not predict which technique would be the most beneficial to that individual; although it should be noted that the study probably did not have enough power to detect such associations given the small sample size.

Finally, the researchers additionally tested a pure acquired prosopagnosia at a later date, who only appeared to benefit from the part-recognition technique. Although this finding was only based on a single case and needs to be replicated with a larger number of individuals, it does raise the possibility that some treatment strategies might be more effective than others with particular cases. Further, there are also practical issues concerned with the application of some of the intervention techniques to a larger number of participants. Indeed, the feature-based strategy used in Powell *et al.*'s study (2008) might not only be the most effective of the three techniques investigated, but might also be the least labour-intensive method for the researcher. For example, providing a personalized training regime with specific semantic information or caricatures of a particular set of faces would be much more difficult than the initiation of a general feature-based processing strategy in each individual. As a final point, the Powell *et al.* study (2008) was designed to be a 'proof-of-point' investigation, and as

Figure 15.1   *Data presented by Powell et al. (2008).*

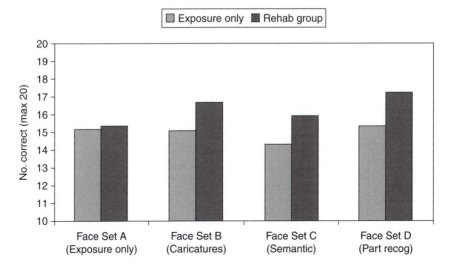

The figure summarizes the number of correct responses achieved by participants after each type of training (the black bars), and those achieved by control participants who did not undergo training (the grey bars). It can be seen that all three training conditions brought about improved face recognition performance compared to both the no-training condition and the control participants.

such no data were provided on whether the improvements extended to new sets of faces or were maintained over time. Thus, although providing promising evidence that face-processing deficits may be treatable in at least acquired cases of prosopagnosia, much work is still needed to determine the optimum intervention strategy with the most long-lasting effects.

15.1.2. Attempts to remedy face recognition deficits in developmental prosopagnosia

Although there have also been few attempts to improve face-processing skills in cases of developmental prosopagnosia (DP), those that have been reported have met with some success. Further, these studies also report follow-up data that provides promising evidence that the benefits gained through training can be both generalized to new sets of faces, and maintained at least in the short-term once intervention has ceased.

Two recent studies have attempted to improve face recognition skills in children with DP. First, Brunsdon *et al.* (2006) attempted to improve face recognition in an eight-year-old child, AL, who appeared to have problems at the level of structural encoding. The researchers gave AL a set of 17 personally known faces (i.e., those of family and friends) to learn on stimuli cards. Six pieces of information were written on the back of each card: the person's name, age, gender and three defining facial features (e.g., wide nostrils, large eyes). AL was shown each card one at a time, and asked to identify the person. He was given feedback about his response, and provided with the correct name if he failed to identify the face correctly. The researchers then explained to AL how he could use the distinguishing facial features to remember each person. AL continued the training at home using the stimuli cards, until he reached 100 per cent accuracy in recognizing the faces in four consecutive sessions. This occurred after 14 sessions, within a one-month period. Encouragingly, AL's improvement in face recognition was generalized to the recognition of a new set of faces, and his family reported anecdotal evidence of improvements in everyday face recognition. Further, the improvement was maintained at a three month follow-up testing session.

A similar study was performed by Schmalzl, Palermo, Green *et al.* (2008). These authors investigated K, a four-year-old girl with DP. Initial assessment found that K also had a problem at the level of structural encoding, particularly in processing the features of a face. Before beginning the training programme, the researchers monitored K's eye movements while she viewed facial stimuli, and found that she tended to focus on the external rather than internal features of the face, and particularly avoided looking at the eyes. Using a similar procedure to Brunsdon *et al.* (2006), K was taught to recognize a set of familiar face photographs, by directing her attention towards distinctive characteristics of each face. After each training session, K was tested on her ability to recognize the faces from the both the training photographs and an additional set of images that displayed the faces from novel viewpoints. Again, training was discontinued once K achieved 100 per cent accuracy in recognizing the training photographs in four consecutive sessions, and this occurred after nine training sessions. Although the improvement did not generalize to the stimuli set that displayed the faces from different viewpoints immediately after training, a significant improvement was noted for these faces at a one-month follow-up. Further, eye movement recordings performed after training showed a significant increase in the percentage of fixations directed to the internal features of the face, and particularly the eye region. Importantly, this effect also generalized to a new set of faces that had not been seen in training.

Finally, a different method was used by DeGutis *et al.* (2007). These authors attempted to improve face recognition in an adult with DP, MZ, who had severe impairments in face perception. The training task was administered over 14 months in two separate intervals. Training required MZ to perform a perceptual classification task repetitively over large numbers of trials. Specifically, facial stimuli were adjusted to vary in 2 mm increments according to eyebrow height and mouth height. MZ was required to classify each face into one of two categories: those faces with higher eyebrows and lower mouths, and those faces with lower eyebrows and higher mouths.

After training, behavioural evidence indicated that MZ's face-processing ability improved on a range of behavioural tasks. However, the most pertinent findings of this study came from changes in neurophysiological measures that were taken before and after training. Specifically, the authors used electroencapholography to investigate whether MZ displayed a selective N170 response (see Chapter 2) for faces compared with watches. Although this face-selective component was not evident before training, its selectivity after training was normal. Further, the authors used functional neuroimaging techniques to measure the functional connectivity between neural regions thought to underpin the face-processing system. Encouragingly, it was found that levels of functional connectivity between these key neural areas were increased after training. Hence, this study provides exciting evidence that face recognition cannot only be improved on a behavioural level in DP, but that intervention can actually modify the neural mechanisms underpinning the face-processing system. This suggests long-lasting improvements might be achievable, at least in developmental forms of prosopagnosia.

15.1.3. Attempts to remedy face recognition deficits in autistic spectrum disorders

Some researchers have also attempted to improve face recognition in autistic spectrum disorder (ASD). In a recent study, Faja *et al.* (2008) developed a computerized training programme that aimed to promote the use of configural processing in adolescents and young adults with ASD. The training programme was designed to parallel the Greeble expertise training developed by Gauthier and colleagues (1997, 1998) (see Chapter 4), and aimed to promote (1) the use of configural processing, (2) attention to the inner features of the face and (3) the use of low spatial frequency information in face processing. Positive reinforcement was provided throughout treatment to increase motivation and attention to the task, and participants were also asked to complete a rule-based tutorial on face processing before each training session, which emphasized strategies for processing faces in a 'normal' manner. Participants completed a maximum of eight training sessions lasting 30–60 minutes during a three-week period. Training was discontinued as soon as the behavioural criterion for expertise was met (i.e., participants became as efficient at recognizing individuals faces as they were at identifying gender), or when eight hours of training was completed. After training, all participants were better at detecting differences in configural information (i.e., second-order relations) than controls with ASD who did not receive training.

Another group has developed a comprehensive package of computerized games, called Let's Face It (Tanaka, Lincoln and Hegg, 2003), aimed at children with ASD. The games are separated into three theoretical domains: those that aim to address the child's ability to (1) attend to faces, (2) recognize facial identity and expressions, and (3) interpret facial cues in a social context. Each game has an original music track, engaging graphics and at least 24 levels of increasing difficulty. Tanaka *et al.* (2010) asked 42 ASD children with face-processing deficits to complete 20 hours of training using the Let's Face It software. Relative to a control group of 37 children who did not receive the training, the experimental group demonstrated reliable improvements in the recognition of both eyes and mouths in part-based and holistic tasks. However, the largest improvement was noted in the part-based rather than holistic task, supporting previous work that suggests these individuals are biased towards a featural processing strategy (e.g., Joseph and Tanaka, 2003) (see Chapter 11). Overall, the authors concluded that these results suggest that children with ASD also exhibit plasticity in their behavioural response to faces, and a short-term intervention programme can produce measurable improvements in face recognition skills in children with this disorder.

15.2. TREATMENT OF EMOTIONAL EXPRESSION IMPAIRMENTS

15.2.1. ASDs

Other studies have attempted to improve the recognition of emotional expressions using a variety of techniques. Some studies have successfully improved emotional expression recognition in ASD using intervention programmes that aim to improve general social skills, rather than just focusing on faces (Bauminger, 2002; Solomon, Goodlin-Jones and Anders, 2004). However, many more researchers have attempted to develop computerized intervention programmes, such as the Let's Face It programme discussed previously.

For example, Silver and Oakes (2001) developed a computerized intervention programme, Emotion Trainer, which provides approximately five hours of training in emotional expression recognition. The authors reported that children and adolescents with ASD who received the training improved in their ability to recognize emotional expressions compared with those in a control group. Bölte *et al.* (2002, 2006) developed another computerized programme, the Frankfurt Test and Training of Facial Affect Recognition (FEFA). They found that the adults with ASD who completed the training improved in their recognition of emotional expressions both within whole faces and within the eye region of a face, when presented in isolation. Golan and Baron-Cohen (2006) also tested the effects of a computerized intervention for emotion recognition, Mind Reading, in adults with high-functioning autism. Although participants who completed the programme improved in their ability to recognize emotional expressions compared with control participants, these benefits did not generalize to novel stimuli that were not presented during training. Finally, Baron-Cohen's group have also created a DVD ('The Transporters') that aims to improve emotional expression recognition in young children with ASD, by superimposing facial stimuli onto vehicles such as trains.

15.2.2. Schizophrenia

Some authors have also attempted to improve emotional expression recognition deficits in individuals with schizophrenia, particularly by directing participants' attention to critical features of facial stimuli. For example, Combs *et al.* (2008) superimposed a visual cue over the eyes and mouths of emotional faces, to direct participants' attention to those particular features. Further, participants were rewarded with 10 cents every time they correctly identified an emotional expression. The authors reported that training improved expression recognition compared with a control group who received the same training without the visual cue, and the effect was maintained at a one-week follow-up assessment. In another study, Russell, Chu and Phillips (2006) demonstrated that emotional expression recognition could be improved in individuals with schizophrenia after just one training session, using a computerized training programme, the Micro-Expression Training Tool. Similar to the technique used by Combs *et al.* (2008), this directs participants' attention to the inner features of the face (i.e., the eyes, nose and mouth). In a follow-up study, the researchers again found that the Micro-Expression Training Tool improved expression recognition in 26 individuals with schizophrenia, and used eye movement analyses to demonstrate that the participants spent more time examining the inner facial features after training (Russell *et al.*, 2008). This finding was maintained at a one-week follow-up.

15.3. A QUICK FIX: INTRANASAL INHALATION OF OXYTOCIN

Very recent research has indicated an alternative manner in which face-processing skills can temporarily be improved: using intranasal inhalation of the hormone oxytocin. Oxytocin is naturally produced and broken down within the human body, and is involved in the regulation of basic social and reproductive behaviours, such as cohabitation, gestation and breastfeeding (Kosfeld *et al.*, 2005). Research with rats has demonstrated that oxytocin is also involved in social but not non-social memory (Huber, Veinante and Stoop, 2005). Recently, synthetic forms of oxytocin have been manufactured that can be nasally inhaled, and these sprays have been used in studies that have examined whether oxytocin can improve face-processing abilities in both healthy and impaired participants.

In the first study to examine the effects of oxytocin on face recognition ability, Rimmele *et al.* (2009) found that healthy undergraduate participants who inhaled an oxytocin nasal spray correctly recalled more newly encoded faces than participants in a placebo condition. However, no difference between the two groups was observed for memory for sculptures and landscapes, supporting the hypothesis that the hormone only improves memory for social stimuli. Some insight into the basis of this improvement in face recognition ability was provided by Guastella, Mitchell and Dadds (2008), who found that intranasal inhalation of oxytocin increases the time spent on the eye region of the face. Andari *et al.* (2010) reported a similar finding in participants with ASD. Although they did not examine whether oxytocin improved the recognition of facial identity, they did observe an increase in the number of fixations to the eye region of the face in their ASD participants. In another paper, Guastella *et al.* (2010) found that oxytocin also improved performance on the Reading the Mind in the Eyes Test (Baron-Cohen *et al.*, 2001) (see Chapter 14) in adolescents with ASD.

There have also been reports that oxytocin can improve emotional expression recognition in schizophrenia. Indeed, oxytocin has been found to decrease amygdala activation when inhaled before the viewing of fearful faces (Kirsch *et al.*, 2005), suggesting this technique might be particularly beneficial in situations where over-activation of the amygdala interferes with the recognition of emotional facial expressions (see Chapter 7). Finally, recent evidence suggests that low oxytocin levels might be related to negative symptoms in schizophrenia, such as social withdrawal and isolation (Keri, Kiss and Kelemen, 2009), and repeated inhalation of oxytocin might relieve such symptoms.

CHAPTER SUMMARY

- Early attempts to improve face recognition in acquired prosopagnosia met with little success (Ellis and Young, 1988; De Haan Young and Newcombe, 1991), although a recent study by Powell *et al.* (2008) suggests that it might be possible to remedy face recognition impairments in this disorder, particularly using a part-based training technique.
- Three investigations have had success in improving face recognition in DP, using different types of intervention strategy (Brunsdon *et al.*, 2006; Schmalzl, Palermo, Green, *et al.*, 2008; DeGutis *et al.*, 2007). These studies provide promising evidence that we can do something to help individuals with this condition.
- Attempts to improve both facial identity and facial expression recognition deficits in ASD using computerized intervention programmes have met with much success (Tanaka, Lincoln and Hegg, 2003; Silver and Oakes, 2001); and similar attention-shaping programmes have also proved successful in treating emotional expression deficits in schizophrenia (Combs *et al.*, 2008; Russell, Chu and Phillips, 2006; Russell *et al.*, 2008).
- Very recent evidence raises the exciting possibility that intranasal inhalation of oxytocin might improve a variety of face-processing deficits on a temporary basis (Andari *et al.*, 2010; Guastella *et al.*, 2010; Kirsch *et al.*, 2005).

FURTHER READING

DeGutis, J. M., Bentin, S., Robertson, L. C., and D'Esposito, M. (2007) 'Functional Plasticity in Ventral Temporal Cortex Following Cognitive Rehabilitation of a Congenital Prosopagnosic', *Journal of Cognitive Neuroscience,* 19, 1790–1802.

Powell, J., Letson, S., Davidoff, J., Valentine, T. and Greenwood, R. (2008) 'Enhancement of Face Recognition Learning in Patients with Brain Injury Using Three Cognitive Training Procedures', *Neuropsychological Rehabilitation,* 18, 182–203.

Rimmele, U., Hediger, K., Heinrichs, M. and Klaver, P. (2009) 'Oxytocin Makes a Face in Memory Familiar', *The Journal of Neuroscience,* 29, 38–42.

Tanaka, J. W., Wolf, J. M., Klaiman, C., Koenig, K., Cockburn, J., *et al.* (2010) 'Using Computerized Games to Teach Face Recognition Skills to Children with Autism Spectrum Disorder: The *Let's Face It!* Program', *Journal of Child Psychology and Psychiatry,* 51, 944–52.

GUIDANCE QUESTIONS

Use the following questions to guide your reading of this chapter and the recommended papers.

1. Evaluate the extent to which face recognition ability can be improved in both acquired and developmental prosopagnosia. How useful are the studies that have been performed up to now in determining whether face recognition can be improved in these disorders?
2. Summarize the techniques that have been used in computerized intervention programmes aimed at both individuals with ASD and those with schizophrenia. Do you think any particular technique is more effective than the others?
3. What is oxytocin and why might it improve an individual's face-processing abilities?

16 Focus Chapter: Integration of Theory and Practice

16.1. THE CLINICAL IMPACT OF DISORDERS OF FACE PROCESSING

It is clear from the discussions throughout this book that face-processing impairments present in a range of acquired, neuropsychiatric and developmental disorders, and are perhaps much more common than originally thought. In recent decades, much research has examined the nature of face-processing impairments in these disorders, and findings have been used to further our theoretical understanding of the human face-processing system.

What has received considerably less attention, however, is the clinical impact of these disorders, and the need to develop effective assessment and treatment tools that are suitable for a range of ages and conditions. Indeed, Chapter 13 discussed the psychosocial impact of face-processing deficits, with a particular focus on developmental prosopagnosia. The chapter described how many prosopagnosics continue to experience frequent failures of recognition despite attempts to use self-developed compensatory strategies, although these experiences do not always have a negative psychosocial impact on individuals with the condition. However, the paper presented by Yardley et al. (2008) raises the issue that prosopagnosia can have a substantial effect on a person's psychosocial well-being. To address this issue, public awareness of the existence of face-processing disorders needs to be dramatically increased, alongside the proportion of research that is being directed to more clinical aspects of face processing.

Perhaps the most concerning issue refers to the suspected number of children who suffer from face-processing deficits. Although we know that many children particularly experience problems in recognizing emotional expressions as a result of a socio-developmental disorder (e.g., autistic spectrum disorders, Turner's syndrome, Williams syndrome), it is largely unknown how many children might suffer from developmental forms of prosopagnosia. However, given recent studies have suggested that developmental prosopagnosia affects around two per cent of the population (Bowles *et al.*, 2009; Kennerknecht *et al.*, 2006), we can translate this figure into an estimation that 700 000 children in the UK alone might suffer from the disorder.

This issue becomes particularly pertinent when we consider the combined effects of several factors. First, the lack of public awareness of prosopagnosia means that most parents and educational professionals are not aware that the disorder exists. This might lead to prosopagnosic children being mis-labelled as 'difficult' or 'lonesome'. Second, although some laboratories are currently developing face-processing tests that are suitable for use in children, no appropriate tools are currently publicly available. This means diagnosis of face recognition deficits in young children has to rely solely on the use of tailor-made tests using personally familiar faces (i.e., those of family and friends), or attempt to interpret scores achieved on adult tests of face-processing ability. Third, in the same context that no treatment regime is currently publicly available for use by adults with prosopagnosia, no such programme is available for children.

Finally, although very few case reports of children with prosopagnosia have been reported, it would not be surprising if the disorder can have just as devastating an impact in children as it can in adults. Indeed, adults have had years to develop and refine compensatory strategies that might help them both to cope with their impairment on a day-to-day basis, and to understand the negativity that others feel when a person fails to recognize them. Further, at least in the UK, children attend schools where uniform is mandatory and rules are strict about personal appearance. Thus, children are forbidden to change characteristics about their appearance that would make them more distinctive, such as hair colour or style, clothing, jewellery or facial piercings. Hence, it is not difficult to imagine that face-processing difficulties might have particularly negative psychosocial consequences in childhood.

16.2. A THEORETICAL BASIS FOR TREATMENT

The above discussion highlights the need for more research that aims to remedy face-processing impairments in both adults and children. Indeed, little existing research has addressed this issue, possibly because most investigations aim to investigate more theoretical aspects of face processing. However, it is not necessarily the case that investigation of intervention strategies has to exist in a theoretical vacuum, and research that targets this issue can simultaneously progress our theoretical understanding of the face-processing system.

Indeed, one does not have to look far from the literature that has been discussed in this book to find a theoretical basis for such investigations. For instance, in Chapter 9, the developmental trajectory of face processing was discussed, including the concept of 'perceptual narrowing' (Nelson, 2001).

Specifically, this theory assumes that we are born with an undefined crude face-processing system that undergoes a process of refinement in response to experience with faces. Indeed, it has been found that very young infants can discriminate between monkey and other-race faces, whereas older infants and adults no longer have this ability (see, for example, Kelly *et al.*, 2007; Pascalis, de Haan and Nelson, 2002). Although these findings suggest some plasticity (the ability of the brain to change as a result of one's experience) in the face-processing system in the first few months of life, Nelson (2001) suggests that early specialization of neural tissue for face processing may lead to a lack of plasticity in later years.

Encouragingly though, other research indicates that the face-processing system may retain some plasticity through to adulthood. For instance, much research has investigated the 'other-race effect', or the finding that we are better at recognizing faces from our own race than those from other races (e.g., Malpass and Kravitz, 1969). One of the explanations for this effect is based on the presumption that the phenomenon reflects the lack of experience the viewer has had with faces from the other race. Indeed, Meissner and Brigham (2001) report a correlation between the level of self-reported contact participants have with another race and the size of the other-race effect as observed in a face recognition task. Further, Elliott, Wills and Goldstein (1973) trained Caucasian students to discriminate between Japanese faces, and reported an improvement in the recognition of both the trained faces and a novel set of stimuli. Hence, evidence suggests that the face-processing system can be tuned to process unfamiliar categories of faces, even in adulthood. It is therefore theoretically possible that intervention might be fruitful even in adults with face-processing deficits.

However, it should be noted that alternative hypotheses have attempted to account for the other-race effect, suggesting some limitations in the implications that can be drawn for the success of adult intervention. Indeed, social categorization accounts of the phenomenon posit that we are simply better at recognizing individuals from our in-group as opposed to our out-group (Bernstein, Young and Hugenberg, 2007). Further, Sangrigoli *et al.* (2005) reported that increased contact with another race does not always eliminate the effect when it begins in adulthood as opposed to childhood.

On the other hand, evidence of an 'own-age bias' in face recognition bolsters the evidence that has emerged from the other-race phenomenon. Indeed, adults are better at recognizing the faces of other adults than those of children or infants, and evidence of this effect has only been noted for upright faces, indicating the involvement of face-selective mechanisms (e.g., Kuefner *et al.*, 2008; Macchi Cassia *et al.*, 2009). Further, it is notable that the same effect has not been observed for pre-school teachers (see, for example, Kuefner *et al.*, 2008), indicating that the face-processing systems of these individuals have adapted in response to the nature of the faces that they most commonly encounter. Interestingly, the size of the composite effect observed in pre-school teachers viewing children's faces is also correlated with the length of their career (De Heering and Rossion, 2008); and Macchi Cassia *et al.* (2009) reported a similar effect in nurses working on a maternity ward.

In sum, the evidence reviewed above demonstrates that theoretical investigations of face processing using unimpaired participants also have practical implications that suggest the face-processing system may remain suitably plastic from birth through to adulthood. Indeed, although there may be some constraints on the system's ability to adapt to new types of facial stimuli (i.e., in duration of exposure), these findings nevertheless provide an encouraging basis for the development of intervention strategies that might be used by individuals with face-processing disorders.

16.3. FUTURE DIRECTIONS

Importantly then, given that theoretical investigations also have practical implications, it must also be the case that practical investigations have implications for theory. Indeed, the development of intervention programmes that aim to improve face processing can speak to important issues about the neural plasticity of the human brain, both in general and about the face-processing system itself. Further, such work also has the potential to shed light on the developmental trajectory of face-processing abilities. To conclude this chapter and indeed the book, the following suggestions for future research may further inform our knowledge about the development of the face-processing system, and its ability to repair or compensate itself across the lifespan.

- Can face-processing deficits in all disorders be treated? Might more success be achieved in the remediation of acquired, developmental or neuropsychiatric deficits?
- Might different intervention strategies be needed for different disorders depending on the aetiological underpinnings of each condition? If so, we need a firm understanding of the causal factors and their interaction in different disorders (see Chapter 12).
- Can all subtypes of prosopagnosia be treated? Can the same intervention programme be used for each subtype? All the intervention attempts reported in the literature so far have investigated individuals with the apperceptive type of prosopagnosia, and some differences in treatment strategy might be needed for associative patients (see Chapter 15). Why did some of these treatment strategies fail?
- Can face-processing deficits be treated at any age? Is there a critical window where treatment is likely to be more successful?

To conclude, further investigation of the relationship between different patterns of cognitive deficits, socio-emotional functioning and genetic and neurological abnormalities will no doubt inform the development of effective treatment strategies that are tailored to particular disorders of face processing. However, the reverse statement is also true, in that assessment of the efficacy of particular intervention techniques has the potential to enhance our knowledge about the nature of disorders of face processing and the theoretical frameworks that are thought to underpin this complex system.

CHAPTER SUMMARY

- Face-processing deficits present in a range of acquired, neuropsychiatric and developmental disorders. Thus, these impairments affect large numbers of adults and children (see Kennerknecht *et al.*, 2006), and can have a profound impact on everyday social and occupational functioning (Yardley *et al.*, 2008).
- Theories about the state of the face-processing system at birth and during infancy suggest an initial period of plasticity that concludes within the first year of life (Kelly *et al.*, 2007; Nelson, 2001).
- However, demonstrations of the other-race (Elliott, Wills and Goldstein, 1973; Meissner and Brigham, 2001) and other-age (Kuefner *et al.*, 2008; Macchi Cassia *et al.*, 2009) effects indicate that the face-processing system may remain plastic throughout life, subject to certain conditions.
- Although few researchers have attempted to improve face-processing deficits, such attempts will not only have important practical benefits, but will also inform our knowledge about particular disorders and the unimpaired face-processing system.

FURTHER READING

Nelson, C. A. (2001) 'The Development and Neural Bases of Face Recognition', *Infant and Child Development,* 10, 3–18.

Sangrigoli, S., Pallier, C., Argenti, A.-M., Ventureyra, V.A.G. and de Schonen, S. (2005) 'Reversibility of the Other-Race Effect in Face Recognition during Childhood', *Psychological Science,* 16, 440–4.

Kuefner, D., Macchi Cassia, V., Picozzi, M. and Bricolo, E. (2008) 'Do all Kids Look Alike? Evidence for an Other-Age Effect in Adults', *Journal of Experimental Psychology: Human Perception and Performance,* 34, 811–17.

Macchi Cassia, V., Picozzi, M., Kuefner, D. and Casati, M. (2009) 'Why Mix-Ups Don't Happen in the Nursery: Evidence for an Experience-Based Interpretation of the Other-Age Effect', *Quarterly Journal of Experimental Psychology,* 62, 1099–107.

De Heering, A. and Rossion, B. (2008) 'Prolonged Visual Experience in Adulthood Modulates Holistic Face Perception', *PLoS One,* 3, e2317.

DISCUSSION QUESTIONS

1. To what extent does evidence from healthy participants indicate that face-processing deficits can be improved?
2. How can intervention studies inform our theoretical knowledge about the healthy face-processing system?
3. What factors might you take into consideration when designing an intervention programme that aims to improve face-processing deficits?

References

Adams, R. B., Gordon, H. L., Baird, A. A., Ambady, N. and Kleck, R. E. (2003) 'Effects of Gaze on Amygdala Sensitivity to Anger and Fear Faces', *Science, 300*, 1536.

Adams, R. B. and Kleck, R. E. (2005) 'Effects of Direct and Averted Gaze on the Perception of Facially Communicated Emotion', *Emotion, 5*, 3–11.

Adolphs, R., Sears, L. and Piven, J. (2001) 'Abnormal Processing of Social Information from Faces in Autism', *Journal of Cognitive Neuroscience, 13*, 232–40.

Aggleton, J. P. (1993) 'The Contribution of the Amygdala to Normal and Abnormal Emotional States', *Trends in Neurosciences, 16*, 328–33.

Aharon, I., Etcoff, N. L., Ariely, D., Chabris, C.F., O'Connor, E. and Breiter, H. C. (2001) 'Beautiful Faces Have Variable Reward Value: fMRI and Behavioral Evidence', *Neuron, 32*, 537–51.

Alexander, M. P., Stuss, D. T. and Benton, D. F. (1979) 'Capgras Syndrome: A Reduplicative Phenomenon', *Neurology, 29*, 334–9.

American Psychiatric Association (2000) *Diagnostic and Statistical Manual of Mental Disorders: DSM-IV-TR* (Washington DC: American Psychiatric Association).

Anand, A., Li, Y. and Wang, Y., (2005) 'Activity and Connectivity of Brain Mood Regulating Circuit in Depression: A Functional Magnetic Resonance Study', *Biological Psychiatry, 57*, 1079–88.

Andari, E., Duhamel., J.-R., Zalla, T., Herbrecht, E., Leboyer, M. and Sirigu, M. (2010) 'Promoting Social Behaviour with Oxytocin in High-Functioning Autism Spectrum Disorders', *Proceedings of the National Academy of Sciences of the USA, 107*, 4389–94.

Ando, S. (2002) 'Luminance-Induced Shift in the Apparent Direction of Gaze', *Perception, 31*, 657–74.

Andrade, L., Caraveo-Anduaga, J. J., Berglund, P., Bijl, R. V., De Graaf, R., Vollebergh, W., *et al.* (2003) 'The Epidemiology of Major Depressive Episodes: Results from the International Consortium of Psychiatric Epidemiology (ICPE) Surveys', *International Journal of Methods in Psychiatric Research, 12*, 165.

Anilkumar, A. P. P., Kumari, V., Mehrotra, R., Aasen, I., Mitterschiffthaler, M. T. and Sharma, T. (2008) 'An fMRI Study of Face Encoding and Recognition in First-Episode Schizophrenia', *Acta Neuropsychiatrica, 20*, 129–38.

Anstis, S. M., Mayhew, J. W. and Morley, T. (1969), 'The Perception of Where a Face or Television 'Portrait' is Looking', *American Journal of Psychology, 82*, 474–89.

Arnott, S. R., Heywood, C. A., Kentridge, R. W. and Goodale, M. A. (2008) 'Voice Recognition and the Posterior Cingulate: An fMRI Study of Prosopagnosia', *Journal of Neuropsychology, 2*, 269–86.

Ashwin, C., Baron-Cohen, S., Wheelwright, S., O'Riordan, M. and Bullmore, E. T. (2007) 'Differential Activation of the Amygdala and the "Social Brain" during Fearful Face-Processing in Asperger Syndrome', *Neuropsychologia, 45*, 2–14.

Assal, G., Favre, C. and Anderes, J. P. (1984) 'Nonrecognition of Farm Animals by a Farmer: Zooagnosia or Prosopagnosia for Animals', *Revue Neurologique, 140*, 580–4.

Assal, F. and Mendez, M. F. (2003) 'Intermetamorphosis in a Patient with Alzheimer's Disease', *The Journal of Neuropsychiatry and Clinical Neurosciences,* 15, 246–7.

Avidan, G., Hasson, U., Malach, R. and Behrmann, M. (2005), 'Detailed Exploration of Face-Related Processing in Congenital Prosopagnosia: 2. Functional Neuroimaging Findings', *Journal of Cognitive Neuroscience,* 17, 1150–67.

Bailey, A. J., Braeutigam, S., Jousmaki, V. and Swithenby, S. J. (2005) 'Abnormal Activation of Face Processing Systems at Early and Intermediate Latency in Individuals with Autism Spectrum Disorder: A Magnetoencephalographic Study', *European Journal of Neuroscience,* 21, 2575–85.

Baranek, G. T. (1999) 'Autism during Infancy: A Retrospective Video Analysis of Sensory Motor and Social Behaviors at 9–12 Months of Age', *Journal of Autism and Developmental Disorders,* 29, 213–24.

Baron-Cohen, S. (1995) 'The Eye Direction Detector (EDD) and the Shared Attention Mechanism (SAM): Two Cases for Evolutionary Psychology', in C. Moore and P. J. Dunham (eds), *Joint Attention: Its Origins and Role in Development* (Hillsdale, NJ: Lawrence Erlbaum Associates Inc), 41–59.

Baron-Cohen, S., Jolliffe, T., Mortimore, C. and Robertson, M. (1997) 'Another Advanced Test of Theory of Mind: Evidence from Very High-Functioning Adults with Autism or Asperger Syndrome', *Journal of Child Psychology and Psychiatry,* 38, 813–22.

Baron-Cohen, S., Ring, H. A., Bullmore, E. T., Wheelwright, S., Ashwin, C. and Williams, S. C. R. (2000) 'The Amygdala Theory of Autism', *Neuroscience and Biobehavioral Reviews,* 24, 355–64.

Baron-Cohen, S., Spitz, A. and Cross, P. (1993) 'Do Children with Autism Recognize Surprise? A Research Note', *Cognition and Emotion,* 7, 507.

Baron-Cohen, S., Wheelwright, S., Hill, J., Raste, Y. and Plumb, I. (2001) 'The "Reading the Mind in the Eyes" Test Revised Version: A Study with Normal Adults, and Adults with Asperger Syndrome or High-Functioning Autism', *Journal of Child Psychology and Psychiatry,* 42, 241–52.

Barton, J. J. S. (2003) 'Disorders of Face Perception and Recognition', *Neurologic Clinics,* 21, 521–48.

Barton, J. J. S. (2008) 'Structure and Function in Acquired Prosopagnosia: Lessons from a Series of 10 Patients with Brain Damage', *Journal of Neuropsychology,* 2197–225.

Barton, J. J. S., Cherkasova, M. V., Hefter, R., Cox, T. A., O'Connor, M. and Manoach, D. S. (2004) 'Are Patients with Social Developmental Disorders Prosopagnosic? Perceptual Heterogeneity in the Asperger and Socio-Emotional Processing Disorders', *Brain,* 127, 1706–16.

Barton, J. J. S., Cherkasova, M. and O'Connor, M. (2001) 'Covert Recognition in Acquired and Developmental Prosopagnosia', *Neurology,* 57, 1161–8.

Barton, J. J. S., Cherkasova, M., Press, D. Z., Intriligator, J. and O'Connor, M. (2004) 'Perceptual Function in Prosopagnosia', *Perception,* 33, 939–56.

Barton, J. J., Press, D. Z., Keenan, J. P. and O'Connor, M. (2002) 'Lesions of the Fusiform Face Area Impair Perception of Facial Configuration in Prosopagnosia', *Neurology,* 58, 71–8.

Bate, S., Haslam, S. and Hodgson, T. L. (2009) 'Angry Faces are Special too: Evidence from the Visual Scanpath', *Neuropsychology,* 23, 658–67.

Bate, S., Haslam, C., Jansari, A. and Hodgson, T. L. (2009) 'Covert Face Recognition Relies on Affective Valence in Congenital Prosopagnosia', *Cognitive Neuropsychology,* 26, 391–411.

Bate, S., Haslam, C., Tree, J. J. and Hodgson, T. L. (2008) 'Evidence of an Eye Movement-Based Memory Effect in Congenital Prosopagnosia', *Cortex,* 44, 806–19.

Bate, S., Parris, B., Haslam, C. and Kay, J. (2010) 'Socio-Emotional Functioning and Face Recognition Ability in the Normal Population', *Personality and Individual Differences,* 48, 239–42.

Batki, A., Baron-Cohen, S., Wheelwright, S., Connellan, J. and Ahluwalia, J. (2000) 'Is There an Innate Gaze Module? Evidence from Human Neonates', *Infant Behavior and Development*, 23, 223–9.

Baudouin, J.-Y., Gilbert, D., Sansone, S. and Tiberghien, G. (2000) 'When the Smile is a Cue to Familiarity', *Memory*, 8, 285–92.

Baudouin, J.-Y. and Humphreys, G. W. (2006) 'Compensatory Strategies in Processing Facial Emotions: Evidence from Prosopagnosia', *Neuropsychologia*, 44, 1361–9.

Baudouin, J.-Y., Vernet, M. and Franck, N. (2008) 'Second-Order Facial Information Processing in Schizophrenia', *Neuropsychology*, 22, 313–20.

Bauer, R. M. (1984) 'Autonomic Recognition of Names and Faces in Prosopagnosia: A Neuropsychological Application of the Guilty Knowledge Test', *Neuropsychologia*, 22, 457–69.

Baum, K. M. and Walker, E. F. (1995) 'Childhood Behavioral Precursors of Adult Symptom Dimensions in Schizophrenia', *Schizophrenia Research*, 16, 111–20.

Bauminger, N. (2002) 'The Facilitation of Social-Emotional Understanding and Social Interaction in High-Functioning Children with Autism: Intervention Outcomes', *Journal of Autism and Developmental Disorders*, 32, 283–98.

Bayliss, A. P., di Pellegrino, G. and Tipper, S. P. (2004) 'Orienting of Attention via Observed Eye Gaze is Head-Centred', *Cognition*, 94, B1-B10.

Bayliss, A. P., Frischen, A., Fenske, M. J. and Tipper, S. P. (2007) 'Affective Evaluations of Objects are Influenced by Observed Gaze Direction and Emotional Expression', *Cognition*, 104, 644–53.

Bayliss, A. P., Paul, M. A., Cannon, P. R. and Tipper, S. P. (2006) 'Gaze Cueing and Affective Judgments of Objects: I Like What You Look at', *Psychonomic Bulletin and Review*, 13, 1061–6.

Bayliss, A. P. and Tipper, S. P. (2005) 'Gaze and Arrow Cueing of Attention Reveals Individual Differences along the Autism Spectrum as a Function of Target Context', *British Journal of Psychology*, 96, 95–114.

Beck, A. T. (1976) *Cognitive Therapy and the Emotional Disorders* (New York: International Universities Press).

Behrmann, M., Avidan, G., Gao, F. and Black. S. (2007) 'Structural Imaging Reveals Anatomical Alterations in Inferotemporal Cortex in Congenital Prosopagnosia', *Cerebral Cortex*, 17, 2354–63.

Behrmann, M., Avidan, G., Marotta, J. J. and Kimchi, R. (2005) 'Detailed Exploration of Face-Related Processing in Congenital Prosopagnosia: 1. Behavioral Findings', *Journal of Cognitive Neuroscience*, 8, 551–65.

Behrmann, M., Marotta, J., Gauthier, I., Tarr, M. J. and McKeeff, T. J. (2005) 'Behavioral Change and its Neural Correlates in Visual Agnosia after Expertise Training', *Journal of Cognitive Neuroscience*, 17, 554–68.

Behrmann, M., Thomas, C. and Humphreys, K. (2006) 'Seeing it Differently: Visual Processing in Autism', *Trends in Cognitive Sciences*, 10, 258–64.

Beidel, D. C., Turner, S. M. and Morris, T. L. (1999) 'Psychopathology of Childhood Social Phobia', *Journal of the American Academy of Child and Adolescent Psychiatry*, 38, 643–50.

Bellugi, U., Sabo, H. and Vaid, J. (1988) 'Spatial Deficits in Children with Williams Syndrome', in J. Stiles-Davis, M. Kritchevsky and U. Bellugi (eds), *Spatial Cognition: Brain Bases and Development* (Hillsdale, NJ: Lawrence Erlbaum Associates), 273–98.

Bellugi, U., Wang, P. P. and Jernigan, T. L. (1994) 'Williams Syndrome: An Unusual Neuropsychological Profile', in S. H. Broman and J. Grafman (eds), *Atypical Cognitive Deficits in Developmental Disorders: Implications for Brain Function* (Hillsdale: NJ: Lawrence Erlbaum Associates, Inc), 23–56.

Benson, P. J. and Perrett, D. I. (1991) Perception and recognition of photographic quality facial caricatures: Implication for the recognition of natural images. *European Journal of Cognitive Psychology,* 3, 105–135.

Benson, P. and Perrett, D. I. (1994) Visual processing of facial distinctiveness. *Perception,* 23, 75–93.

Bentin, S., Allison, T., Puce, A., Perez, E. and McCarthy, G. (1996) 'Electrophysiological Studies of Face Perception in Humans', *Journal of Cognitive Neuroscience,* 8, 551–65.

Bentin, S., DeGutis, J. M., D'Esposito, M. and Robertson, L. C. (2007) 'Too Many Trees to See the Forest: Performance, ERP and fMRI Manifestations of Integrative Congenital Prosopagnosia', *Journal of Cognitive Neuroscience,* 19, 132–46.

Bentin, S. and Deouell, L. Y. (2000) 'Structural Encoding and Identification in Face Processing: ERP Evidence for Separate Mechanisms', *Cognitive Neuropsychology,* 17, 35–54.

Bentin, S., Deouell, L. Y. and Soroker, N. (1999) 'Selective Visual Streaming in Face Recognition: Evidence from Developmental Prosopagnosia', *NeuroReport,* 10, 823–7.

Benton, A. L. and Van Allen, M. W. (1968) 'Impairment in Facial Recognition in Patients with Cerebral Disease', *Cortex,* 4, 344–58.

Bernstein, M. J., Young, S. G. and Hugenberg, K. (2007) 'The Cross-Category Effect: Mere Social Categorization is Sufficient to Elicit an Own-Group Bias in Face Recognition', *Psychological Science,* 18, 706–12.

Bindemann, M., Brown, C., Koyas, T. and Russ, A. (2012) 'Individual Differences in Face Identification Postdict Eyewitness Accuracy', *Applied Research in Memory and Cognition,* 1, 96–103.

Bindemann, M., Burton, A. M. and Langton, S. R. H. (2008) 'How Do Eye-Gaze and Facial Expression Interact?', *Visual Cognition,* 16, 708–33.

Birmingham, E., Bischof, W. F. and Kingstone, A. (2009) 'Get Real! Resolving the Debate about Equivalent Social Stimuli', *Visual Cognition,* 17, 904–24.

Bishop, D. V. M. (1997) 'Cognitive Neuropsychology and Developmental Disorders: Uncomfortable Bedfellows', *The Quarterly Journal of Experimental Psychology A: Human Experimental Psychology,* 50, 899–923.

Blair, R., Frith, U., Smith, N., Abell, F. and Cipolotti, L. (2002) 'Fractionation of Visual Memory: Agency Detection and its Impairment in Autism', *Neuropsychologia,* 40, 108–18.

Bobes, M. A., Lopera, F., Garcia, M., Déaz-Comas, L., Galan, L. and Valdes-Sosa, M. (2003) 'Covert Matching of Unfamiliar Faces in a Case of Prosopagnosia: An ERP Study', *Cortex,* 39, 41–56.

Bobes, M. A., Martin, M., Olivares, E. and Valdes-Sosa, M. (2000) 'Different Scalp Topography of Brain Potentials Related to Expression and Identity Matching of Faces', *Cognitive Brain Research,* 9, 249–60.

Bodamer, J. (1947) Die Prosop-Agnosie (Die Agnosie des Physiognomieerkennens) *Archiv für Psychiatrie und Nervenkrankheiten,* 179, 6–54.

Boeri, R. and Salmaggi, A. (1994) 'Prosopagnosia: Commentary', *Current Opinion in Neurology,* 7, 61–4.

Bölte, S., Feineis-Matthews, S., Leber, S., Dierks, T., Hubl, D. and Poustka, F. (2002) 'The Development and Evaluation of a Computer-Based Program to Test and to Teach the Recognition of Facial Affect', *International Journal of Circumpolar Health,* 61, 61–8.

Bölte, S., Hubl, D., Feineis-Matthews, S., Prvulovic, D., Dierks, T. and Poustka, F. (2006) 'Facial Affect Recognition Training in Autism: Can We Animate the Fusiform Gyrus?', *Behavioral Neuroscience,* 120, 211–16.

Bonner, L. and Burton, A. M. (2004) '7–11-Year-Old Children Show an Advantage for Matching and Recognizing the Internal Features of Familiar Faces: Evidence against a Developmental Shift', *Quarterly Journal of Experimental Psychology*, 57A, 1019–29.

Bookheimer, S., Wang, A., Scott, A., Sigman, M. and Dapretto, M. (2008) 'Frontal Contributions to Face Processing Differences in Autism: Evidence from fMRI of Inverted Face Processing', *Journal of the International Neuropsychological Society*, 14, 922–32.

Boucher, J. and Lewis, V. (1992) 'Unfamiliar Face Recognition in Relatively Able Autistic Children', *Journal of Child Psychology and Psychiatry*, 33, 843–59.

Boucher, J., Lewis, V. and Collis, G. (1998) 'Familiar Face and Voice Matching and Recognition in Children with Autism', *Journal of Child Psychology and Psychiatry*, 39, 171–81.

Boucher, J. and Warrington, E. K. (1976) 'Memory Deficits in Early Infantile Autism: Some Similarities to the Amnesic Syndrome', *British Journal of Psychology*, 67, 73–87.

Boutsen, L. and Humphreys, G. W. (2002) 'Face Context Interferes with Local Part Processing in a Prosopagnosic Patient', *Neuropsychologia*, 40, 2305–13.

Bouvier, S. E. and Engel, S. A. (2006) 'Behavioral Deficits and Cortical Damage Loci in Cerebral Achromatopsia', *Cerberal Cortex*, 16, 183–91.

Bowles, D., McKone, E., Dawel, A., Duchaine, B., Schmalzl, L., Palermo, R., *et al.* (2009) 'Diagnosing Prosopagnosia: Effects of Aging and Participant-Stimulus Ethnic Match on the Cambridge Face Memory Test and the Cambridge Face Perception Test', *Cognitive Neuropsychology*, 26, 423–455.

Bozikas, V. P., Kosmidis, M. H., Anezoulaki, D., Giannakou, M. and Karavatos, A. (2004) 'Relationship of Affect Recognition with Psychopathology and Cognitive Performance in Schizophrenia', *Journal of the International Neuropsychological Society*, 10, 549–58.

Breen, N., Caine, D. and Coltheart, M. (2000) 'Models of Face Recognition and Delusional Misidentification: A Critical Review', *Cognitive Neuropsychology*, 17, 55–71.

Breen, N., Coltheart, M. and Caine, D. (2001) 'A Two-Way Window on Face Recognition', *Trends in Cognitive Sciences*, 5, 234–235.

Bruce, V. (1986) 'Influences of Familiarity on the Processing of Faces', *Perception*, 15, 387–97.

Bruce, V. and Valentine, T. (1985) 'Identity Priming in the Recognition of Familiar Faces', *British Journal of Psychology*, 76, 363–83.

Bruce, V. and Valentine, T. (1986) 'Semantic Priming of Familiar Faces', *Quarterly Journal of Experimental Psychology*, 38A, 125–50.

Bruce, V., Valentine, T. and Baddeley, A. (1987) 'The Basis of the Three-Quarters View Advantage in Face Recognition', *Applied Cognitive Psychology*, 1, 109–20.

Bruce, V. and Young, A. (1986) 'Understanding Face Recognition', *British Journal of Psychology*, 77, 305–27.

Brune, M. (2005) 'Emotion Recognition, "Theory of Mind", and Social Behavior in Schizophrenia', *Psychiatry Research*, 133, 135–47.

Brunsdon, R., Coltheart, M., Nickels, L. and Joy, P. (2006) 'Developmental Prosopagnosia: A Case Analysis and Treatment Study', *Cognitive Neuropsychology*, 23, 822–40.

Bruyer, R., Laterre, C., Seron, X., Feyereisen, P., Strypstein, E., Pierrard, E., *et al.* (1983) 'A Case of Prosopagnosia with Some Preserved Covert Remembrance of Familiar Faces', *Brain and Cognition*, 2, 257–84.

Buchanan, L., Pavlovic, J. and Rovet, J. (1998. 'The Contribution of Visuospatial Working Memory to Impairments in Facial Processing and Arithmetic in Turner Syndrome', *Brain and Cognition*, 37, 72–5.

Bukach, C. M., Gauthier, I. and Tarr, M. J. (2006) 'Beyond Faces and Modularity: The Power of an Expertise Framework', *Trends in Cognitive Science*, 10, 159–66.

Burton, A. M., Bruce, V. and Johnston, R. A. (1990) 'Understanding Face Recognition with an Interactive Activation Model', *British Journal of Psychology,* 81, 361–80.

Burton, A. M., Jenkins, R., Hancock, P. B. J. and White, D. (2005) Robust representations for face recognition. *Cognitive Psychology,* 51, 256–284.

Burton, A. M., White, D. and McNeil, A. (2010) 'The Glasgow Face Matching Test', *Behavior Research Methods,* 42, 286–91.

Burton, A. M., Young, A. W., Bruce, V., Johnston, R. A. and Ellis, A. W. (1991) 'Understanding Covert Recognition', *Cognition,* 39, 129–66.

Busey, T. A. and Vanderkolk, J. R. (2005) 'Behavioral and Electrophysiological Evidence for Configural Processing in Fingerprint Experts', *Vision Research,* 45, 431–48.

Bushnell, I. W. R. (2001) 'Mother's Face Recognition in Newborn Infants: Learning and Memory', *Infant and Child Development,* 10, 67–74.

Cacioppo, J. T. and Gardner, W. L. (1999) 'Emotions', *Annual Review of Psychology,* 50, 191–214.

Caharel, S., Courtay, N., Bernard, C., Lalonde, R. and Rebai, M. (2005) 'Familiarity and Emotional Expression Influence an Early Stage of Face Processing: An Electrophysiological Study', *Brain and Cognition,* 59, 96–100.

Caldara, R., Schyns, P., Mayer, E., Smith, M. Z., Gosselin, F. and Rossion, B. (2005) 'Does Prosopagnosia Take the Eyes Out of Face Representations? Evidence for a Defect in Representing Diagnostic Facial Information Following Brain Damage', *Journal of Cognitive Neuroscience,* 17, 1652–66.

Calder, A. J., Lawrence, A. D., Keane, J., Scott, S. K., Owen, A. M., Christoffels, I. and Young, A. W. (2002) 'Reading the Mind from Eye Gaze', *Neuropsychologia,* 40, 1129–38.

Calder, A. J. and Young, A. W. (2005) 'Understanding Facial Identity and Facial Expression Recognition', *Nature Neuroscience Reviews,* 6, 641–53.

Calder, A. J., Young, A. W., Rowland, D., Perrett, D. I., Hodges, J. R. and Etcoff, N. L. (1996) 'Facial Emotion Recognition after Bilateral Amygdala Damage: Differentially Severe Impairment of Fear', *Cognitive Neuropsychology,* 13, 699–745.

Caldera, R., Seghier, M. L., Rossion, B., Lazeyras, F., Michel, C. and Havert, C. A. (2006) 'The Fusiform Face Area is Tuned for Curvilinear Patterns with More High-Contrasted Elements in the Upper Part', *NeuroImage,* 31, 313–19.

Campbell, R., Brooks, B., de Haan, E. and Roberts, T. (1996) 'Dissociating Face Processing Skills: Decisions about Lip-Read Speech, Expression, and Identity', *Quarterly Journal of Experimental Psychology, Section A,* 49, 295–314.

Campbell, R., Landis, T. and Regard, M. (1986) Face recognition and lipreading: A neurological dissociation. *Brain,* 109, 509–521.

Campbell, R., Walker, J. and Baron-Cohen, S. (1995) 'The Development of Differential Use of Inner and Outer Face Features in Familiar Face Identification', *Journal of Experimental Child Psychology,* 59, 196–210.

Camras, L. A., Grow, J. G. and Ribordy, S. C. (1983) 'Recognition of Emotional Expression by Abused Children', *Journal of Clinical Child Psychology,* 12, 325–8.

Capgras, J. and Reboul-Lachaux, J. (1923) 'L'illusion des "sosies" dans un delire systematize chronique', *Bulletin de la Société Clinique de Médicine Mentale,* 11, 6–16.

Cassia, V. M., Turati, C. and Simion, F. (2004) 'Can a Nonspecific Bias toward Top-Heavy Patterns Explain Newborns' Face Preference?', *Psychological Science,* 15, 379–83.

Chambon, V., Baudouin, J.-Y. and Franck, N. (2006) 'The Role of Configural Information in Facial Emotion Recognition in Schizophrenia', *Neuropsychologia,* 44, 2437–44.

Chan, D., Anderson, V., Pijnenburg, Y., Whitwell, J., Barnes, J., Scahill, R., *et al.* (2009) 'The Clinical Profile of Right Temporal Lobe Atrophy', *Brain,* 132, 1287–98.

Chapman, L. J. and Chapman, J. P. (1973) *Disordered Thought in Schizophrenia* (New York: Appleton-Century-Crofts).

Charcot, J. M. (1883) 'Un cas de suppression brusque et isolée de la vision mentale des signes et des objets (forms et couleurs)', *Le Progrès Médical*, 11, 568–71.

Chen, C. H., Suckling, J., Ooi, C., Fu, C. H., Williams, S. C., Walsh, N. D., *et al.* (2008) 'Functional Coupling of the Amygdala in Depressed Patients Treated with Antidepressant Medication', *Neuropsychopharmacology*, 33, 1909–18.

Chen, Y., Norton, D., McBain, R., Ongur, D. and Heckers, S. (2009) 'Visual and Cognitive Processing of Face Information in Schizophrenia: Detection, Discrimination and Working Memory', *Schizophrenia Research*, 107, 92–8.

Christodoulou, G. N. (1978) 'Syndrome of Selective Doubles', *American Journal of Psychiatry*, 135, 249–51.

Cline, M. G. (1967) 'The Perception of where a Person is Looking', *American Journal of Psychology*, 80, 41–50.

Collishaw, S. M. and Hole, G. J. (2000) Featural and configurational processes in the recognition of faces of different familiarity. *Perception*, 29, 893–909.

Coltheart, M., Langdon, R. and McKay, R. (2007) 'Schizophrenia and Monothematic Delusions', *Schizophrenia Bulletin*, 33, 642–7.

Combs, D. R. and Gouvier, W. D. (2004) 'The Role of Attention in Affect Perception: An Examination of Mirsky's Four Factor Model of Attention in Chronic Schizophrenia', *Schizophrenia Bulletin*, 30, 727–38.

Combs, D. R., Tosheva, A., Penn, D. L., Basso, M. R., Wanner, J. L. and Laib, K. (2008) 'Attentional-Shaping as a Means to Improve Emotion Perception Deficits in Schizophrenia', *Schizophrenia Research*, 105, 68–77.

Cooney, R. E., Atlas, L. Y., Joormann, J., Eugène, F. and Gotlib, I. H. (2006) 'Amygdala Activation in the Processing of Neutral Faces in Social Anxiety Disorder: Is Neutral Really Neutral?', *Psychiatry Research*, 148, 55–9.

Costafreda, S. G., Khanna, A., Mourao-Miranda, J. and Fu, C. H. Y. (2009) 'Neural Correlates of Sad Faces Predicts Clinical Remission to Cognitive Behavioural Therapy in Depression', *NeuroReport*, 20, 637–41.

Courbon, P. and Fail, G. (1927) 'Syndrome "d'illusion de Fregoli" et schizophrenie', *Bulletin de la Société Clinique de Médicine Mentale*, 15, 121–5.

Courbon, P. and Tusques, J., (1932) 'Illusions d'intermetamorphose et de la charme', *Annales Médico-Psycholiques*, 901, 401–6.

Cox, D., Meyers, E. and Sinha, P. (2004) 'Contextually Evoked Object-Specific Responses in Human Ventral Cortex'; *Science*, 303, 115–17.

Crane, J. and Milner, B. (2002) 'Do I Know You? Face Perception and Memory in Patients with Selective Amygdalo-Hippocampectomy', *Neuropsychologia*, 40, 530–8.

Critchley, H. D., Daly, E. M., Bullmore, E. T., Williams, S. C., Van Amelsvoort, T., Robertson, D. M., *et al.* (2000) 'The Functional Neuroanatomy of Social Behaviour: Changes in Cerebral Blood Flow when People with Autistic Disorder Process Facial Expressions', *Brain*, 123, 2203–12.

Critchley, H., Daly, E., Phillips, M., Brammer, M., Bullmore, E., Williams, S., *et al.* (2000) 'Explicit and Implicit Neural Mechanisms for Processing of Social Information from Facial Expressions: A Functional Magnetic Resonance Imaging Study', *Human Brain Mapping*, 9, 93–105.

D'Argembeau, A. and Van der Linden, M. (2007) 'Facial Expressions of Emotion Influence Memory for Facial Identity in an Automatic Way', *Emotion*, 7, 507–15.

Da Costa, A. P., Leigh, A. E., Man, M. S. and Kendrick, K. M. (2004) 'Face Pictures Reduce Behavioural, Autonomic, Endocrine and Neural Indices of Stress and Fear in Sheep', *Proceedings of the Royal Society B: Biological Sciences*, 271, 2077–84.

Dalton, K. M., Nacewicz, B. M., Johnstone, T., Schaefer, H. S., Gernsbacher, M. A., Goldsmith, H. H., *et al.* (2005) 'Gaze Fixation and the Neural Circuitry of Face Processing in Autism', *Nature Neuroscience,* 8, 519–26.

Damasio, A. R., Damasio, H. and Van Hoesen, G. W. (1982) 'Prosopagnosia: Anatomic Basis and Behavioural Mechanisms', *Neurology,* 32, 331–41.

Darling, S., Martin, D., Hellmann, J. H. and Memon, A. (2009) 'Some Witnesses are Better than Others', *Personality and Individual Differences,* 47, 369–73.

Davidoff, J. and Landis, T. (1990) 'Recognition of Unfamiliar Faces in Prosopagnosia', *Neuropsychologia,* 28, 1143–61.

Dawson, G., Webb, S. J., Carver, L., Panagiotides, H. and McPartland, J. (2004) 'Young Children with Autism Show Atypical Brain Responses to Fearful Versus Neutral Facial Expressions of Emotion', *Developmental Science,* 7, 340–59.

Dawson, G., Webb, S. J. and McPartl and, J. (2005) 'Understanding the Nature of Face Processing Impairments in Autism: Insights from Behavioural and Electrophysiological Studies', *Developmental Neuropsychology,* 27, 403–24.

De Gelder, B., Bachoud-Lévi, A.-C. and Degos, J.-D. (1998) 'Inversion Superiority in Visual Agnosia May Be Common to a Variety of Orientation Polarised Objects Besides Faces', *Vision Research,* 38, 2855–61.

De Gelder, B., Frissen, I., Barton, J. and Hadjikhani, N. (2003) 'A Modulatory Role for Facial Expressions in Prosopagnosia', *Proceedings of the National Academy of Sciences of the USA,* 100, 13105–13110.

De Gelder, B. and Rouw, R. (2000a) 'Configural Face Processes in Acquired and Developmental Prosopagnosia: Evidence for Two Separate Face Systems?', *NeuroReport,* 11, 3145–50.

De Gelder, B. and Rouw, R. (2000b) Paradoxical configuration effects for faces and objects in prosopagnosia. *Neuropsychologia, 38,* 1271–1279.

De Haan, E. H. (1999) 'A Familial Factor in the Development of Face Processing Deficits', *Journal of Clinical and Experimental Neuropsychology,* 21, 312–15.

De Haan, E. H., Bauer, R. M. and Greve, K. W. (1992) 'Behavioural and Physiological Evidence for Covert Face Recognition in a Prosopagnosic Patient', *Cortex,* 28, 77–95.

De Haan, E. H. and Campbell, R. (1991) 'A Fifteen Year Follow-Up of a Case of Developmental Prosopagnosia', *Cortex,* 27, 489–509.

De Haan, E. H., Young, A. W. and Newcombe, F. (1987) 'Face Recognition without Awareness', *Cognitive Neuropsychology,* 4, 385–415.

De Haan, E. H. F., Young, A. W. and Newcombe, F. (1991) 'Covert and Overt Recognition in Prosopagnosia', *Brain,* 114, 2575–91.

De Heering, A., Houthuys, S. and Rossion, B. (2007) 'Holistic Face Processing is Mature at 4 Years of Age: Evidence from the Composite Face Effect', *Journal of Experimental Child Psychology,* 96, 57–70.

De Heering, A. and Rossion, B. (2008) 'Prolonged Visual Experience in Adulthood Modulates Holistic Face Perception', *PLOS One,* 3, e2317.

De Renzi, E., Faglioni, P., Grossi, D. and Nichelli, P. (1991) 'Apperceptive and Associative Forms of Prosopagnosia', *Cortex,* 27, 213–21.

De Renzi, E., Perani, D., Carlesimo, G. A., Silveri, M. C. and Fazio, F. (1994) 'Prosopagnosia can be Associated with Damage Confined to the Right Hemisphere – an MRI and PET Study and a Review of the Literature', *Neuropsychologia,* 8, 893–902.

De Renzi, E., Zambolin, A. and Crisi, G. (1987) 'The pattern of Neuropsychological Impairment Associated with Left Posterior Cerebral Artery Infarction', *Brain,* 110, 1099–16.

De Schonen, S. and Mathivet, E. (1989) 'First Come First Served: A Scenario about Development of Hemispheric Specialization in Face Recognition During Infancy', *European Bulletin of Cognitive Psychology (CPC),* 9, 3–44.

De Wit, T. C. J., Falck-Ytter, T. and von Hofsten, C. (2008) 'Young Children with Autism Spectrum Disorder Look Differently at Positive versus Negative Emotional Faces', *Research in Autism Spectrum Disorders*, 2, 651–9.

Deeley, Q., Daly, E. M., Surguladze, S., Page, L., Toal, F., Robertson, D., *et al.* (2007) 'An Event Related Functional Magnetic Resonance Imaging Study of Facial Emotion Processing in Asperger Syndrome', *Biological Psychiatry*, 62, 207–17.

DeGutis, J. M., Bentin, S., Robertson, L. C. and D'Esposito, M. (2007) 'Functional Plasticity in Ventral Temporal Cortex Following Cognitive Rehabilitation of a Congenital Prosopagnosic', *Journal of Cognitive Neuroscience*, 19, 1790–1802.

Delvenne, J.-F., Seron, X., Coyette, F. and Rossion, B. (2004) 'Evidence for Perceptual Deficits in Associative Visual (prosop)Agnosia: A Single-Case Study', *Neuropsychologia*, 42, 597–612.

Dennett, H. W., McKone, E., Tavashmi, R., Hall, A., Pidcock, M., Edwards, M., *et al.* (2012) 'The Cambridge Car Memory Test: A Task Matched in Format to the Cambridge Face Memory Test, with Norms, Reliability, Sex Differences, Dissociations from Face Memory, and Expertise Effects', *Behavior Research Methods*, 44, 587–605.

Deruelle, C., Mancini, J., Livet, M., Casse-Perrot, C. and de Schonen, S. (1999) 'Configural and Local Processing of Faces in Children with Williams Syndrome', *Brain and Cognition*, 41, 276–98.

Dereulle, C., Rondan, C., Gepner, B. and Tardif, C. (2004) 'Spatial Frequency and Face Processing in Children with Autism and Asperger Syndrome', *Journal of Autism and Developmental Disorders*, 34, 199–210.

Dereulle, C., Rondan, C., Mancini, J. and Livet, M. (2003) 'Exploring Face Processing in Williams Syndrome', *Cognitie, Creier, Comportanent*, 7, 157–71.

Desimone, R., Albright, T. D., Gross, C. G. and Bruce, C. (1984) 'Stimulus-Selective Properties of Inferior Temporal Neurons in the Macaque', *Journal of Neuroscience*, 4, 2051–62.

Diamond, R. and Carey, S. (1977) 'Developmental Changes in the Representation of Faces', *Journal of Experimental Child Psychology*, 23, 1–22.

Diamond, R. and Carey, S. (1986) 'Why Faces are and are Not Special: An Effect of Expertise', *Journal of Experimental Psychology: General*, 115, 107–17.

Dion, K., Berscheid, E. and Walster, E. (1972) 'What is Beautiful is Good', *Journal of Personality and Social Psychology*, 24, 285–90.

Dobel, C., Geiger, L., Bruchmann, M., Putsche, C., Schweinberger, S. R. and Junghofer, M. (2008) 'On the Interplay between Familiarity and Emotional Expression in Face Perception', *Psychological Research*, 72, 580–6.

Doherty-Sneddon, G., Riby, D. M., Calderwood, L. and Ainswirth, L. (2009) 'Stuck on You: Face-to-Face Arousal and Gaze Aversion in Williams Syndrome', *Cognitive Neuropsychiatry*, 14, 1–14.

Dohn, H. and Crews, E., (1986) 'Capgras Syndrome: A Literature Review and Case Series', *Hillside Journal of Clinical Psychiatry*, 8, 56–74.

Downing, P. E. (2007) 'Face Perception: Broken into Parts', *Current Biology*, 17, R888-R889.

Driver, J., Davis, G., Ricciardelli, P., Kidd, P., Maxwell, E. and Baron-Cohen, S. (1999) 'Gaze Perception Triggers Reflexive Visuospatial Orienting', *Visual Cognition*, 6, 509–40.

Duchaine, B. (2000) 'Developmental Prosopagnosia with Normal Configural Processing', *NeuroReport*, 11, 79–83.

Duchaine, B. (2008) 'Editorial Comment on "Prevalence of Hereditary Prosopagnosia (HPA) in Hong Kong Chinese Population"', *American Journal of Medical Genetics Part A*, 140A, 2860–2.

Duchaine, B. C., Dingle, K., Butterworth, E. and Nakayama, K. (2004) 'Normal Greeble Learning in a Severe Case of Developmental Prosopagnosia', *Neuron*, 43, 469–73.

Duchaine, B., Germine, L. and Nakayama, K. (2007) 'Family Resemblance: Ten Family Members with Prosopagnosia and Within-Class Object Agnosia', *Cognitive Neuropsychology*, 24, 419–30.

Duchaine, B., Murray, H., Turner, M., White, S. and Garrido, L. (2010) 'Normal Social Cognition in Developmental Prosopagnosia', *Cognitive Neuropsychology*, 25, 1–15.

Duchaine, B. and Nakayama, K. (2004) 'Developmental Prosopagnosia and the Benton Facial Recognition Test', *Neurology*, 62, 1219–20.

Duchaine, B. C. and Nakayama, K. (2005) 'Dissociations of Face and Object Recognition in Developmental Prosopagnosia', *Journal of Cognitive Neuroscience*, 17, 249–61.

Duchaine, B. C. and Nakayama, K. (2006a) 'Developmental Prosopagnosia: A Window to Content-Specific Face Processing', *Current Opinion in Neurobiology*, 16, 166–73.

Duchaine, B. and Nakayama, K. (2006b) 'The Cambridge Face Memory Test: Results for Neurologically Intact Individuals and an Investigation of its Validity Using Inverted Face Stimuli and Prosopagnosic Subjects', *Neuropsychologia*, 44, 576–85.

Duchaine, B., Nieminen-von Wendt, T., New, J. and Kulomaki, T. (2003) 'Dissociation of Visual Recognition in A Developmental Prosopagnosic: Evidence for Separable Developmental Processes', *Neurocase*, 9, 380–9.

Duchaine, B., Parker, H. and Nakayama, K. (2003) 'Normal Emotion Recognition in a Prosopagnosic', *Perception*, 32, 827–38.

Duchaine, B. C. and Weidenfeld, A. (2003) 'An Evaluation of Two Commonly Used Tests of Unfamiliar Face Recognition', *Neuropsychologia*, 41, 713–20.

Duchaine, B., Yovel, G., Butterworth, E. and Nakayama, K. (2006) 'Prosopagnosia as an Impairment to Face-Specific Mechanisms: Elimination of the Alternative Hypothesis in A Developmental Case', *Cognitive Neuropsychology*, 23, 714–47.

Duchaine, B., Yovel, G. and Nakayama, K. (2007) 'No Global Processing Deficit in the Navon Task in 14 Developmental Prosopagnosics'., *Social, Cognitive and Affective Neuroscience*, 2, 104–13.

Edwards, J., Jackson, H. J. and Pattison, P. E. (2002) 'Emotion Recognition via Facial Expression and Affective Prosody in Schizophrenia: A Methodological Review', *Clinical Psychology Review*, 22, 789–832.

Edwards, J., Pattison, P. E., Jackson, H. J. and Wales, R. J. (2001) 'Facial Affect and Affective Prosody Recognition in First-Episode Schizophrenia', *Schizophrenia Research*, 48, 235–53.

Eimer, M. (2000) 'The Face-Specific N170 Component Reflects Late Stages in the Structural Encoding of Faces', *NeuroReport*, 11, 2319–24.

Ekman, P. (1971) 'Universals and Cultural Differences in Facial Expressions of Emotion', in J. K. Cole (ed.), *Nebraska Symposium on Motivation* (Lincoln, NE: University of Nebraska Press), 207–83.

Ekman, P. and Friesen, W. V. (1971) 'Constants across Cultures in the Face and Emotion', *Journal of Personality and Social Psychology*, 17, 124–9.

Ekman, P. and Friesen, W. L. (1976) *Pictures of Facial Affect* (Palo Alto, CA: Consulting Psychologist Press).

Ekman, P., Sorenson, E. R. and Friesen, W. V. (1969) 'Pan-Cultural Elements in Facial Displays of Emotions', *Science*, 164, 86–8.

Elfenbein, H. A. and Ambady, N. (2002) 'On the Universality and Cultural Specificity of Emotion Recognition: A Meta-Analysis', *Psychological Bulletin*, 128, 203–35.

Elfenbein, H. A. and Ambady, N. (2003a) 'Cultural Similarity's Consequences: A Distance Perspective on Cross-Cultural Differences in Emotion Recognition', *Journal of Cross Cultural Psychology*, 34, 92–109.

Elfenbein, H. A. and Ambady, N. (2003b) 'Universals and Cultural Differences in Recognizing Emotions', *Current Directions in Psychological Science*, 12, 159–64.

Elfenbein, H. A., Beaupre, M., Levesque, M. and Hess, U. (2007) 'Toward a Dialect Theory: Cultural Differences in the Expression and Recognition of Posed Facial Expressions', *Emotion*, 7, 131–46.

Elliott, E. A., Wills, E. J. and Goldstein, A. G. (1973) 'The Effects of Discrimination Training on the Recognition of White and Oriental Faces', *Bulletin of the Psychonomic Society*, 2, 71–3.

Ellis, A. W., Young, A. W. and Flude, B. M. (1990) 'Repetition Priming and Face Processing: Priming Occurs within the System that Responds to the Identity of a Face', *Quarterly Journal of Experimental Psychology A: Human Experimental Psychology*, 42, 495–512.

Ellis, H. D. and Lewis, M. B. (2001) 'Capgras Delusion: A Window on Face Recognition', *Trends in Cognitive Sciences*, 5, 149–56.

Ellis, H. D., Lewis, M. B., Moselhy, H. F. and Young, A. W. (2000) 'Automatic without Autonomic Responses to Familiar Faces: Differential Components of Covert Face Recognition in a Case of Capgras Delusion', *Cognitive Neuropsychiatry*, 5, 255–69.

Ellis, H. D., Shepherd, J. W. and Davies, G. M. (1979) 'Identification of Familiar and Unfamiliar Faces from Internal and External Features: Some Implications for Theories of Face Recognition', *Perception*, 8, 431–39.

Ellis, H. D., Whitley, J. and Luauté, J. -P. (1994) 'Delusional Misidentification: The Three Original Papers on the Capgras, Frégoli and Intermetamorphosis Delusions', *History of Psychiatry*, 5, 117–46.

Ellis, H. and Young, A. (1988) 'Training in Face-Processing Skills for a Child with Acquired Prosopagnosia', *Developmental Neuropsychology*, 4, 283–94.

Ellis, H. D. and Young, A. W., (1990) 'Accounting for Delusional Misidentifications', *British Journal of Psychiatry*, 157, 239–48.

Ellis, H. D., Young, A. W., Quayle, A. H. and De Pauw, K. W. (1997) 'Reduced Autonomic Responses to Faces in Capgras Delusion', *Proceedings of the Royal Society B: Biological Science*, 264, 1085–92.

Endo, N., Endo, M., Kirita, T. and Maruyama, K. (1992) 'The Effects of Expression on Face Recognition', *Tohoku Psychologica Folia*, 51, 37–44.

Etcoff, N. (1984) 'Selective Attention to Facial Identity and Facial Emotion', *Neuropsychologia*, 22, 281–95.

Evangeli, M. and Broks, M. E. (2000) 'Face Processing in Schizophrenia: Parallels with the Effects of Amygdala Damage', *Cognitive Neuropsychiatry*, 5, 81–104.

Evans, J. J., Heggs, A. J., Antoun, N. and Hodges, J. R. (1995) 'Progressive Prosopagnosia Associated with Selective Right Temporal-Lobe Atrophy – a New Syndrome', *Brain*, 118, 1–13.

Faja, S., Aylward, E., Bernier, R. and Dawson, G. (2008) 'Becoming a Face Expert: A Computerized Face-Training Program for High-Functioning Individuals with Autism Spectrum Disorders', *Developmental Neuropsychology*, 33, 1–24.

Fakra, E., Salgado-Pineda, P., Delaveau, P., Hariri, A. R. and Blin, O. (2008) 'Neural Bases of Different Cognitive Strategies for Facial Affect Processing in Schizophrenia', *Schizophrenia Research*, 100, 191–205.

Farah, M. J. (1990) *Visual Agnosia* (Cambridge: MIT Press).

Farah, M. J., Levinson, K. L. and Klein, K. L. (1995) 'Face Perception and within-Category Discrimination in Prosopagnosia', *Neuropsychologia*, 33, 661–74.

Farah, M. J., O'Reilly, R. C. and Vecera, S. P. (1993) 'Dissociated Overt and Covert Recognition as an Emergent Property of a Lesioned Neural Network', *Psychological Review*, 100, 571–88.

Farroni, T., Csibra, G., Simion, F. and Johnson, M. H. (2002) 'Eye Contact Detection in Humans from Birth', *Proceedings of the National Academy of Sciences of the USA*, 99, 9602–5.

Feinberg, T. E., DeLuca, J., Giacino, J. T., Roane, D. M. and Solms, M. (2005) 'Right Hemisphere Pathology and the Self', in T. E. Feinberg and J. P. Keenan (eds), *The Lost Self: Pathologies of the Brain and Identity* (New York: Oxford University Press).

Feinberg, T. E., Rifkin, A., Schaffer, C. and Walker, E. (1986) 'Facial Discrimination and Emotional Recognition in Schizophrenia and Affective Disorders', *Archives of General Psychiatry*, 43, 276–9.

Feinberg, T. E. and Roane, D. M. (2005) 'Delusional Misidentification', *Psychiatric Clinics of North America*, 28, 665–83.

Fiorentini, A., Maffei, L. and Sandini, G. (1983) 'The Role of High Spatial Frequencies in Face Perception', *Perception*, 12, 195–201.

Fleminger, S. and Burns, A. (1993) 'The Delusional Misidentification Syndromes in Patients with and without Evidence of Organic Cerebral Disease: A Structured Review of Case Reports', *Biological Psychiatry*, 33, 22–32.

Flin, R. H. (1980) 'Age Effects in Children's Memory for Unfamiliar Faces', *Developmental Psychology*, 16, 373–4.

Flude, B. M., Ellis, A. W. and Kay, J. (1989) 'Face Processing and Name Retrieval in an Anomic Aphasic – Names are Stored Separately from Semantic Information about Familiar People', *Brain and Cognition*, 11, 60–72.

Foa, E. B., Gilboa-Schectman, E., Amir, N. and Freshman, M. (2000) 'Memory Bias in Generalized Social Phobia: Remembering Negative Emotional Expressions', *Journal of Anxiety Disorders*, 14, 501–19.

Foldiak, P., Xiao, D., Keysers, C., Edwards, R. and Perrett, D. I. (2004) 'Rapid Serial Visual Presentation for the Determination of Neural Selectivity in area STSa', *Progress in Brain Research*, 144, 107–16.

Förstl, H., Almeida, O. P., Owen, A., Burns, A. and Howard, R. (1991) 'Psychiatric, Neurological and Medical Aspects of Misidentification Syndromes: A Review of 260 Cases', *Psychological Medicine*, 21, 905–10.

Förstl, H., Burns, A., Jacoby, R. and Levy, R. (1991) 'Neuroanatomical Correlates of Clinical Misidentification and Misperception in Senile Dementia of the Alzheimer Type', *Journal of Clinical Psychiatry*, 52, 268–71.

Fortune, S. (1992) Voronoi diagrams and Delaunay triangulations. In D. Z. Du and F. K. Hwang (Eds.), *Computing in Euclidean geometry*. Singapore: World Scientific Publishing Company.

Freire, A. and Lee, K. (2001) 'Face Recognition in 4- to 7-Year-Olds: Processing of Configural, Featural, and Paraphernalia Information', *Journal of Experimental Child Psychology*, 80, 347–71.

Freire, A., Lee, K. and Symons, L. A. (2000) 'The Face-Inversion Effect as a Deficit in the Encoding of Configural Information: Direct Evidence', *Perception*, 29, 159–70.

Friesen, C. K. and Kingstone, A. (1998) 'The Eyes Have it! Reflexive Orienting is Triggered by Nonpredictive Gaze', *Psychonomic Bulletin and Review*, 5, 490–5.

Frigerio, E., Burt, D. M., Gagliardi, C., Cioffi, G., Martelli, S., Perrett, D. I., *et al.* (2006) 'Is Everybody Always My Friend? Perception of Approachability in Williams Syndrome', *Neuropsychologia*, 44, 254–9.

Fu, C. H., Williams, S. C., Brammer, M. J., Suckling, J., Kim, J., Cleare, A. J., *et al.* (2007) 'Neural Responses to Happy Facial Expressions in Major Depression Following Antidepressant Treatment', *American Journal of Psychiatry*, 164, 599–607.

Fu, C. H., Williams, S. C., Cleare, A. J., Brammer, M. J., Walsh, N. D., Kim, J., *et al.* (2004) 'Attenuation of the Neural Responses to Sad Faces in Major Depression by Antidepressant Treatment', *Archives of General Psychiatry*, 61, 877–89.

Fu, C. H., Williams, S. C., Cleare, A. J., Scott, J., Mitterschiffthaler, M. T., Walsh, N. D., *et al.* (2008) 'Neural Responses to Sad Facial Expressions in Major Depression Following Cognitive Behavioral Therapy', *Biological Psychiatry*, 64, 505–12.

Gagliardi, C., Frigerio, E., Burt, D. M., Cazzaniga, I., Perrett, D. I. and Borgatti, R. (2003) 'Facial Recognition in Williams Syndrome', *Neuropsychologia*, 41, 733–8.

Galaburda, A. M. and Bellugi, U. (2000) 'Multi-Level Analysis of Cortical Neuroanatomy in Williams Syndrome', *Journal of Cognitive Neuroscience*, 12, 74–88.

Gallant, J. L., Connor, C. E., Rakshit, S., Lewis, J. W. and Van Essen, D. C. (1996) 'Neural Responses to Polar, Hyperbolic, and Cartesian Gratings in Area V4 of the Macaque Monkey', *Journal of Neurophysiology*, 76, 2718–39.

Gallegos, D. R. and Tranel, D. (2005) 'Positive Facial Affect Facilitates the Identification of Famous Faces', *Brain and Language*, 93, 338–48.

Galton, F. (1879) Composite portraits, made by combining those of many different persons into a single resultant figure. *Journal of the Anthropological Institute of Great Britain and Ireland*, 8, 132–144.

Garner, M., Baldwin, D. S., Bradley, B. P. and Mogg, K. (2009) 'Impaired Identification of Fearful Faces in Generalised Social Phobia', *Journal of Affective Disorders*, 115, 460–5.

Garrido, L., Duchaine, B. and Nakayama, K. (2008) 'Face Detection in Normal and Prosopagnosic Individuals', *Journal of Neuropsychology*, 2, 219–40.

Garrido, L., Furl, N., Draganski, B., Weiskopf, N., Stevens, J., Tan, G. C. -Y., *et al.* (2009) 'VBM Reveals Reduced Grey Matter Volume in the Temporal Cortex of DPs', *Brain*, 132, 3443–55.

Gathers, A. D., Bhatt, R., Corbly, C. R., Farley, A. B. and Joseph, J. E. (2004) 'Developmental Shifts in Cortical Loci for Face and Object Recognition', *NeuroReport*, 15, 1549–53.

Gauthier, I., Curran, T., Curby, K. M. and Collins, D. (2003) 'Perceptual Interference Supports a Non-Modular Account of Face Processing', *Nature Neuroscience*, 6, 428–32.

Gauthier, I., Skudlarksi, P., Gore, J. C. and Anderson, A. W. (2000) 'Expertise for Cars and Birds Recruit Brain Areas Involved in Face Recognition', *Nature Neuroscience*, 3, 191–7.

Gauthier, I. and Tarr, M. J. (1997) 'Becoming a "Greeble" Expert: Exploring Mechanisms for Face Recognition', *Vision Research*, 37, 1673–82.

Gauthier, I. and Tarr, M. J. (2002) 'Unravelling Mechanisms for Expert Object Recognition: Bridging Brain Activity and Behaviour', *Journal of Experimental Psychology: Human Perception and Performance*, 28, 431–46.

Gauthier, I., Tarr, M. J., Anderson, A. W., Skudlarski, P. and Gore, J. C. (1999) 'Activation of the Middle Fusiform "Face Area" Increases with Expertise in Recognizing Novel Objects', *Nature Neuroscience*, 2, 568–73.

Gauthier, I., Williams, P. C., Tarr, M. J. and Tanaka, J. W. (1998) 'Training "Greeble" Experts: A Framework for Studying Expert Object Recognition Processes', *Vision Research*, 38, 2401–28.

Ge, L., Anzures, G., Wang, Z., Kelly, D. J., Pascalis, O., Quinn, P. C., *et al.* (2008) 'An Inner Face Advantage in Children's Recognition of Familiar Peers', *Journal of Experimental Child Psychology*, 101, 124–36.

Geldart, S., Mondloch, C. J., Maurer, D., De Schonen, S. and Brent, H. P. (2002) 'The Effect of Early Visual Deprivation on the Development of Face Processing', *Developmental Science*, 5, 490–501.

Gentili, C., Gobbini, M. I., Ricciardi, E., Vanello, N., Pietrini, P., Haxby, J. V., *et al.* (2008) 'Differential Modulation of Neural Activity throughout the Distributed Neural System for Face Perception in Patients with Social Phobia and Healthy Subjects', *Brain Research Bulletin*, 77, 286–92.

George, N., Driver, J. and Dolan, R. (2001) 'Seeing Gaze-Direction Modulates Fusiform Activity and its Coupling with other Brain Areas during Face Processing', *NeuroImage*, 13, 1102–12.

Germine, L. T., Duchaine, B. and Nakayama, K. (2011) 'Where Cognitive Development and Aging Meet: Face Learning Ability Peaks after Age 30', *Cognition,* 118, 201–10.

Gilboa-Schechtman, E., Ben-Artzi, E., Jeczemien, P., Marom, S. and Hermesh, H. (2004) 'Depression Impairs the Ability to Ignore the Emotional Aspects of Facial Expression: Evidence from the Garner Task', *Cognition and Emotion,* 18, 209–31.

Glass, L. (1969) 'Moire Effect from Random Dots', *Nature,* 223, 578–80.

Gloning, I., Gloning, K. and Hoff, H. (1967) 'On Optic Hallucinations. A Study Based on 241 Patients with Lesions of the Occipital Lobe and its Surrounding Regions Verified by Autopsy or Surgery', *Wiener Zeitschrift für Nervenheilkunde und deren Grenzgebiete,* 25, 1–19.

Gobbini, M. I. and Haxby, J. V. (2007) 'Neural Systems for Recognition of Familiar Faces', *Neuropsychologia,* 45, 32–41.

Gobbini, M. I., Leibenluft, E., Santiago, N. and Haxby, J. V. (2004) 'Social and Emotional Attachment in the Neural Representation of Faces', *NeuroImage,* 22, 1628–35.

Goffaux, V. and Rossion, B. (2007) Face inversion disproportionately impairs the perception of vertical but not horizontal relations between features. *Journal of Experimental Psychology: Human Perception and Performance,* 33, 995–1002.

Golan, O. and Baron-Cohen, S. (2006) 'Systemizing Empathy: Teaching Adults with Asperger Syndrome or High-Functioning Autism to Recognize Complex Emotions Using Interactive Multimedia', *Development and Psychopathology,* 18, 591–617.

Golarai, G., Ghahremani, D. G., Whitfield-Gabrieli, S., Reiss, A., Eberhardt, J. L., Gabrieli, J. D., *et al.* (2007) 'Differential Development of High-Level Visual Cortex Correlates with Category-Specific Recognition Memory', *Nature Neuroscience,* 10, 512–22.

Golarai, G., Hong, S., Haas, B. W., Galaburda, A. M., Mills, D. L., Bellugi, U., *et al.* (2010) 'The Fusiform Face Area is Enlarged in Williams Syndrome', *The Journal of Neuroscience,* 30, 6700–12.

Goldstein, A. G. and Chance, J. E. (1980) Memory for faces and schema theory. *Journal of Psychology,* 105, 47–59.

Good, C. D., Lawrence, K., Thomas, N. S., Price, C. J., Ashburner, J., Friston, K. J., *et al.* (2003) 'Dosage-Sensitive X-Linked Locus Influences the Development of Amygdala and Orbitofrontal Cortex, and Fear Recognition in Humans', *Brain,* 126, 2431–46.

Goren, C., Sarty, M. and Wu, P. Y. (1975) 'Abstract Visual Following and Pattern Discrimination of Face-Like Stimuli by Newborn Infants', *Pediatrics,* 56, 544–9.

Gotlib, I. H. and Hammen, C. L. (1992) *Psychological Aspects of Depression: Toward a Cognitive-Interpersonal Integration* (Oxford, England: John Wiley and Sons).

Grill-Spector, K., Golarai, G. and Gabrieli, J. (2008) 'Developmental Neuroimaging of the Human Ventral Visual Cortex', *Trends in Cognitive Science,* 12, 152–62.

Grill-Spector, K., Knouf, N. and Kanwisher, N. (2004) 'The Fusiform Face Area Subserves Face Perception, Not Generic within-Category Identification', *Nature Neuroscience,* 7, 555–62.

Gross, C. G. (2005) 'Processing the Facial Image: A Brief History', *American Psychologist,* 60, 755–63.

Gross, C. G., Rocha-Miranda, C. E. and Bender, D. B. (1972) 'Visual Receptive Fields of Neurons in Inferotemporal Cortex of the Monkey', *Science,* 166, 1303–6.

Grossman, J. B., Klin, A., Carter, A. S. and Volkmar, F. R. (2000) 'Verbal Bias in Recognition of Facial Emotions in Children with Asperger Syndrome', *Journal of Child Psychology and Psychiatry,* 41, 369–79.

Grueter, M., Grueter, T., Bell, V., Horst, J., Laskowski, W., Sperling, K., *et al.* (2007) 'Hereditary Prosopagnosia: The First Case Series', *Cortex,* 43, 734–49.

Grüsser, O. J. and Landis, T. (1991) *Visual Agnosias and Other Disturbances of Visual Perception and Cognition* (London: Macmillan).

Guastella, A. J., Einfeld, S. L., Gray, K. M., Rinehart, N. J., Tonge, B. J., Lambert, T. J., *et al.* (2010) 'Intranasal Oxytocin Improves Emotion Recognition for Youth with Autism Spectrum Disorders', *Biological Psychiatry,* 67, 692–4.

Guastella, A. J., Mitchell, P. B. and Dadds, M. R. (2008) 'Oxytocin Increases Gaze to the Eye Region of Human Faces', *Biological Psychiatry,* 63, 3–5.

Gupta, R. (2011) 'Attentional, Visual, and Emotional Mechanisms of Face Processing Proficiency in Williams Syndrome', *Frontiers in Behavioral Neuroscience,* 5, 18.

Gur, R. C., Erwin, R. J., Gur, R. E., Zwil, A. S., Heimberg, C. and Kraemar, H. C. (1992) 'Facial Emotion Discrimination II: Behavioral Findings in Depression', *Psychiatry Research,* 42, 241–51.

Gur, R. E., Loughead, J., Kohler, C. G., Elliott, M. A., Lesko, K., Ruparel, K., *et al.* (2007) 'Limbic Activation Associated with Misidentification of Fearful Faces and Flat Affect in Schizophrenia', *Archives of General Psychiatry,* 64, 1356–66.

Gur, R. E., Mcgrath, C., Chan, R. M., Schroeder, L., Turner, T., Turetsky, B. I., *et al.* (2002) 'An fMRI Study of Facial Emotion Processing in Patients with Schizophrenia', *American Journal of Psychiatry,* 161, 1806–13.

Haas, B. W., Hoeft, E., Searcy, Y. M., Mills, D., Bellugi, U. and Reiss, A. (2010) 'Individual Differences in Social Behaviour Predict Amygdala Response to Fearful Facial Expressions in Williams ', *Neuropsychologia,* 48, 1283–8.

Habel, U., Klein, M., Shah, N. J., Toni, I., Zilles, K., Falkai, P., *et al.* (2004) 'Genetic Load on Amygdala Hypofunction during Sadness in Nonaffected Brothers of Schizophrenia Patients', *American Journal of Psychiatry,* 161, 1806–13.

Hadjikhani, N. and de Gelder, B. (2002) 'Neural Basis of Prosopagnosia: An fMRI Study', *Human Brain Mapping,* 16, 176–82.

Hadjikhani, N., Joseph, R. M., Snyder, J., Chabris, C. F., Clark, J., Steele, S., *et al.* (2004) 'Activation of the Fusiform Gyrus when Individuals with Autism Spectrum Disorder View Faces', *NeuroImage,* 22, 1141–50.

Haig, N. D. (1984) The effect of feature displacement on face recognition. *Perception,* 13, 505–512.

Hall, J., Harris, J. M., Sprengelmeyer, R., Sprengelmeyer, A., Young, A. W., Santos, I. M., *et al.* (2004) 'Social Cognition and Face Processing in Schizophrenia', *British Journal of Psychiatry,* 185, 169–70.

Hall, J., Whalley, H. C., McKirdy, J. W., Romaniuk, L., McGonigle, D., McIntosh, A. M., *et al.* (2008) 'Overactivation of Fear Systems to Neutral Faces in Schizophrenia', *Biological Psychiatry,* 64, 70–3.

Harris, A. M. and Aguirre, G. K. (2008) 'The Effects of Parts, Wholes, and Familiarity on Face-Selective Responses in MEG', *Journal of Vision,* 8, 1–12.

Harris, A., Duchaine, B. and Nakayama, K. (2005) 'Normal and Abnormal Face Selectivity of the M170 Response in Developmental Prosopagnosics', *Neuropsychologia,* 43, 2125–36.

Harwood, D. G., Barker, W. W., Ownby, R. L. and Duara, R. (1999) 'Prevalence and Correlates of Capgras Syndrome in Alzheimer's Disease', *International Journal of Geriatric Psychiatry,* 14, 415–20.

Hasselmo, M. E., Rolls, E. T. and Baylis, G. C. (1986) 'Selectivity between Facial Expressions in the Responses of a Population of Neurons in the Superior Temporal Sulcus of the Monkey', *Neuroscience Letters,* 26, 571.

Hasselmo, M. E., Rolls, E. T. and Baylis, G. C. (1989) 'The Role of Expression and Identity in the Face-Selective Responses of Neurons in the Temporal Visual Cortex of the Monkey', *Behavioural Brain Research,* 32, 203–18.

Hasson, U., Avidan, G., Deouell, L. Y., Bentin, S. and Malach, R. (2003) 'Face-Selective Activation in a Congenital Prosopagnosic Subject', *Journal of Cognitive Neuroscience,* 15, 419–31.

Haxby, J. C., Hoffman, E. A. and Gobbini, M. I. (2000) 'The Distributed Human Neural System for Face Perception', *Trends in Cognitive Sciences,* 4, 223–33.

Hay, D. C. and Cox, R. (2000) 'Developmental Changes in the Recognition of Faces and Facial Features', *Infant and Child Development,* 9, 199–212.

Hay, D. C. and Young, A. W. (1982) 'The Human Face', in A. W. Ellis (ed.), *Normality and Pathology in Cognitive Functions* (London: Academic Press), 173–202.

Hécaen, H. and Angelergues, R. (1962) 'Agnosia for Faces (Prosopagnosia)', *Archives of Neurology,* 7, 92–100.

Hécaen, H. and Angelergues, R. (1963) *La cécité psychique* (Paris: Masson).

Hempel, A., Hempel, E., Schonknecht, P., Stippich, C. and Schroder, J. (2003) 'Impairment in Basal Limbic Function in Schizophrenia during Affect Recognition', *Psychiatry Research: Neuroimaging,* 122, 115–24.

Henson, R. N., Shallice, T., Gorno-Tempini, M. L. and Dolan, R. J. (2002) 'Face Repetition Effects in Implicit and Explicit Memory Tests as Measured by fMRI', *Cerebral Cortex,* 12, 178–86.

Hernandez, N., Metzger, A., Magne, R., Bonnet-Brilhault, F., Rouz, S., Barthelemy, C., et al. (2009) 'Exploration of Core Features of A Human Face by Healthy and Autistic Adults Analysed by Visual Scanning', *Neuropsychologia,* 47, 1004–12.

Herzmann, G., Danthiir, V., Schacht, A., Sommer, W. and Wilhelm, O. (2008) 'Toward a Comprehensive Test Battery for Face Processing: Assessment of the Tasks', *Behavior Research Methods,* 40, 840–57.

Hietanen, J. K. and Leppänen, J. M. (2003) 'Does Facial Expression Affect Attention Orienting by Gaze Direction Cues?', *Journal of Experimental Psychology: Human Perception and Performance,* 29, 1228–43.

Hobson, R. P., Ouston, J. and Lee, A. (1988) 'What's in a Face? The Case of Autism', *The British Journal of Psychology,* 79, 441–53.

Hoff, H. and Pötzl, O. (1937) 'Über eine optisch-agnostische Störung des "Physiognomie-Gedächtnisses"', *Zeitschrift für die Gesamte Neurologie und Psychiatrie,* 159, 367–95.

Hoffman, E. A. and Haxby, J. V. (2000) 'Distinct Representations of Eye Gaze and Identity in the Distributed Human Neural System for Face Perception', *Nature Neuroscience,* 3, 80–4.

Holt, D., Kunkel, L., Weiss, A. P., (2006) 'Increased Medial Temporal Lobe Activation During the Passive Viewing of Emotional and Neutral Facial Expressions in Schizophrenia', *Schizophrenia Research,* 82, 153–62.

Hooker, C. I. L., Paller, K. A., Gitelman, D. R., Parrish, T. B., Mesulam, M. -M. and Reber, P. J. (2003) 'Brain Networks for Analysing Eye Gaze', *Cognitive Brain Research,* 17, 406–18.

Hooker, C. and Park, S. (2002) 'Emotion Processing and its Relationship in Schizophrenia Patients', *Psychiatry Research,* 112, 41–50.

Horley, K., Williams, L. M., Gonsalvez, C. and Gordon, E. (2004) 'Face to Face: Visual Scanpath Evidence of Abnormal Processing of Facial Expressions in Social Phobia', *Psychiatry Research,* 127, 43–53.

Hornak, J., Rolls, E. T. and Wade, D. (1996) 'Face and Voice Expression Identification in Patients with Emotional and Behavioural Changes Following Ventral Frontal Lobe Damage', *Neuropsychologia,* 34, 247–61.

Hosoda, M., Stone-Romero, E. F. and Coats, G. (2003) 'The Effects of Physical Attractiveness on Job-Related Outcomes: A Meta-Analysis of Experimental Studies', *Personnel Psychology,* 56, 431–62.

Huber, D., Veinante, P. and Stoop, R. (2005) 'Vasopressin and Oxytocin Excite Distinct Neuronal Populations in the Central Amygdala'., *Science,* 308, 245–8.

Hubl, D., Bolte, S., Feineis-Matthews, S., Lanfermann, H., Federspiel, A., Strik, W., et al. (2003) 'Functional Imbalance of Visual Pathways Indicates Alternative Face Processing Strategies in Autism', *Neurology,* 61, 1232–7.

Hudson, A. J. and Grace, G. M. (2000) 'Misidentification Syndromes Related to Face Specific Area in the Fusiform Gyrus', *Journal of Neurology, Neurosurgery and Psychiatry,* 69, 645–58.

Humphreys, G. and Riddoch, M. J. (1993) *Birmingham Object Recognition Battery* (Hove, UK: Lawrence Erlbaum Associates).

Humphreys, K., Minshew, N., Leonard, G. L. and Behrmann, M. (2007) 'A Fine-Grained Analysis of Facial Expression Processing in High-Functioning Adults with Autism', *Neuropsychologia,* 45, 685–95.

Iaria, G., Bogod, N., Fox, C. J. and Barton, J. J. (2009) 'Developmental Topographical Disorientation: Case One', *Neuropsychologia,* 47, 30–40.

Ingram, R. E. (1984) 'Information Processing and Feedback: Effects of Mood and Information Favorability on the Cognitive Processing of Personally Relevant Information', *Cognitive Therapy and Research,* 8, 371–86.

Itier, R. J. and Taylor, M. J. (2004) 'Effects of Repetition Learning on Upright, Inverted and Contrast-Reversed Face Processing Using ERPs', *NeuroImage,* 21, 1518–32.

Jackson, J. H. (1876) 'Case of Large Cerebral Tumour without Optic Neuritis, and with Left Hemiplegia and Imperceptions', *Royal London Ophthalmic Hospital Reports,* 8, 434–44.

Jacques, C., d'Arripe, O. and Rossion, B. (2007) 'The Time Course of the Inversion Effect During Individual Face Discrimination', *Journal of Vision,* 7, 1–9.

Jacques, C. and Rossion, B. (2004) 'Concurrent Processing Reveals Competition between Visual Representations of Faces', *NeuroReport,* 15, 2417–21.

Johnson, M. H. (2001) 'Functional Brain Development in Humans', *Nature Reviews Neuroscience,* 2, 475–83.

Johnson, M. H. (2005) 'Sub-Cortical Face Processing', *Nature Reviews Neuroscience,* 6, 766–74.

Johnson, M. H. and de Haan, M. (2001) 'Developing Cortical Specialization for Visual-Cognitive Function: The Case of Face Recognition', in J. L. McClelland and R. S. Seigler (eds), *Mechanisms of Cognitive Development: Behavioral and Neural Perspectives* (Mahwah, NJ: Erlbaum), 253–27.

Johnson, M. H., Dziurawiec, S., Ellis, H. and Morton, J. (1991) 'Newborns' Preferential Tracking of Face-Like Stimuli and its Subsequent Decline', *Cognition,* 40, 1–19.

Johnson, M. and Morton, J. (1991) *Biology and Cognitive Development: The Case of Face Recognition* (Oxford: Blackwell).

Jones, B. C., DeBruine, L. M., Little, A. C., Conway, C. A. and Feinberg, D. R. (2006) 'Integrating Gaze Direction and Expression in Preferences For Attractive Faces', *Psychological Science,* 17, 588–91.

Jones, R. D. and Tranel, D. (2001) 'Severe Developmental Prosopagnosia in a Child with Superior Intellect', *Journal of Clinical and Experimental Neuropsychology,* 23, 265–73.

Jones, W., Bellugi, U., Lai, Z. and Chiles, M. (2000) 'Hypersociability in Williams Syndrome', *Journal of Cognitive Neuroscience,* 12, 30–46.

Jones, W., Carr, K. and Klin, A. (2008) 'Absence of Preferential Looking to the Eyes of Approaching Adults Predicts Level of Social Disability in 2-Year-Old Toddlers with Autism Spectrum Disorder', *Archives of General Psychiatry,* 65, 946–54.

Joormann, J. and Gotlib, I. H. (2006) 'Is this Happiness I See? Biases in the Identification of Emotional Facial Expressions in Depression and Social Phobia', *Journal of Abnormal Psychology,* 115, 705–14.

Joseph, R. M. and Tanaka, J. (2003) 'Holistic and Part-Based Face Recognition in Children with Autism', *Journal of Child Psychology and Psychiatry,* 44, 529–42.

Josephs, K. A., Whitwell, J. L., Knopman, D. S., Boeve, B. F., Vemuri, P., Senjem, M. L., et al. (2009) 'Two Distinct Subtypes of Right Temporal Variant Frontotemporal Dementia', *Neurology,* 73, 1443–50.

Joshua, N. and Rossell, S. (2009) 'Configural Face Processing in Schizophrenia', *Schizophrenia Research*, 112, 99–103.

Joubert, S., Felician, O., Barbeau, E., Sontheimer, A., Barton, J. J., Ceccaldi, M., *et al.* (2003) 'Impaired Configurational Processing in a Case of Progressive Prosopagnosia Associated with Predominant Right Temporal Lobe Atrophy', *Brain*, 126, 2537–2550.

Kampe, K. K., Frith, C. D., Dolan, R. J. and Frith, U. (2001) 'Reward Value of Attractiveness and Gaze', *Nature*, 413, 589.

Kan, Y., Mimura, M., Kamijima, K. and Kawamura, M. (2004) 'Recognition of Emotion from Moving Facial and Prosodic Stimuli in Depressed Patients', *Journal of Neurology, Neurosurgery and Psychiatry*, 75, 1667–71.

Kanwisher, N., McDermott, J. and Chun, M. (1997) 'The Fusiform Face Area: A Module in Human Extrastriate Cortex Specialized for Face Perception', *Journal of Neuroscience*, 17, 4302–11.

Kanwisher, N. and Yovel, G. (2006) 'The Fusiform Face Area: A Cortical Region Specialized for the Perception of Faces', *Proceedings of the Royal Society B: Biological Sciences*, 361, 2109–28.

Kapur, S. (2003) 'Psychosis as a State of Aberrant Salience: A Framework Linking Biology, Phenomenology, and Pharmacology in Schizophrenia', *American Journal of Psychiatry*, 160, 13–23.

Karmiloff-Smith, A. (1997) 'Crucial Differences between Developmental Cognitive Neuroscience and Adult Neuropsychology', *Developmental Neuropsychology*, 13, 513–24.

Karmiloff-Smith, A., Scerif, G. and Ansari, D. (2003) 'Double Dissociation in Developmental Disorders? Theoretically Misconceived, Empirically Dubious', *Cortex*, 39, 161–3.

Karmiloff-Smith, A., Thomas, M., Annaz, D., Humphreys, K., Ewing, S., Brace, N., *et al.* (2004) 'Exploring the Williams Syndrome Face Processing Debate: The Importance of Building Developmental Trajectories', *Journal of Child Psychology and Psychiatry*, 45, 1258–74.

Katsyri, J., Tippana, K., Sams, M., Saalasti, S. and von Wendt, L. (2008) 'Impaired Recognition of Facial Emotions from Low-Spatial Frequencies in Asperger Syndrome', *Neuropsychologia*, 47, 1888–97.

Kaufmann, J. M. and Schweinberger, S. R. (2004) 'Expression Influences the Recognition of Familiar Faces', *Perception*, 33, 399–408.

Keedwell, P. A., Andrew, C., Williams, S. C. R., Brammer, M. J. and Phillips, M. L. (2005a) 'A Double Dissociation of Ventromedial Prefrontal Cortical Responses to Sad and Happy Stimuli in Depressed and Healthy Individuals', *Biological Psychiatry*, 58, 495–503.

Keedwell, P. A., Andrew, C., Williams, S. C. R., Brammer, M. J. and Phillips, M. L. (2005b) 'The Neural Correlates of Anhedemia in Major Depressive Disorder', *Biological Psychiatry*, 58, 843–53.

Keedwell, P., Drapier, D., Surguladze, S., Giampietro, V., Brammer, M. and Phillips, M. (2009) 'Neural Markers of Symptomatic Improvement during Antidepressant Therapy in Severe Depression: Subgenual Cingulate and Visual Cortical Responses to Sad, but not Happy, Facial Stimuli are Correlated with Changes in Symptom Score', *Journal of Psychopharmacology*, 23, 775–88.

Kelly, D. J., Quinn, P. C., Slater, A. M., Lee, K., Ge, L. and Pascalis, O. (2007) 'The Other-Race Effect Develops During Infancy: Evidence of Perceptual Narrowing', *Psychological Science*, 18, 1084–9.

Kennerknecht, I., Grueter, T., Welling, B., Wentzek, S., Horst, J., Edwards, S., *et al.* (2006) 'First Report of Prevalence of Non-Syndromic Hereditary Prosopagnosia (HPA)', *American Journal of Medical Genetics*, 140, 1617–22.

Kennerknecht, I., Yee-Ho, N. and Wong, V. C. N. (2008) 'Prevalence of Hereditary Prosopagnosia (HPA) in Hong Kong Chinese Population', *American Journal of Medical Genetics Part A*, 146A, 2863–70.

Keri, S., Kiss, I. and Kelemen, O. (2009) 'Sharing Secrets: Oxytocin and Trust in Schizophrenia', *Social Neuroscience*, 4, 287–93.

Kessler, R. C., Stein, M. B. and Berglund, P. A. (1998) 'Social Phobia Subtypes in the National Comorbidity Survey', *American Journal of Psychiatry*, 155, 613–19.

Kingstone, A., Friesen, C. K. and Gazzaniga, M. S. (2000) 'Reflexive Joint Attention Depends on Lateralized Cortical Connections', *Psychological Science*, 11, 159–66.

Kirsch, P., Esslinger, C., Chen, Q., Mier, D., Lis, S., Siddhanti, S., *et al.* (2005) 'Oxytocin Modulates Neural Circuitry for Social Cognition and Fear in Humans', *The Journal of Neuroscience*, 25, 11489–93.

Kleiner, K. A. and Banks, M. S. (1987) 'Stimulus Energy Does not Account for 2-Month-Old's Preferences', *Journal of Experimental Psychology: Human Perception and Performance*, 13, 594–600.

Kleinhans, N. M., Richards, T., Sterling, L., Stegbauer, K. C., Mahurin, R., Johnson, L. C., *et al.* (2008) 'Abnormal Functional Connectivity in Autism Spectrum Disorders during Face Processing', *Brain*, 131, 1000–12.

Klin, A., Jones, W., Schiltz, R., Volkmar, F. and Cohen, D. (2002) 'Visual Fixation Patterns During Viewing of Naturalistic Social Situations as Predictors of Social Competence in Individuals with Autism', *Archives of General Psychiatry*, 59, 809–16.

Klin, A., Sparrow, S. S., de Bildt, A., Cicchetti, D. V., Cohen, D. J. and Volkmar, F. R. (1999) 'A Normed Study of Face Recognition in Autism and Related Disorders', *Journal of Autism and Developmental Disorders*, 29, 499–508.

Kobatake, E. and Tanaka, K. (1994) 'Neuronal Selectivites to Complex Object Features in the Ventral Visual Pathway of the Macaque Cerebral Cortex', *Journal of Neurophysiology*, 71, 2269–80.

Kohler, C. G., Bilker, W., Hagendoorn, M., Gur, R. E. and Gur, R. C. (2000) 'Emotion Recognition Deficit in Schizophrenia: Association with Symptomology and Cognition', *Biological Psychiatry*, 48, 127–36.

Kohler, C. G., Turner, T. H., Bilker, W. B., Bresinger, C. M., Siegel, S. J., Kanes, S. J., *et al.* (2003) 'Facial Emotion Recognition in Schizophrenia: Intensity Effects and Error Pattern', *The American Journal of Psychiatry*, 160, 1768–74.

Kolassa, I. T., Kolassa, S., Musial, F. and Miltner, W. H. R. (2007) 'Event-Related Potentials to Schematic Faces in Social Phobia', *Cognition and Emotion*, 21, 1721–44.

Kolassa, I. T. and Miltner, W. H. R. (2006) 'Psychophysiological Correlates of Face Processing in Social Phobia', *Brain Research*, 1118, 130–41.

Kosfeld, M., Heinrichs, M., Zak, P. J., Fischbacher, U. and Fehr, E. (2005) 'Oxytocin Increases Trust in Humans', *Nature*, 435, 673–6.

Kottoor, T. M. (1989) 'Recognition of Faces by Adults', *Psychological Studies*, 34, 102–5.

Krabbendam, L. and van Os, J. (2005) 'Schizophrenia and Urbanicity: A Major Environmental Influence – Conditional on Genetic Risk', *Schizophrenia Bulletin*, 31, 795–9.

Kracke, I. (1994) 'Developmental Prosopagnosia in Asperger Syndrome: Presentation and Discussion of an Individual Case', *Developmental Medicine and Child Neurology*, 36, 873–86.

Kress, T. and Daum, I. (2003) 'Event-Related Potentials Reflect Impaired Face Recognition in Patients with Congenital Prosopagnosia', *Neuroscience Letters*, 352, 133–6.

Krolak-Salmon, P., Henaff, M. A., Isnard, J., Tallon-Baudry, C., Guenot, M., Vighetto, A., *et al.* (2003) 'An Attention Modulated Response to Disgust in Human Ventral Anterior Insula', *Annals of Neurology*, 53, 446–53.

Kucharska-Pietura, K., David, A. S., Masiak, M. and Phillips, M. L. (2005) 'Perception of Facial and Vocal Affect by People with Schizophrenia in Early and Late Stages of Illness', *British Journal of Psychiatry*, 187, 523–8.

Kuefner, D., Macchi Cassia, V., Picozzi, M. and Bricolo, E. (2008) 'Do All Kids Look Alike? Evidence for an other-Age Effect in Adults', *Journal of Experimental Psychology: Human Perception and Performance*, 34, 811–17.

Kuhl, P. K. (1998) 'The Development of Speech and Language', in T. J. Carew, R. Menzel, and C. J. Schatz (eds), *Mechanistic Relationships between Development and Learning* (New York: Wiley), 53–73.

Kurucz, J. and Feldmar, G. (1979) Prosopo-affective agnosia as a symptom of cerebral organic disease. *Journal of the American Geriatrics Society*, 27, 91–95.

Laeng, B. and Caviness, V. S. (2001) 'Prosopagnosia as a Deficit in Encoding Curved Surface', *Journal of Cognitive Neuroscience*, 13, 556–76.

Lahaie, A., Mottron, L., Arguin, M., Berthiaume, C., Jemel, B. and Saumier, D. (2006) 'Face Perception in High-Functioning Autistic Adults: Evidence for Superior Processing of Face Parts, Not for a Configural Face-Processing Deficit', *Neuropsychology*, 20, 30–41.

Lander, K. and Metcalfe, S. (2007) 'The Influence of Positive and Negative Facial Expressions on Face Familiarity', *Memory*, 15, 63–9.

Landis, T. (2004) 'Désorientation topographique'. in A. B. Safran, A. Vighetto, T. Landis and E. A. Cabanis (eds), *Neuro-ophtalmologie* (Paris: Masson), 130–4.

Landis, T., Cummings, J. L., Benson, D. F. and Palmer, E. P. (1986) 'Loss of Topographic Form: An Environmental Agnosia', *Archives of Neurology*, 43, 132–6.

Landis, T., Cummings, J. L., Christen, L., Bogen, J. E. and Imhof, H. G. (1986) 'Are Unilateral Right Posterior Cerebral Lesions Sufficient to Cause Prosopagnosia? Clinical and Radiological Findings in Six Additional Patients', *Cortex*, 22, 243–52.

Lange, C. and Irle, E. (2004) 'Enlarged Amygdala Volume and Reduced Hippocampal Volume in Young Women with Major Depression', *Psychological Medicine*, 34, 1059–64.

Langenecker, S. A., Bieliauskas, L. A., Rapport, L. J., Zubieta, J. -K., Wilde, E. A. and Berent, S. (2005) 'Face Emotion Perception and Executive Functioning Deficits in Depression', *Journal of Clinical and Experimental Neuropsychology*, 27, 320–33.

Langlois, J. H., Kalakanis, L., Rubenstein, A. J., Larson, A., Hallam, M. and Smoot, M. (2000) 'Maxims or Myths of Beauty? A Meta-Analytic and Theoretical Review', *Psychological Bulletin*, 126, 390–423.

Langton, S. R. H., Watt, R. J. and Bruce, V. (2000) 'Do the Eyes Have it? Cues to the Direction of Social Attention', *Trends in Cognitive Sciences*, 4, 50–9.

Lawrence, K., Kuntsi, J., Coleman, M., Campbell, R. and Skuse, D. (2003) 'Face and Emotion Recognition Deficits in Turner Syndrome: A Possible Role for X-Linked Genes in Amygdala Development', *Neurophysiology*, 17, 39–49.

Lê, S., Raufaste, E. and Démonet, J. F. (2003) 'Processing of Normal, Inverted, and Scrambled Faces in a Patient with Prosopagnosia: Behavioural and Eye Tracking Data', *Cognitive Brain Research*, 17, 26–35.

Le Grand, R., Barrie, J. and Tanaka, J. (2005) 'Testing the Face-Like versus Geometric Properties of the N170 Component', *Journal of Cognitive Neuroscience*, 12 (Suppl.), 112.

Le Grand, R., Cooper, P., Mondloch, C. J., Lewis, T. L., Sagiv, N., de Gelder, B. and Maurer, D. (2006) 'What Aspects of Face Processing are Impaired in Developmental Prosopagnosia?', *Brain and Cognition*, 61, 139–58.

Le Grand, R., Mondloch, C. J., Maurer, D. and Brent, H. P. (2001) 'Neuroperception: Early Visual Experience and Face Processing', *Nature*, 410, 890.

Leder, H. and Bruce, V. (2000) 'When Inverted Faces are Recognized: The Role of Configural Information in Face Recognition', *Quarterly Journal of Experimental Psychology A*, 53, 513–36.

Lee, C. U., Shenton, M. E., Salisbury, D. F., Kasai, K., Onitsuka, T., Dickey, C. C., et al. (2002) 'Fusiform Gyrus Volume Reduction in First-Episode Schizophrenia: A Magnetic Resonance Imaging Study', *Archives of General Psychiatry*, 59, 775–81.

Lee, Y., Duchaine, B., Nakayama, K. and Wilson, H. (2010) 'Three Cases of Developmental Prosopagnosia from One Family: Detailed Neuropsychological and Psychophysical Investigation of Face Processing', *Cortex*, 46, 949–64.

Leppänen, J. M., Milders, M., Bell, J. S., Terriere, E. and Hietanen, J. K. (2004) 'Depression Biases the Recognition of Neutral Faces', *Psychiatry Research*, 128, 123–33.

Leppänen, J. M. and Nelson, C. A. (2009) 'Tuning the Developing Brain to Social Signals of Emotions', *Nature Reviews Neuroscience*, 10, 37–47.

Lewis, M. B. and Ellis, H. D. (2001) 'A Two-Way Window on Face Recognition', *Trends in Cognitive Sciences*, 5, 235.

Lewis, M. B. and Johnston, R. A. (1999) A unified account of the effects of caricaturing faces. *Visual Cognition*, 6, 1–42.

Lewis, M. B. and Sherwood, S. (2001) 'Autonomic Responses to Familiar Faces without Autonomic Responses to Familiar Voices: Evidence for Voice-Specific Capgras Delusion', *Cognitive Neuropsychiatry*, 6, 217–28.

Lewis, T. L., Ellemberg, D., Maurer, D., Dirks, M., Wilkinson, F. and Wilkinson, H. R. (2004) 'A Window on the Normal Development of Sensitivity to Global Form in Glass Patterns', *Perception*, 33, 409–18.

Li, J., Tian, M., Fang, H., Xu, M., Li, H. and Liu, J. (2010) 'Extraversion Predicts Individual Differences in Face Recognition', *Communicative and Integrative Biology*, 3, 295–8.

Lieb, R., Wittchen, H. U., Höfler, M., Fuetsch, M., Stein, M. B. and Merikangas, K. R. (2000) 'Parental Psychopathology, Parenting Styles and the Risk of Social Phobia in Offspring: A Prospective-Longitudinal Community Study', *Archives of General Psychiatry*, 57, 859–66.

Light, L. L., Kayra-Stuart, F. and Hollander, S. (1979) Recognition memory for typical and unusual faces. *Journal of Experimental Psychology: Human Learning and Memory*, 5, 212–228.

Lissauer, H. (1890) 'Ein Fall von Seelenblindheit nebst einem beitrage zur Theorie derselben', *Archiv für Psychiatrie und Nervenkrankheiten*, 21, 222–70.

Liu, J., Harris, A. and Kanwisher, N. (2002) 'Stages of Processing in Face Perception: An MEG Study', *Nature Neuroscience*, 5, 910–16.

Liu, J., Harris, A. and Kanwisher, N. (2010) 'Perception of Face Parts and Face Configurations: An fMRI Study', *Journal of Cognitive Neuroscience*, 22, 203–11.

Liu, J., Higuchi, M., Marantz, A. and Kanwisher, N. (2000) 'The Selectivity of the Occipitotemporal M170 for Faces', *NeuroReport*, 11, 337–41.

Loughland, C. M., Williams, L. M. and Gordon, E. (2002) 'Visual Scanpaths to Positive and Negative Facial Emotions in an Outpatient Schizophrenic Sample', *Schizophrenia Research*, 55, 159–70.

Loveland, K., Tunali-Kotoski, B., Chen, Y., Ortegon, J., Pearson, D., Brelsford, K. and Gibbs, M. (1997) 'Emotion Regulation in Autism: Verbal and Nonverbal Information', *Developmental Psychopathology*, 9, 579–93.

Lynn, S. K. and Salisbury, D. F. (2008) 'Attenuated Modulation of the N170 ERP by Facial Expressions in Schizophrenia', *Clinical EEG and Neuroscience*, 39, 108–11.

Macchi Cassia, V., Picozzi, M., Kuefner, D. and Casati, M. (2009) 'Why Mix-Ups Don't Happen in the Nursery: Evidence for an Experience-Based Interpretation of the other-Age Effect', *Quarterly Journal of Experimental Psychology*, 62, 1099–107.

Macchi Cassia, V., Turati, C. and Simion, F. (2004) 'Can a Nonspecific Bias toward Top-Heavy Patterns Explain Newborns' Face Preference?', *Psychological Science*, 15, 379–83.

Magee, W. J., Eaton, W. W., Wittchen, H. U., McGonagle, K. A. and Kessler, R. C. (1996) 'Agoraphobia, Simple Phobia, and Social Phobia in the National Comorbidity Survey', *Archives of General Psychiatry*, 53, 159–68.

Malpass, R. S. and Kravitz, J. (1996) 'Recognition for Faces of Own and other Race', *Journal of Personality and Social Psychology*, 13, 330–4.

Mandal, M. K. (1987) 'Decoding of Facial Emotions, in Terms of Expressiveness, by Schizophrenics and Depressives', *Psychiatry*, 50, 371–6.

Mandal, M. K., Pandey, R. and Prasad, A. B. (1998) 'Facial Expressions of Emotions and Schizophrenia: A Review', *Schizophrenia Bulletin*, 24, 399–412.

Marotta, J. J., Genovese, C. R. and Behrmann, M. (2001) 'A Functional MRI Study of Face Recognition in Patients with Prosopagnosia', *NeuroReport*, 12, 1581–7.

Marotta, J. J., McKeeff, T. J. and Behrmann, M. (2002) 'The effects of Rotation and Inversion on Face Processing in Prosopagnosia', *Cognitive Neuropsychology*, 19, 31–47.

Marsh, P. J. and Williams, L. M. (2006) 'ADHD and Schizophrenia Phenomenology: Visual Scanpaths to Emotional Faces as a Potential Psychophysiological Marker?', *Neuroscience and Biobehavioral Reviews*, 30, 651–65.

Mason, M. F., Hood, B. M. and Macrae, C. N. (2004) 'Look into My Eyes: Gaze Direction and Person Memory', *Memory*, 12, 637–43.

Mathews, A., Fox, E., Yiend, J. and Calder, A. (2003) 'The Face of Fear: Effects of Eye Gaze and Emotion on Visual Attention', *Visual Cognition*, 10, 823–35.

Mattson, A. J., Levin, H. S. and Grafman, J. (2000) 'A Case of Prosopagnosia Following Moderate Closed Head Injury with Left Hemisphere Focal Lesion', *Cortex*, 36, 125–37.

Maurer, D., Le Grand, R. and Mondloch, C. J. (2002) The many faces of configural processing. *Trends in Cognitive Science*, 6, 255–260.

McCarthy, G., Puce, A., Gore, J. C. and Allison, T. (1997) 'Face-Specific Processing in the Human Fusiform Gyrus', *Journal of Cognitive Neuroscience*, 9, 605–10.

McClelland, J. L. and Rumelhart, D. E. (1988) *Explorations in parallel distributed processing*. Cambridge, MA: Bradford Books.

McConachie, H. R. (1976) 'Developmental Prosopagnosia: A Single Case Report', *Cortex*, 12, 76–82.

McGivern, R. F., Andersen, J., Byrd, D., Mutter, K. L. and Reilly, J. (2002) 'Cognitive Efficiency on a Match to Sample Task Decreases at the Onset of Puberty in Children', *Brain and Cognition*, 50, 73–89.

McGrath, J., Saha, S., Chant, D. and Welham, J. (2008) 'Schizophrenia: A Concise Overview of Incidence, Prevalence, and Mortality', *Epidemiologic Reviews*, 30, 67–76.

McKenna, P. J. (2007) *Schizophrenia and* related syndromes (2nd edn) (HoveL Routledge).

McKone, E. and Kanwisher, N. (2005) 'Does the Human Brain Process Objects of Expertise Like Faces? A Review of the Evidence', in S. Dehaene, J. -R. Duhamel, M. Hauser, and G. Rizzolatti (eds), *From Monkey Brain to Human Brain* (Cambridge, MA: The MIT Press), 339–56.

McKone, E., Kanwisher, N. and Duchaine, B. C. (2007) 'Can Generic Expertise Explain Special Processing for Faces?', *Trends in Cognitive Sciences*, 11, 8–15.

McNeil, J. and Warrington, E. (1993) 'Prosopagnosia: A Face-Specific Disorder', *Quarterly Journal of Experimental Psychology A*, 46, 1–10.

McPartland, J., Dawson, G., Webb, S., Panagiotides, H. and Carver, L. (2004) 'Event-Related Brain Potentials Reveal Anomalies in Temporal Processing of Faces in Autism Spectrum Disorder', *Journal of Child Psychology and Psychiatry*, 45, 1235–45.

Meadows, J. C. (1974) 'The Anatomical Basis of Prosopagnosia', *Journal of Neurology, Neurosurgery and Psychiatry*, 37, 489–501.

Meissner, C. A. and Brigham, J. C. (2001) 'Thirty Years of Investigating the Own-Race Bias in Memory for Faces: A Meta-Analytic Review', *Psychology, Public Policy, and Law*, 7, 3–35.

Merzenich, M., Wright, B., Jenkins, W., Xerri, C., Byl, N., Miller, S., *et al.* (1996) 'Cortical Plasticity Underlying Perceptual, Motor, And Cognitive Skill Development: Implications for Neurorehabilitation', *Cold Spring Harbor Symposia on Quantitative Biology*, 61, 1–8.

Meyer-Lindenberg, A., Hariri, A. R., Munoz, K. E., Mervis, C. B., Mattay, V. S., Morris, C. A., *et al.* (2005) 'Neural Correlates of Genetically Abnormal Social Cognition on Williams Syndrome', *Nature Neuroscience*, 8, 991–3.

Michalopoulou, P. G., Surguladze, S., Morley, L. A., Giampietro, V. P., Murray, R. M. and Shergill, S. S. (2008) 'Facial Fear Processing and Psychotic Symptoms in Schizophrenia: Functional Magnetic Resonance Imaging Study', *British Journal of Psychiatry*, 192, 191–6.

Mills, D. L., Alvarez, T. D., St George, M., Appelbaum, L. G., Bellugi, U. and Neville, H. (2000) 'III. Electrophysiological Studies of Face Processing in Williams Syndrome', *Journal of Cognitive Neuroscience*, 12 (Suppl 1), 47–64.

Mohlman, J., Carmin, C. N. and Price, R. B. (2007) 'Jumping to Interpretations: Social Anxiety Disorder and the Identification of Emotional Facial Expressions', *Behaviour Research and Therapy*, 45, 591–9.

Mondloch, C. J., Le Grand, R. and Maurer, D. (2002) 'Configural Face Processing Develops More Slowly than Featural Face Processing', *Perception*, 31, 553–66.

Mondloch, C. J., Lewis, T. L., Budreau., D. R., Maurer, D., Dannemiller, J. L., Stephens, B. R., *et al.* (1999) 'Face Perception During Early Infancy', *Psychological Science*, 10, 419–22.

Moore, C. D., Cohen, M. X. and Ranganath, C. (2006) 'Neural Mechanisms of Expert Skills in Visual Working Memory', *Journal of Neuroscience*, 26, 11187–96.

Morris, C. A. and Mervis, C. B. (1999) 'Williams Syndrome', in C. R. Reynolds and S. Goldstein (eds), *Handbook of Neurodevelopmental and Genetic Disorders in Children* (New York, NY, US: Guildford Press), 555–90.

Moscovitch, M. and Moscovitch, D. A. (2000) 'Super Face-Inversion Effects for Isolated Internal or External Features, and for Fractured Faces', *Cognitive Neuropsychology*, 17, 201–19.

Moscovitch, M., Winocur, G. and Behrmann, M. (1997) 'What is Special about Face Recognition? Nineteen Experiments on a Person with Visual Object Agnosia and Dyslexia but Normal Face Recognition', *Journal of Cognitive Neuroscience*, 9, 555–604.

Motley, M. and Camden, C. (1988) 'Facial Expression of Emotion: A Comparison of Posed Expressions versus Spontaneous Expressions in an Interpersonal Communication Setting', *Western Journal of Speech Communication*, 52, 1–22.

Mottron, L., Dawson, M., Soulières, I., Hubert, B. and Burack, J. (2006) 'Enhanced Perceptual Functioning in Autism: An Update, and Eight Principles of Autistic Perception', *Journal of Autism and Developmental Disorders*, 36, 27–43.

Moulson, M. C., Fox, N. A., Zeanah, C. H. and Nelson, C. A. (2009) 'Early Adverse Experiences and the Neurobiology of Facial Emotion Processing', *Developmental Psychology*, 45, 17–30.

Mueser, K. T., Penn, D. L., Blanchard, J. J. and Bellack, A. S. (1997) 'Affect Recognition in Schizophrenia: A Synthesis of Findings across Three Studies', *Psychiatry*, 60, 301–8.

Murphy, D. G., Allen, G., Haxby, J. V., Largay, K. A., Daly, E., White, B. J., *et al.* (1994) 'The Effects of Sex Steroids, and the X Chromosome, on Female Brain Function: A Study of the Neuropsychology of Adult Turner Syndrome', *Neuropsychologia*, 32, 1309–23.

Naab, P. J. and Russell, J. A. (2007) 'Judgments of Emotion from Spontaneous Facial Expressions of New Guineans', *Emotion*, 7, 736–44.

Namiki, C., Hirao, K., Yamada, M., Hanakawa, T., Fukuyama, H., Hayashi, T., *et al.* (2007) 'Impaired Facial Emotion Recognition and Reduced Amygdalar Volume in Schizophrenia', *Psychiatry Research*, 156, 23–32.

Navon, D. (1977) 'Forest before Trees: The Precedence of Global Features in Visual Perception', *Cognitive Psychology*, 9, 353–83.

Nelson, C. A. (2001) 'The Development and Neural Bases of Face Recognition', *Infant and Child Development*, 10, 3–18.

Norton, D., McBain, R., Holt, D. J., Ongur, D. and Chen, Y. (2009) 'Association of Impaired Facial Affect Recognition with Basic Facial and Visual Processing Deficits in Schizophrenia', *Biological Psychiatry*, 65, 1094–8.

Nunn, J. A., Postma, P. and Pearson, R. (2001) 'Developmental Prosopagnosia: Should it be Taken at Face Value?', *Neurocase*, 7, 15–27.

O'Craven, K. M. and Kanwisher, N. (2000) 'Mental Imagery of Faces and Places Activates Corresponding Stimulus-Specific Brain Regions', *Journal of Cognitive Neuroscience*, 12, 1013–23.

O'Doherty, J., Winston, J., Critchley, H., Perrett, D., Burt, D. M. and Dolan, R. J. (2003) 'Beauty in a Smile: The Role of Medial Orbitofrontal Cortex in Facial Attractiveness', *Neuropsychologia*, 41, 147–55.

Ogai, M., Matsumoto, H., Suzuki, K., Ozawa, F., Fukuda, R., Uchiyama, I., *et al.* (2003) 'fMRI Study of Recognition of Facial Expressions in High-Functioning Autistic Patients', *NeuroReport*, 14, 559–63.

Olsson, N. and Juslin, P. (1999) 'Can Self-Reported Encoding Strategy and Recognition Skill be Diagnostic of Performance in Eyewitness Identifications?', *Journal of Applied Psychology*, 84, 42–9.

Onitsuka, T., Niznikiewicz, M. A., Spencer, K. M., Frumin, M., Kuroki, N., Lucia, L. C., *et al.* (2006) 'Functional and Structural Deficits in Brain Regions Subserving Face Perception in Schizophrenia', *American Journal of Psychiatry*, 163, 455–62.

Op De Beeck, H., Baker, C., Dicarlo, J. and Kanwisher, N. (2006) 'Discrimination Training Alters Objects Representations in Human Extrastriate Cortex', *Journal of Neuroscience*, 26, 13025–36.

Osterling, J. A., Dawson, G. and Munson, J. A. (2002) 'Early Recognition of One Year Old Infants with Autism Spectrum Disorder versus Mental Retardation', *Development and Psychopathology*, 14, 239–52.

Pascalis, O., de Haan, M. and Nelson, C. A. (2002) 'Is Face Processing Species-Specific During the First Year of Life?', *Science*, 296, 1321–3.

Passarotti, A. M., Paul, B. M., Bussiere, J. R., Buxton, R. B., Wong, E. C. and Stiles, J. (2003) 'The Development of Face and Location Processing: An fMRI Study', *Developmental Science*, 6, 100–17.

Pelli, D. G., Robson, J. G. and Wilkins, A. J. (1998) 'The Design of a New Letter Chart for Measuring Contrast Sensitivity', *Clinical Vision Sciences*, 2, 187–99.

Pellicano, E., Rhodes, G. and Peters, M. (2006) 'Are Preschoolers Sensitive to Configural Information in Faces?', *Developmental Science*, 9, 270–7.

Pelphrey, K., Morris, J., McCarthy, G. and LaBar, K. (2007) 'Perception of Dynamic Changes in Facial Affect and Identity in Autism', *Social, Cognitive and Affective Neuroscience*, 2, 140–9.

Pelphrey, K. A., Sasson, N. J., Reznich, J. S., Paul, G., Goldman, B. D. and Piven, J. (2002) 'Visual Scanning of Faces in Autism', *Journal of Autism and Developmental Disorders*, 32, 249–61.

Pelphrey, K. A., Singerman, J. D., Allison, T. and McGarthy, G. (2003) 'Brain Activation Evoked by Perception of Gaze Shifts: The Influence of Context', *Neuropsychologia*, 41, 156–70.

Penn, D. L., Combs, D. R., Ritchie, M., Franics, J., Cassisi, J., Morris, S., *et al.* (2000) 'Emotion Recognition in Schizophrenia: Further Investigation of Generalized versus Specific Deficit Models', *Journal of Abnormal Psychology,* 109, 512–16.

Perlman, W. R., Webster, M. J., Kleinman, J. E. and Weickert, C. S. (2004) 'Reduced Glucocorticoid and Estrogen Receptor Alpha Messenger Ribonucleic Acid Levels in the Amygdala of Patients with Major Mental Illness', *Biological Psychiatry,* 56, 844–52.

Perrett, D. I., Hietanen, J. K., Oram, M. W. and Benson, P. J. (1992) 'Organization and Functions of Cells Responsive to Faces in the Temporal Cortex', *Philosophical Transactions of the Royal Society of London B,* 335, 23–30.

Perrett, D. I., Rolls, E. T. and Caan, W. (1982) 'Visual Neurones Responsive to Faces in the Monkey Temporal Cortex', *Experimental Brain Research,* 47, 329–42.

Pessoa, L. (2009) 'How Do Emotion and Motivation Direct Executive Control?', *Trends in Cognitive Science,* 13, 160–6.

Phan, K. L., Fitzgerald, D. A., Nathan, P. J. and Tancer, M. E. (2006) 'Association between Amygdala Hyperactivity to Harsh Faces and Severity of Social Anxiety in Generalized Social Phobia', *Biological Psychiatry,* 59, 424–9.

Phillips, M. L., Williams, L., Senior, C., Bullmore, E. T., Brammer, M. J., Andrew, C., *et al.* (1999) 'A Differential Neural Response to Threatenings and Non-Threatening Negative Facial Expressions in Paranoid and Non-Paranoid Schizophrenics', *Psychiatry Research,* 92, 11–31.

Picozzi, M., Macchi Cassia, V., Turati, C. and Vescovo, E. (2009) 'The Effect of Inversion on 3- to 5-Year-Olds' Recognition of Face and Nonface Visual Objects', *Journal of Experimental Child Psychology,* 102, 487–502.

Pierce, K., Muller, R. A., Ambrose, J., Allen, G. and Courchesne, E. (2001) 'Face Processing Occurs Outside the Fusiform "Face Area" in Autism: Evidence from Functional MRI', *Brain,* 124, 2059–73.

Pinsk, M. A., DeSimone, K., Morre, T., Gross, C.G. and Kastner, S. (2005) 'Representations of Faces and Body Parts in Macaque Temporal Cortex: A Functional MRI Study', *Proceedings of the National Academy of Sciences of the USA,* 102, 6996–7001.

Pitcher, D., Charles, L., Devlin, J. T., Walsh, V. and Duchaine, B. (2009) 'Triple Dissociation of Faces, Bodies, and Objects in Extrastriate Cortex', *Current Biology,* 19, 319–24.

Pitcher, D., Walsh, V. and Duchaine, B. (2011) 'The Role of the Occipital Face Area in the Cortical Face Perception Network', *Experimental Brain Research,* 209, 481–93.

Pitcher, D., Walsh, V., Yovel, G. and Duchaine, B. (2007) 'TMS Evidence for the Involvement of the Right Occipital Face Area in Early Face Processing', *Current Biology,* 17, 1568–73.

Pollak, S. D., Cicchetti, D., Hornung, K. and Reed, A. (2000) 'Recognizing Emotion in Faces: Developmental Effects of Child Abuse and Neglect', *Developmental Psychology,* 36, 679–88.

Pollak, S. D., Messner, M., Kistler, D. J. and Cohn, J. F. (2009) 'Development of Perceptual Expertise in Emotion Recognition', *Cognition,* 110, 242–7.

Porter, M. A., Shaw, T. and Marsh, P. J. (2010) 'An Unusual Attraction to the Eyes in Williams-Beuren Syndrome: A Manipulation of Facial Affect while Measuring Face Scanpaths', *Cognitive Neuropsychiatry,* 15, 505–30.

Posner, M. I. (1980) 'Orienting of attention', *Quarterly Journal of Experimental Psychology,* 32, 3–25.

Pourtois, G., Sander, D., Andres, M., Grandjean, D., Reveret, L., Olivier, E., *et al.* (2004) 'Dissociable Roles of the Human Somatosensory and Superior Temporal Cortices for Processing Social Face Signals', *European Journal of Neuroscience,* 20, 3507–15.

Pourtois, G., Schwarz, S., Seghier, M. L., Lazeyras, F. and Vuilleumier, P. (2005) 'Portraits or People? Distinct Representations of Face Identity in the Human Visual Cortex', *Journal of Cognitive Neuroscience,* 17, 1043–57.

Powell, J., Letson, S., Davidoff, J., Valentine, T. and Greenwood, R. (2008) 'Enhancement of Face Recognition Learning in Patients with Brain Injury Using Three Cognitive Training Procedures', *Neuropsychological Rehabilitation*, 18, 182–203.

Pozzulo, J. D. and Lindsay, R. C. L. (1998) 'Identification Accuracy of Children versus Adults: A Meta-Analysis', *Law and Human Behavior*, 22, 549–70.

Puce, A., Allison, T., Bentin, S., Gore, J. C. and McGarthy, G. (1998) 'Temporal Cortex Activation in Humans Viewing Eye and Mouth Movements', *Journal of Neuroscience*, 18, 2188–99.

Quaglino, A. and Borelli, G. (1867) 'Emiplegia sinistra con amaurosi – guarigione – perdita totale della percezione dei colori e della memoria della configurazione degli oggetti', *Giornale d'Oftalmologia Italiano*, 10, 106–17.

Quinn, P. C. and Slater, A. (2003) 'Face Perception at Birth and Beyond', in O. Pascalis and A. Slater (eds), *The Development of Face Processing in Infancy and Early Childhood: Current Perspectives* (New York: Nova Science Publisher, 3–12.

Quinn, P. C. and Tanaka, J. W. (2009) 'Infants' Processing of Featural and Configural Information in the Upper and Lower Halves of the Face', *Infancy*, 14, 474–87.

Reed, C. L., Stone, V. E., Bozova, S. and Tanaka, J. (2003) 'The Body-Inversion Effect', *Psychological Science*, 14, 302–8.

Reed, C. L., Stone, V. E., Grubb, J. D. and McGoldrick, J. E. (2006) 'Turning Configural Processing Upside Down: Part and Whole Body Postures', *Journal of Experimental Psychology: Human Perception and Performance*, 32, 73–87.

Reid, I., Young, A. W. and Hellawell, D. J. (1993) 'Voice Recognition Impairment in a Blind Capgras Patient', *Behavioral Neurology*, 6, 225–8.

Reiss, A. L., Eckert, M. A., Rose, F. E., Karchemskiy, A., Kesler, S., Chang, M., Reynolds, M. F., Kwon, H. and Galaburda, A. (2004) 'An Experiment of Nature: Brain Anatomy Parallels Cognition and Behaviour in Williams Syndrome', *Journal of Neuroscience*, 24, 5009–15.

Reiss, A. L., Freund, L., Plotnick, L., Baumgardner, T., Green, K., Sozer, A. C., Reader, M., Boehm, C. and Denokla, M. B. (1993) 'The Effects of X Monosomy on Brain Development: Monozygotic Twins Discordant for Turner's Syndrome', *Annals of Neurology*, 34, 95–107.

Rhodes, G., Brennan, S. and Carey, S. (1987) Identification and ratings of caricatures: Implications for mental representations of faces. *Cognitive Psychology*, 19, 473–497.

Rhodes, G., Byatt, G., Michie, P. T. and Puce, A. (2004) 'Is the Fusiform Face Area Specialized for Faces, Individuation, or Expert Identification?', *Journal of Cognitive Neuroscience*, 16, 189–203.

Rhodes, G., Harwood, K., Yoshikawa, S., Nishitani, M. and McLean, I. (2002) 'The Attractiveness of Average Faces: Cross-Cultural Evidence and Possible Biological Basis', in G. Rhodes and L. A. Zebrowitz (eds), *Facial Attractiveness Evolutionary, Cognitive and Social Perspectives* (Westport, CT: Ablex), 35–58.

Riddoch, M. J., Johnston, R. A., Bracewell, R. M., Boutsen, R. and Humphreys, G. W. (2008) 'Are Faces Special? A Case of Pure Prosopagnosia', *Cognitive Neuropsychology*, 25, 3–26.

Ridout, N., Dritschel, B., Matthews, K., McVicar, M., Reid, I. C. and O'Carroll, R. E. (2009) 'Memory for Emotional Faces in Major Depression Following Judgment of Physical Facial Characteristics at Encoding', *Cognition and Emotion*, 23, 739–52.

Rimmele, U., Hediger, K., Heinrichs, M. and Klaver, P. (2009) 'Oxytocin Makes a Face in Memory Familiar', *The Journal of Neuroscience*, 29, 38–42.

Ristic, J., Friesen, C. K. and Kingstone, A. (2002) 'Are Eyes Special? It Depends on How You Look at it', *Psychonomic Bulletin and Review*, 9, 507–13.

Rizzo, M., Hurtig, R. and Damasio, A. R. (1987) 'The Role of Scanpaths in Facial Recognition and Learning', *Annals of Neurology*, 22, 41–5.

Robbins, R. and McKone, E. (2003) 'Can Holistic Processing be Learned for Inverted Faces?', *Cognition,* 88, 79–107.

Robbins, R. and McKone, E. (2007) No face-like processing of objects-of-expertise in three behavioural tasks. *Cognition,* 103, 34–79.

Rojo, V. I., Caballero, L., Irvela, L. M. and Baca, E. (1991) 'Capgras' Syndrome in a Blind Patient', *American Journal of Psychiatry,* 148, 1272.

Romans, S. M., Stefanatos, G., Roeltgen, D. P., Kushner, H. and Ross, J. L. (1998) 'Transition to Young Adulthood in Ullrich-Turner Syndrome: Neurodevelopmental Changes', *American Journal of Medical Genetics,* 79, 140–7.

Rose, F. E., Lincoln, A. J., Lai, Z., Ene, M., Searcy, Y. M. and Bellugi, U. (2007) 'Orientation and Affective Expression Effects on Face Recognition in Williams Syndrome and Autism', *Journal of Autism and Developmental Disorders,* 37, 513–22.

Ross, J. L., Kushner, H. and Zinn, A. R. (1997) 'Discriminant Analysis of the Ullrich-Turner Syndrome Neurocognitive Profile', *American Journal of Medical Genetics,* 72, 275–80.

Ross, J. L., Stefanatos, G., Roeltgen, D., Kushner, H. and Cutler, G. B., Jr. (1995) 'Ullrich-Turner Syndrome: Neurodevelopmental Changes from Childhood through Adolescence', *American Journal of Medical Genetics,* 58, 74–82.

Rossion, B., Caldara, R., Segnier, M., Schuller, A. -M., Lazeyras, F. and Mayer, E. (2003) 'A Network of Occipito-Temporal Face-Sensitive Areas Besides the Right Middle Fusiform Gyrus is Necessary for Normal Face Processing', *Brain,* 126, 2381–95.

Rossion, B., Gauthier, I., Goffaux, V., Tarr, M. J. and Crommelinck, M. (2002) 'Expertise Training with Novel Objects Leads to Left-Lateralized Facelike Electrophysiological Responses', *Psychological Science,* 13, 250–7.

Rossion, B., Joyce, C. A., Cottrell, G. W. and Tarr, M. J. (2003) 'Early Lateralization and Orientation Tuning for Face, Word, and Object Processing in the Visual Cortex', *NeuroImage,* 20, 1609–24.

Rossion, B., Kaiser, M. D., Bub, D. and Tanaka, J. W. (2009) 'Is the Loss of Diagnosticity of the Eye Region a Common Feature of Acquired Prosopagnosia?', *Journal of Neuropsychology,* 3, 69–78.

Rosso, I. M., Cintron, C. M., Steingard, R. J., Renshaw, P. F., Young, A. D. and Yurgelun-Todd, D. A. (2005) 'Amygdala and Hippocampus Volumes in Pediatric Major Depression', *Biological Psychiatry,* 57, 21–6.

Rouse, H., Donnelly, N., Hadwin, J. A. and Brown, T. (2004) 'Do Children with Autism Perceive Second-Order Relational Features? The Case of the Thatcher Illusion', *Journal of Child Psychology and Psychiatry,* 45, 1246–57.

Russell, J. A. (1994) 'Is there Universal Recognition of Emotion from Facial Expressions? A Review of the Cross-Cultural Studies', *Psychological Review,* 115, 102–41.

Russell, R., Duchaine, B. and Nakayama, K. (2009) 'Super-Recognizers: People with Extraordinary Face Recognition Ability', *Psychonomic Bulletin and Review,* 16, 252–7.

Russell, T. A., Chu, E. and Phillips, M. L. (2006) 'An Investigation of the Effectiveness of Emotion Recognition Remediation in Schizophrenia Using the Micro-Expression Training Tool', *British Journal of Clinical Psychology,* 45, 579–83.

Russell, T. A., Green, M. J., Simpson, I. and Coltheart, M. (2008) 'Remediation of Facial Emotion Perception in Schizophrenia: Concomitant Changes in Visual Attention', *Schizophrenia Research,* 103, 248–56.

Russell, T. A., Reynaud, E., Kucharska-Pietura, K., Ecker, C., Benson, P. J., Zelaya, F., et al. (2007) 'Neural Responses to Dynamic Expressions of Fear in Schizophrenia', *Neuropsychologia,* 45, 107–23.

Sachs, G., Steger-Wuchse, D., Kryspin-Exner, I., Gur, R. C. and Katschnig, H. (2004) 'Facial Recognition Deficits and Cognition in Schizophrenia', *Schizophrenia Research,* 68, 27–35.

Sangrigoli, S., Pallier, C., Argenti, A. -M., Ventureyra, V. A. G. and de Schonen, S. (2005) 'Reversibility of the other-Race Effect in Face Recognition During Childhood', *Psychological Science,* 16, 440–4.

Scherf, K. S., Behrmann, M., Humphreys, K. and Luna, B. (2007) 'Visual Category-Selectivity for Faces, Places and Objects Emerges along Different Developmental Trajectories', *Developmental Science,* 10, F15–F31.

Schiltz, C. and Rossion, B. (2006) 'Faces are Represented Holistically in the Human Occipito-Temporal Cortex', *NeuroImage,* 32, 1385–94.

Schiltz, C., Sorger, B., Caldara, R., Ahmed, F., Mayer, E., Goebel, R. and Rossion, B. (2006) 'Impaired Face Discrimination in Acquired Prosopagnosia is Associated with Abnormal Response to Individuals Faces in the Right Middle Fusiform Gyrus', *Cerebral Cortex,* 16, 574–86.

Schmalzl, L., Palermo, R. and Coltheart, M. (2008) 'Cognitive Heterogeneity in Genetically-Based Prosopagnosia: A Family Study', *Journal of Neuropsychology,* 2, 99–117.

Schmalzl, L., Palermo, R., Green, M., Brunsdon, R. and Coltheart, M. (2008) 'Training of Familiar Face Recognition and Visual Scan Paths for Faces in a Child with Congenital Prosopagnosia', *Cognitive Neuropsychology,* 25, 704–29.

Schneider, F., Gur, R. C., Gur, R. E. and Shtasel, D. L. (1995) 'Emotional Processing in Schizophrenia: Neurobehavioral Probes in Relation to Psychopathology', *Schizophrenia Research,* 17, 67–75.

Schultz, R. T. (2005) 'Developmental Deficits in Social Perception in Autism: The Role of the Amygdala and Fusiform Face Area', *International Journal of Developmental Neuroscience,* 23, 125–41.

Schultz, R. T., Gauthier, I., Klin, A., Fulbright, R. K., Anderson, A. W., Volkmar, F., *et al.* (2000) 'Abnormal Ventral Temporal Cortical Activity during Face Discrimination among Individuals with Autism and Asperger Syndrome', *Archives of General Psychiatry,* 57, 331–43.

Schwarz, B. L., Marvel, C. L., Drapalski, A., Rosse, R. B. and Deutsch, S. I. (2002) 'Configural Processing in Face Recognition in Schizophrenia', *Cognitive Neuropsychiatry,* 7, 15–39.

Schwarzer, G., Huber, S., Grueter, M., Grueter, T., Groβ, C., Hipfel, M., *et al.* (2007) 'Gaze Behaviour in Hereditary Prosopagnosia', *Psychological Research,* 71, 583–90.

Schwarzlose, R. F., Baker, C. I. and Kanwisher, N. (2005) 'Separate Face and Body Selectivity on the Fusiform Gyrus', *The Journal of Neuroscience,* 25, 11055–9.

Schyns, P. G. and Oliva, A. (1999) 'Dr. Angry and Mr. Smile: When Categorization Flexibly Modifies the Perception of Faces in Rapid Visual Presentations', *Cognition,* 69, 243–65.

Scott, L. S., Pascalis, O. and Nelson, C. A. (2007) 'A Domain-General Theory of the Development of Perceptual Discrimination', *Current Directions in Psychological Science,* 16, 197–201.

Searcy, Y. M., Lincoln, A. J., Rose, F. E., Klima, E. S., Bavar, N. and Korenberg, J. R. (2004) 'The Relationship between Age and IQ in Adults with Williams Syndrome', *American Journal on Mental Retardation,* 109, 231–6.

Sergent, J., Ohta, S., MacDonald, B. and Zuck, E. (1994) 'Segregated Processing of Facial Identity and Emotion in the Human Brain', *Visual Cognition,* 1, 349–69.

Sergent, J. and Signoret, J. -L. (1992) 'Varieties of Functional Deficits in Prosopagnosia', *Cerebral Cortex,* 2, 375–88.

Seron, X., Mataigne, F., Coyette, F., Rectem, D., Bruyer, R. and Laterre, E. C. (1995) 'A Case of Metamorphopsia Restricted to Faces and Different Familiar Objects', *Revue Neurologique,* 151, 691–8.

Shallice, T. (1988) *From Neuropsychology to Mental Structure* (Cambridge: Cambridge University Press).

Sheline, Y. I., Barch, D. M., Donnelly, J. M., Ollinger, J. M., Snyder, A. Z. and Mintun, M. A. (2001) 'Increased Amygdala Response to Masked Emotional Faces in Depressed Subjects Resolves with Antidepressant Treatment: An fMRI Study', *Biological Psychiatry*, 50, 651–8.

Shin, Y. -W., Na, M. H., Ha, T. H., Kang, D. -H., Yoo, S. -Y. and Kwon, J. S. (2008) 'Dysfunction In Configural Processing in Patients with Schizophrenia', *Schizophrenia Bulletin*, 34, 538–43.

Signer, S. F., Van Ness, P. C. and Davis, R. J. (1990) 'Capgras' Syndrome Associated with Sensory Loss', *Western Journal of Medicine*, 152, 719–20.

Silva, J. A. and Leong, G. B. (1991) 'A Case of "subjective" Frégoli Syndrome', *Journal of Psychiatry and Neuroscience*, 16, 103–5.

Silva, J. A., Leong, G. B., Weinstock, R. and Ruiz-Sweeney, M. (2001) 'Delusional Misidentification and Aggression in Alzheimer's Disease', *Journal of Forensic Science*, 46, 581–5.

Silver, H., Goodman, R., Biker, W., Gur, R. C., Isakov, V., Knoll, G., *et al.* (2006) 'Impaired Error Monitoring Contributes to Face Recognition Deficit in Schizophrenic Patients', *Schizophrenia research*, 85, 151–61.

Silver, H., Shlomo, N., Turner, T. and Gur, R. C. (2002) 'Perception of Happy and Sad Facial Expressions in Chronic Schizophrenia: Evidence for Two Evaluative Systems', *Schizophrenia Research*, 55, 171–7.

Silver, M. and Oakes, P. (2001) 'Evaluation of a New Computer Intervention to Teach People with Autism or Asperger Syndrome to Recognize and Predict Emotions in Others', *Autism*, 5, 299–316.

Simion, F., Valenza, E., Macchi Cassia, V., Turati, C. and Umilta, C. (2002) 'Newborns' Preference of Up-Down Asymmetrical Configurations', *Developmental Science*, 5, 427–34.

Skuse, D. H., James, R. S., Bishop, D. V., Coppin, B., Dalton, P., Aamodt-Leeper, G., *et al.* (1997) 'Evidence from Turner's Syndrome of an Imprinted X-Linked Locus Affecting Cognitive Function', *Nature*, 387, 705–8.

Slater, A., Van der Schulenberg, C., Brown, E., Badenoch, M., Butterworth, G., *et al.* (1998) 'Newborn Infants Prefer Attractive Faces', *Infant Behavior and Development*, 21, 345–4.

Slaughter, V., Heron, M. and Sim, S. (2002) 'Development of Preferences for the Human Body Shape in Infancy', *Cognition*, 85, B71–B81.

Snodgrass, J. G. and Vanderwort, M. (1980) 'A Standardized Set of 160 Pictures: Norms for Name Agreement, Image Agreement, Familiarity, and Visual Complexity', *Journal of Experimental Psychology: Human Perception and Performance*, 6, 174–215.

Solomon, M., Goodlin-Jones, B. L. and Anders, T. F. (2004) 'A Social Adjustment Enhancement Intervention for High Functioning Autism', Asperger's Syndrome, and Pervasive Developmental Disorder NOS. *Journal of Autism and Developmental Disorders*, 34, 649–68.

Sorger, B., Goebel, R., Schiltz, C. and Rossion, B. (2007) 'Understanding the Functional Neuroanatomy of Acquired Prosopagnosia', *NeuroImage*, 35, 836–52.

Staton, R. D., Brunback, R. A. and Wilson, H. (1982) 'Reduplicative Paramnesia: A Disconnection Syndrome of Memory', *Cortex*, 18, 23–36.

Steeves, J. E., Culham, J. C., Duchaine, B. C., Cavina Pratesi, C., Valyear, K. F., Schindler, I., *et al.* (2006) 'The Fusiform Face Area is not Sufficient for Face Recognition: Evidence from a Patient with Dense Prosopagnosia and no Occipital Face Area. *Neuropsychologia*, 44, 594–609.

Steeves, J., Dricot, L., Goltz, H. C., Sorger, B., Peters, J., Milner, A. D., *et al.* (2009) 'Abnormal Face Identity Coding in the Middle Fusiform Gyrus of Two Brain-Damaged Prosopagnosic Patients', *Neuropsychologia*, 47, 2584–92.

Stephan, B. C. and Caine, D. (2009) 'Aberrant Pattern of Scanning in Prosopagnosia Reflects Impaired Face Processing', *Brain and Cognition*, 69, 262–8.

Sterling, L., Dawson, G., Webb, S. J., Murias, M., Munson, J., Panagiotides, H., *et al.* (2008) 'The Role of Face Familiarity in Eye Tracking of Faces by Individuals with Autism Spectrum Disorders', *Journal of Autism and Developmental Disorders*, 38, 1666–75.

Stollhoff, R., Jost, J., Elze, T. and Kennerknecht, I. (2011) 'Deficits in Long-Term Recognition Memory Reveal Dissociated Subtypes in Congenital Prosopagnosia', *PLoS One*, 6, e15702.

Striano, T. and Reid, V. M. (2006) 'Social Cognition in the First Year', *Trends in Cognitive Sciences*, 10, 471–6.

Stromme, P., Bjornstad, P. G. and Ramstad, K. (2002) 'Prevalence Estimation of Williams Syndrome', *Journal of Child Neurology*, 17, 269–71.

Sugita, Y. (2009) 'Innate Face Processing', *Current Opinion in Neurobiology*, 19, 39–44.

Surguladze, S., Brammer, M. J., Keedwell, P., Giampietro, V., Young, A. W., Travis, M. J., *et al.* (2005) 'A Differential Pattern of Neural Response toward Sad versus Happy Facial Expressions in Major Depressive Disorder', *Biological Psychiatry*, 57, 201–9.

Surguladze, S., Russell, T., Kucharska-Pietura, K., Travis, M. J., Giampietro, V., David, A. S., *et al.* (2006) 'A Reversal of the Normal Pattern of Parahippocampal Response to Neutral and Fearful Faces is Associated with Reality Distortion in Schizophrenia', *Biological Psychiatry*, 57, 201–9.

Surguladze, S. A., Young, A., Senior, C., Brébion, G., Travis, M. J. and Phillips, M. L. (2004) 'Recognition Accuracy and Response Bias to Happy and Sad Facial Expressions in Patients with Major Depression', *Neuropsychology*, 18, 212–18.

Tager-Flusberg, H., Plesa-Skwerer, D., Faja, S. and Joseph, R. M. (2003) 'People with Williams Syndrome Process Faces Holistically', *Cognition*, 89, 11–24.

Tanaka, J. W. and Curran, T. (2001) 'A Neural Basis for Expert Object Recognition', *Psychological Science*, 12, 43–7.

Tanaka, J. W. and Farah, M. J. (1993) Parts and wholes in face recognition. *Quarterly Journal of Experimental Psychology: Human Experimental Psychology*, *46A*, 225–245.

Tanaka, J. W., Lincoln, S. and Hegg, L. (2003) 'A Framework for the Study and Treatment of Face Processing Deficits in Autism', in H. Leider and G. Schwarzer (eds), *The Development of Face Processing* (Berlin: Hogrefe), 101–10.

Tanaka, J. and Porterfield, A. (2002) 'The Own-Face Effect as an Electrophysiological Marker of Self', *Cognitive Neuroscience Society: Ninth Annual Meeting Abstracts*, 66.

Tanaka, J. W., Wolf, J. M., Klaiman, C., Koenig, K., Cockburn, J., Herlihy, L., *et al.* (2010) 'Using Computerized Games to Teach Face Recognition Skills to Children with Autism Spectrum Disorder: The *Let's Face It!* Program', *Journal of Child Psychology and Psychiatry*, 51, 944–52.

Tanskanen, T., Nasanen, R., Ojanpaa, H. and Hari, R. (2007) 'Face Recognition and Cortical Responses: Effect of Stimulus Duration', *NeuroImage*, 35, 1636–44.

Tarr, M. J. and Gauthier, I. (2000) 'FFA: A Flexible Fusiform Area for Subordinate-Level Visual Processing Automatized by Expertise', *Nature Neuroscience*, 3, 764–9.

Tassabehji, M. (2003) 'Williams-Beuren Syndrome: A Challenge for Genotype-Phenotype Correlations', *Human Molecular Genetics*, 12, 229–37.

Taylor, M. J., Batty, M. and Itier, R. J. (2004) 'The Faces of Development: A Review of Early Face Processing Over Childhood', *Journal of Cognitive Neuroscience*, 16, 1426–42.

Temple, C. M. (1992) *Developmental Memory Impairment: Faces and Patterns*, in R. Campbell (ed.), *Mental Lives: Case Studies in Cognition* :(Oxford: Blackwell).

Teunisse, J. P. and de Gelder, B. (2003) 'Face Processing in Adolescents with Autistic Disorder: The Inversion and Composite Effects', *Brain and Cognition*, 51, 285–94.

Thibault, P., Bourgeois, P. and Hess, U. (2006) 'The Effect of Group Identification on Emotion Recognition: The Case of Cats and Basketball Players', *Journal of Experimental and Social Psychology*, 42, 676–83.

Thomas, C., Avidan, G., Humphreys, K., Jung, K. J., Gao, F. and Behrmann, M. (2009) 'Reduced Structural Connectivity in Ventral Visual Cortex in Congenital Prosopagnosia', *Nature Neuroscience*, 29, 29–31.

Thompson, P. (1980) Margaret Thatcher: A new illusion. *Perception*, 9, 483–484.

Thompson, P. M., Lee, A. D., Dutton, R. A., Geaga, J. A., Hayashi, K. M., Eckert, M. A., *et al.* (2005) 'Abnormal Cortical Complexity and Thickness Profiles Mapped in Williams Syndrome', *Journal of Neuroscience*, 25, 4146–58.

Tippett, L. J., Miller, L. A. and Farah, M. J. (2000) 'Prosopamnesia: A Selective Impairment in Face Learning', *Cognitive Neuropsychology*, 17, 241–55.

Tipples, J. (2002) 'Eye Gaze is Not Unique: Automatic Orienting in Response to Uninformative Arrows',. *Psychonomic Bulletin and Review*, 9, 314–18.

Tipples, J. (2005) 'Orienting to Eye Gaze and Face Processing', *Journal of Experimental Psychology: Human Perception and Performance*, 31, 843–56.

Todorov, A. and Duchaine, B. (2008) 'Reading Trustworthiness in Faces without Recognizing Faces', *Cognitive Neuropsychology*, 25, 395–410.

Tranel, D., Damasio, A. R. and Damasio, H. (1988) 'Intact Recognition of Facial Expression, Gender, and Age in Patients with Impaired Recognition of Face Identity', *Neurology*, 38, 690–6.

Tranel, D., Damasio, H. and Damasio, A. R. (1995) 'Double Dissociation between Overt and Covert Face Recognition', *Journal of Cognitive Neuroscience*, 7, 425–32.

Tsao, D. Y., Freiwald, W. A., Knutsen, T. A., Mandeville, J. B. and Tootell, R. B. (2003) 'Faces and Objects in Macaque Cerebral Cortex', *Nature Neuroscience*, 6, 989–95.

Tsao, D. Y., Freiwald, W. A., Tootell, R. B. H. and Livingstone, M. S. (2006) 'A Cortical Region Consisting Entirely of Face-Selective Cells', *Science*, 311, 670–4.

Tsirempolou, E., Lawrence, K., Lee, K., Ewing, S. and Karmiloff-Smith, A. (2006) 'Understanding the Social Meaning of the Eyes: Is Williams Syndrome So Different from Autism?', *World Journal of Pediatrics*, 2, 288–96.

Tsoi, D. T., Lee, K. H., Khokhar, W. A., Mir, N. U., Swalli, J. S., Gee, K. A., *et al.* (2008) 'Is Facial Emotion Recognition Impairment in Schizophrenia Identical for Different Emotions? A Signal Detection Analysis', *Schizophrenia Research*, 99, 263–9.

Turati, C., Bulf, H. and Simion, F. (2008) 'Newborns' Face Recognition Over Changes in Viewpoint', *Cognition*, 106, 1300–21.

Turetsky, B. I., Kohler, C. G., Indersmitten, T., Bhati, M. T., Charbonnier, D. and Gur, R. C. (2007) 'Facial Emotion Recognition in Schizophrenia: When and Why Does it Go Awry?', *Schizophrenia Research*, 94, 253–63.

Valentine, T. (1991) 'A Unified Account of the Effects of Distinctiveness, Inversion and Race in Face Recognition', *Quarterly Journal of Experimental Psychology*, 43A, 161–204.

Valentine, T. and Bruce, V. (1986a) Recognizing familiar faces: The role of distinctiveness and familiarity. *Canadian Journal of Psychology*, 40, 300–305.

Valentine, T. and Bruce, V. (1986b) The effect of distinctiveness in recognizing and classifying faces. *Perception*, 15, 525–535.

Valentine, T. and Endo, M. (1992) Towards an exemplar model of face processing: The effects of race and distinctiveness. *Quarterly Journal of Experimental Psychology*, 44A, 671–703.

Valentine, T., Powell, J., Davidoff, F, Letson, S. and Greenwood, R. (2006) 'Prevalence and Correlates of Face Recognition Impairments after Acquired Brain Injury', *Neuropsychological Rehabilitation*, 16, 272–97.

Valenza, E., Simion, F., Cassia, V. M. and Umilta, C. (1996) 'Face Preference at Birth', *Journal of Experimental Psychology: Human Perception and Performance*, 22, 892–903.

Van Os, J. and Kapur, S. (2009) 'Schizophrenia', *Lancet,* 374, 635–48.

Van't Wout, M., van Dijke, A., Aleman, A., Kessels, R. P., Pijpers, W. and Kahn, R. S. (2007) 'Fearful Faces in Schizophrenia: The Relationship between Patient Characteristics and Facial Affect Recognition', *Journal of Nervous and Mental Disease,* 195, 758–64.

Von Kriegstein, K., Kleinschmidt, A. and Giraud, A. L. (2006) 'Voice Recognition and Cross-Modal Responses to Familiar Speakers' Voices in Prosopagnosia', *Cerebral Cortex,* 16, 1314–22.

Vuilleumier, P., Armony, J. L., Driver, J. and Dolan, R. J. (2001) 'Effects of Attention and Emotion on Face Processing in the Human Brain: An Event-Related fMRI Study', *Neuron,* 30, 829–41.

Walker, E. F., McGuire, M. and Bettes, B. (1984) 'Recognition and Identification of Facial Stimuli by Schizophrenics and Patients with Affective Disorders', *British Journal of Clinical Psychology,* 23, 37–44.

Wallace, S., Coleman, M. and Bailey, A. (2008) 'An Investigation of Basic Facial Expression Recognition in Autism Spectrum Disorders', *Cognition and Emotion,* 22, 1353–80.

Walther, S., Federspiel, A., Horn, H., Bianchi, P., Wiest, R., Wirth, M., *et al.* (2009) 'Encoding Deficit During Face Processing within the Right Fusiform Face Area in Schizophrenia'., *Psychiatry research: Neuroimaging,* 172, 184–91.

Wang, A. T., Dapretto, M., Hariri, A. R., Sigman, M. and Bookheimer, S. Y. (2004) 'Neural Correlates of Facial Affect Processing in Children and Adolescents with Autism Spectrum Disorder', *Journal of the American Academy of Child and Adolescent Psychiatry,* 43, 481–90.

Wang, P. P., Doherty, S., Rourke, S. B. and Bellugi, U. (1995) 'Unique Profile of Visuo-Perceptual Skills in a Genetic Syndrome', *Brain and Cognition,* 29, 54–65.

Warrington, E. K. (1984) *Recognition Memory Test* (Windsor, UK: NFER-Nelson).

Warrington, E. K. and James, M. (1967) 'An Experimental Investigation of Facial Recognition in Patients with Unilateral Cerebral Lesions', *Cortex,* 3, 317–26.

Warrington, E. K. and James, M. (1991) *Visual Object and Space Perception Battery (VOSP)* (Thames Valley Test Company: Bury St Edmunds).

Wechsler, D. (2001) *Wechsler Test of Adult Reading* (San Antonio, TX: The Psychological Corporation).

Weisberg, J., van Turennout, M. and Martin, A. (2007) 'A Neural System for Learning about Object Function', *Cerebral Cortex,* 17, 513–21.

Weniger, G., Lange, C., Ruther, E. and Irle, E. (2004) 'Differential Impairments of Facial Affect Recognition in Schizophrenia Subtypes and Major Depression', *Psychiatry Research,* 128, 135–46.

Whittaker, J. F., Deakin, J. F. and Tomenson, B. (2001) 'Face Processing in Schizophrenia: Defining the Deficit', *Psychological Medicine,* 31, 499–507.

Wigan, A. L. (1844) *A New View of Insanity: The Duality of the Mind* (London: Longman).

Wilbrand, H. (1887) *Die Seelenblindheit als Herderscheinung und ihre Beziehungen zur homonymen Hemianopsie* (Wiesbaden: J.F. Bergmann).

Wilkinson, F., James, T. W., Wilson, H. R., Gati, J. S., Menon, R. S. and Goodale, M. A. (2000) 'An fMRI Study of the Selective Activation of Human Extrastriate Form Vision Areas by Radial and Concentric Gratings', *Current Biology,* 10, 1455–8.

Wilkinson, F., Wilson, H. R. and Habak, C. (1998) 'Detection and Recognition of Radial Frequency Patterns', *Vision Research,* 38, 3555–68.

Williams, L. M., Das, P., Harris, A. W., Liddell, B. B., Brammer, M. J., Olivieri, G., *et al.* (2004) 'Dysregulation of Arousal and Amygdala-Prefrontal Systems in Paranoid Schizophrenia', *American Journal of Psychiatry,* 161, 480–9.

Williams, M. A., Berberovic, N. and Mattingley, J. B. (2007) 'Abnormal fMRI Adaptation to Unfamiliar Faces in a Case of Developmental Prosopamnesia', *Current Biology*, 17, 1259–64.

Wilmer, J. B., Germine, L., Chabris C. F., Chatterjee, G., Williams, M., Loken, E. *et al.* (2010) 'Human Face Recognition is Highly Heritable', *Proceedings of the National Academy of Sciences of the USA*, 107, 5238–41.

Wilson, R. R., Blades, M. and Pascalis, O. (2007) 'What Do Children Look at in an Adult Face with which They are Personally Familiar?',*British Journal of Developmental Psychology*, 25, 375–82.

Winston, J. S., Vuilleumier, P. and Dolan, R. J. (2003) 'Effects of Low-Spatial Frequency Components of Fearful Faces on Fusiform Cortex Activity', *Current Biology*, 13, 1824–29.

Wittchen, H. U., Nelson, C. B. and Lachner, G. (1998) 'Prevalence of Mental Disorders and Psychosocial Impairments in Adolescents and Young Adults', *Psychological Medicine*, 28, 109–6.

Wojciulik, E., Kanwisher, N. and Driver, J. (1998) 'Covert Visual Attention Modulates Face-Specific Activity in the Human Fusiform Gyrus: fMRI Study', *Journal of Neurophysiology*, 79, 1574–8.

Wollaston, W. H. (1824) 'On the Apparent Direction of Eyes in a Portrait', *Philosophical Transactions of the Royal Society of London*, 114, 247–56.

Wong, T. K., Fung, P. C., Chua, S. E. and McAlonan, G. M. (2008) 'Abnormal Spatiotemporal Processing of Emotional Facial Expressions in Childhood Autism: Dipole Source Analysis of Event-Related Potentials', *European Journal of Neuroscience*, 28, 407–16.

Wright, H., Wardlaw, J., Young, A. W. and Zeman, A. (2006) 'Prosopagnosia Following Nonconvulsive Status Epilepticus Associated with a Left Fusiform Gyrus Malformation', *Epilepsy and Behavior*, 9, 197–203.

Wynn, J. K., Lee, J., Huran, W. P. and Green, M. F. (2008) 'Using Event Related Potentials to Explore Stages of Facial Affect Recognition Deficits in Schizophrenia', *Schizophrenia Bulletin*, 34, 679–87.

Xu, Y., Liu, J. and Kanwisher, N. (2005) 'The M170 is Selective for Faces, not for Expertise', *Neuropsychologia*, 43, 558–97.

Yardley, L., McDermott, L., Pisarski, S., Duchaine, B. and Nakayama, K. (2008) 'Psychosocial Consequences of Developmental Prosopagnosia: A Problem of Recognition', *Journal of Psychosomatic Research*, 65, 445–51.

Yin, R. K. (1969) Looking at upside-down faces. *Journal of Experimental Psychology*, 81, 141–145.

Yoon, J. H., D'Esposito, M. and Carter, C. S. (2006) 'Preserved Function of the Fusiform Face Area in Schizophrenia as Revealed by fMRI', *Psychiatry Research*, 148, 205–16.

Young, A. W. (2000) 'Wondrous Strange: The Neuropsychology of Abnormal Beliefs', *Mind and Language*, 15, 47–73.

Young, A. W., Aggleton, J. P., Hellawell, D. J., Johnson, M., Broks, P. and Hanley, J. R. (1995) 'Face Processing Impairments after Amygdalotomy', *Brain*, 118, 15–24.

Young, A. W. and Burton, A. M. (1999) 'Simulating Face Recognition: Implications for Modelling Cognition', *Cognitive Neuropsychology*, 16, 1–48.

Young, A. W., Hay, D. C. and Ellis, A. W. (1985) 'The Faces that Launched a Thousand Slips: Everyday Difficulties and Errors in Recognising People', *British Journal of Psychology*, 76, 495–523.

Young, A. W., Hellawell, D. and de Haan, E. H. F. (1988) 'Cross-Domain Semantic Priming in Normal Subjects and a Prosopagnosic Patient', *Quarterly Journal of Experimental Psychology Section A: Human Experimental Psychology*, 40, 561–80.

Young, A., Hellawell, D. and Hay, D. C. (1987) Configurational information in face perception. *Perception*, 16, 737–759.

Young, A. W., McWeeny, K. H., Hay, D. C. and Ellis, A. W. (1986a) Access to identity-specific semantic codes from familiar faces. *Quarterly Journal of Experimental Psychology A: Human Experimental Psychology*, 38, 271–295.

Young, A. W., McWeeny, K. H., Hay, D. C. and Ellis, A. W. (1986b) 'Matching Familiar and Unfamiliar Faces on Identity and Expression', *Psychological Research*, 48, 63–8.

Young, A. W., Newcombe, F., de Haan, E. H., Small, M. and Hay, D. C. (1993) 'Face Perception after Brain Injury. Selective Impairments Affecting Identity and Expression', *Brain*, 116, 941–59.

Young, A., Perrett, D., Calder, A., Sprengelmeyer, R. and Ekman, P. (2002) *Facial Expressions of Emotion: Stimuli and Tests (FEEST)* (Thames Valley Test Company).

Young, G. (2008) Capgras delusion: An interactionist model. *Consciousness and Cognition*, 17, 863–876.

Yovel, G. and Duchaine, B. (2006) 'Specialized Face Perception Mechanisms Extract Both Part and Spacing Information: Evidence from Developmental Prosopagnosia', *Journal of Cognitive Neuroscience*, 18, 580–93.

Yovel, G. and Kanwisher, N. (2004) Face perception: Domain specific, not person specific. *Neuron*, 44, 889–898.

Yovel, G. and Kanwisher, N. (2005) 'The Neural Basis of the Behavioral Face-Inversion Effect', *Current Biology*, 15, 2256–62.

Yovel, G., Levy, J., Graboweckey, M. and Paller, K. (2003) 'Neural Correlates of the Left-Visual-Field Superiority in Face Perception Appears at Multiple Stages of Face Perception', *Journal of Cognitive Neuroscience*, 15, 462–7.

Yovel, G., Paller, K. A. and Levy, J. (2005) A whole face is more than the sum of its parts: Interactive processing in face perception. *Visual Cognition*, 12, 337–352.

Yue, X., Tjan, B. S. and Biederman, I. (2006) 'What Makes Faces Special', *Vision Research*, 26, 3802–11.

Zangenehpour, S. and Chaudhuri, A. (2005) 'Patchy Organization and Asymmetric Distribution of the Neural Correlates of Face Processing in Monkey Inferotemporal Cortex. *Current Biology*, 15, 993–1005.

Zihl, J. and von Cramon, D. (1986) *Zerebrale Sehstörungen* (Kohlhammer: Stuttgart).

Index